Rehabilitation Counseling Research

Rehabilitation Counseling Research

by
Brian Bolton

with contributions by
Paul Cooper, Daniel Cook, and **Jim Harper**

Arkansas Rehabilitation Research and Training Center
University of Arkansas, Fayetteville

with a foreword by
George Wright

University Park Press
Baltimore

UNIVERSITY PARK PRESS
International Publishers in Science, Medicine, and Education
233 East Redwood Street
Baltimore, Maryland 21202

Composed by University Park Press, Typesetting Division
Manufactured in the United States of America by
The Maple Press Company

Library of Congress Cataloging in Publication Data

Bolton, Brian F
Rehabilitation counseling research.

Earlier ed. published in 1974 under title: Introduction
to rehabilitation research.
Bibliography: p.
Includes indexes.
1.   Rehabilitation research. 2.   Rehabilitation
counseling — Research. I. Title.
HD7255.B63   1979   362.8'5   79-13612
ISBN 0-8391-1501-6

Contents

Foreword

This is an important contribution to the professional education of rehabilitation-ists. The text explains difficult numerical concepts so that they are clear even to people more inclined toward verbal learning. The material is selected and presented for the particular interests and informational needs of the counselor in rehabilitation. Even the examples are prepared for this selected readership. As a consequence of this work it is to be hoped that all rehabilitation students will master these essentials of research design and application so that they can further their learning and keep current on the new knowledge of future research publications. The ability to learn more through independent study is a primary purpose of professional education. In a field such as ours this effort for growth and development depends upon the practitioner's competency in the comprehension of research reports.

When Brian Bolton was a research assistant in the rehabilitation counseling psychology program at the University of Wisconsin-Madison, he and several other Ph.D. degree students worked under my direction in the preparation of *Rehabilitation Research;* published by the university with Ann Trotter as coauthor, that book was an attempt to describe the best research and demonstration projects funded by federal rehabilitation grants through the mid-1960s. Brian even then had the knack of clarifying difficult statistical design problems and of preparing highly readable research papers.

It has been my experience that human service workers use the concepts learned in statistics courses in invaluable, if subtle, ways over and beyond their role as a research consumer and their task of "keeping up with the literature." Even though the rehabilitationist may not conduct scientific studies after graduate school, there are other needs for the knowledge. The first and foremost centers on the understanding of the rehabilitation client: the concepts of deviation, relative chances of success, and client evaluation profiles necessitate this knowledge for an understanding of individual differences. Also I have found that the professional worker or administrator can apply techniques of research design in informal studies of people and situations. They provide objectivity and structure for organizing and analyzing data of all kinds collected from various sources in many different ways. Vocational rehabilitation work is fascinating because every client is different in terms of potentials and needs, necessitating a unique rehabilitative program. The growth aspect of professional practice lies in the opportunity to learn from the longitudinal experience derived from the successes (and failures) of each case — what combinations of people and service characteristics work and why they work. This accumulation of feedback information rapidly builds to such proportions that the mass requires systematic information handling, the techniques of which are found in the mathematics of statistics.

It is inconceivable to me that graduate education in rehabilitation counseling would not require a course on statistics and research design — although a few colleges make it optional. But I also believe that this rehabilitation research course should be particularized for the level, interests, and needs of the students. Herein lies the value of this text.

George Nelson Wright
Madison, Wisconsin

Preface

The ultimate goal of rehabilitation research is the improvement of services to disabled clients. Because rehabilitation counselors are the primary agents in the service-delivery process they are the logical target of research publications. Unfortunately, most research results are disseminated in a form unsuitable for use by the typical practitioner. One solution to this problem is to prepare the counselor to be a research consumer.

The purpose of *Rehabilitation Counseling Research* is to introduce students and practitioners to research methodology so that they can become intelligent consumers of research. By incorporating research-based knowledge into their counseling practice, rehabilitation professionals assure that handicapped persons receive optimal services. The following assumptions underlie the counselor-as-research-consumer approach to research utilization:

1. The effective rehabilitation practitioner's counseling style should be continually evolving as new knowledge extends our capability of improving the life adjustment of disabled clients.
2. Research in rehabilitation and the social sciences produces knowledge and skills that are potentially usable in rehabilitation counseling practice.
3. Rehabilitation practitioners can improve their counseling effectiveness by incorporating new knowledge and techniques into their modes of operation.
4. Each rehabilitation counselor develops a relatively unique counseling style that reflects his/her personality and philosophy; thus, the use of research results is an individualized matter.

The focus of the book is on conceptual understanding and the basic principles of research design as opposed to computational details and the intricacies of implementing and conducting investigations. Summaries of rehabilitation research studies that have been reported in the literature are used to illustrate design strategies and the problems of interpreting results. The specific goals of *Rehabilitation Counseling Research* are to:

1. Develop a level of understanding of statistical procedures, psychometric methods, and research design that will enable the practitioner to read critically the published literature in rehabilitation and related areas.
2. Develop the requisite skills in translating research results into implications for counseling practice that will enable the practitioner to translate empirically derived knowledge and techniques into a form that may be incorporated into his/her unique counseling style.
3. Foster positive attitudes toward the application of scientific methodology in social service settings so that future practitioners may become collaborators in research studies conducted in agency settings.

There are no prerequisites for reading this book although a background in the social and behavioral sciences would be helpful. The intended audiences are students in rehabilitation counselor training programs and practicing rehabilitation counselors. However, students and practitioners in other helping professions should find the book useful. It can serve as a text in a one-semester course in research methods for consumers or as a sourcebook for inservice training programs. As with any text that aims to prepare students to achieve a minimal level of competence in a functional skill, practice is necessary. Journal articles and various types of research reports in rehabilitation, psychology, and special education can serve as practice materials. The matter of practice is discussed further in the next section entitled "To the Student and the Instructor."

Rehabilitation Counseling Research is an extensive revision and expansion of a book that the author wrote in the summer of 1973 *(Introduction to Rehabilitation Research,* Charles C Thomas, 1974). Because of the scope of the revision (approximately 70% of the material is new) and the emphasis on rehabilitation counseling, a new title that more accurately describes the content was selected. The revised book contains 10 chapters that cover major topics and 7 appendices that include reviews of the rehabilitation research literature and overviews of technical issues and procedures.

The additions that are especially noteworthy are as follows. Chapter 1 (Introduction) contains new sections on synthetic or integrative studies in rehabilitation and the evaluation of rehabilitation research. Chapter 3 (Fundamentals of Measurement) includes a lengthy section on sources of information about tests and measures. Appendix 1 contains descriptions of nine tests and inventories that were constructed for use in rehabilitation. Chapter 4 (Research Design) is greatly expanded with more examples and a new section on the concept of control. Chapter 5 (Assessment of Outcomes) includes in-depth discussions of the issues of perspectives and dimensionality and a section on the approaches to inventory construction. Appendix 2 is a review of psychometric studies of the 16PF and Appendix 3 presents a biographical sketch of the eminent quantitative personality theorist R. B. Cattell. Almost one-half of Chapter 6 (Prediction of Outcomes) is devoted to longitudinal follow-up studies. Appendix 4 summarizes the multivariate prediction studies in rehabilitation and Appendix 5 outlines the methodology of prediction research. Chapter 7 (Factor Analysis) is extensively revised with many new sections. Appendix 6 summarizes the factor analytic studies in rehabilitation and Appendix 7 reviews technical procedures and issues in factor analysis. Chapter 8 (Rehabilitation Program Evaluation) and Chapter 9 (Case Weighting Systems) are entirely new. Finally, Chapter 10 (Research Utilization) is greatly expanded to incorporate recent developments, such as the research utilization specialist program, the visiting consultant and RULE projects, and the Florida RRI's extensive work in information retrieval and dissemination.

Three of my colleagues are listed on the title page as collaborators in the authorship of *Rehabilitation Counseling Research.* Paul Cooper and Dan Cook wrote the chapter on program evaluation and Paul Cooper and Jim Harper co-authored the chapter on case weighting systems. They are exceptionally well qualified to write chapters on these subjects for future consumers of rehabilitation research and I thank them for contributing to this volume.

Five individuals have contributed indirectly to the book through their influence on the senior author: Professors Alfred Butler and George Wright of the University of Wisconsin, Professor Henry Kaiser of the University of California

(Berkeley), Professor William Gellman of DePaul University, and Dr. Asher Soloff of the Chicago Jewish Vocational Service. I appreciate their support and assistance during the past 15 years.

Rehabilitation Counseling Research was written with the support of Rehabilitation Services Administration Grant No. 16-P-56812, RT-13 to the Arkansas Rehabilitation Research and Training Center and is a nonprofit endeavor on the part of the authors. Appreciation is expressed to Joan Sanow and the staff at University Park Press for expediting the publication process. Special thanks are given to Connie Akridge for typing the manuscript, to Patty George for assembling the indices, and to David Sigman for the cover design.

To the Student
and the Instructor

I have been concerned with issues and problems in teaching research to rehabilitation counseling students for the past 10 years. During this period I have taught a variety of statistics and research courses, supervised numerous student research projects, written (and revised) an introductory research textbook, and published articles and presented papers summarizing my views on teaching research to rehabilitation counseling students.

While my general position regarding the role of research preparation in rehabilitation counselor training programs is pretty firmly established, I do have occasional doubts about it. Two years ago I received a brief note from the training officer for a state rehabilitation agency to whom we had sent a reprint of an article entitled "Client psychological adjustment associated with three counseling styles" (Bolton, 1977e).

To: Brian Bolton

> After reading a report like this regarding client psychological adjustment, my generally negative view of rehabilitation research is reinforced. I really don't know what you are trying to say. Suggest you take a course in report writing.

John Smith

My response to Mr. Smith (not his real name) indicates the nature of a fundamental issue in the research training of future practitioners.

Dear Mr. Smith:

> Thank you for your brief note of August 11, 1977. I am never happy when I receive such a communication; however, I do realize that your views are not unique. Ironically, in the same issue of the *Rehabilitation Counseling Bulletin* in which the "Client psychological adjustment..." article was published, I stated the opinion that research training in rehabilitation counselor training programs should be optional. When I am confronted with clear evidence that practitioners cannot read simple research reports, I am tempted to revise my position.
>
> In other words, I wonder if you (and many other practitioners) don't need to take a course in *report reading,* as opposed to your suggestion that I take a course in report writing. Several years ago I wrote a book designed to help practitioners become adequate report readers. A descriptive brochure is enclosed.
>
> Again, thank you for taking the time to express your opinion.

Would a course in rehabilitation research help to "straighten out" Mr. Smith's "generally negative view of rehabilitation research"? Or is his unfavorable attitude the result of having been required to take one or more research courses? My position is that *traditional* courses in research methods in the social and behavioral sciences do not prepare students to understand and use the results of research in their work. However, I do believe that a course of study that emphasizes the preparation of future practitioners to be *research consumers* can contribute to the ultimate advancement of rehabilitation counseling practice. Consequently, I designed and organized the present textbook to introduce rehabilitation counseling students to the basic concepts of statistics, measurement, and research design that are essential to becoming effective research consumers.

Rehabilitation Counseling Research provides the core materials for rehabilitation research courses that are planned to satisfy the American Rehabilitation Counseling Association's (1978) policy statement on professional preparation, which includes "techniques for understanding and utilizing research findings" (p. 234) as an area of curricular emphasis. In order for research training to play a significant role in the preparation of "self-developing" rehabilitation practitioners, the following objectives should be stressed:

1. The student should possess the skills necessary to read research publications with a reasonable degree of understanding. The specific skills include basic principles of research design (e.g., ex post facto versus experimental designs) and interpretation (e.g., generalizability), measurement (e.g., reliability), and statistics (e.g., tests of significance versus size of effect).

2. The student should develop the habit of reading the academic journals that are relevant to rehabilitation practice. Since the only way to develop the habit of reading is to read, research training should be designed around a structured reading schedule. After a brief introduction to research methodology, all teaching of conceptual tools should take place in conjunction with the analysis and interpretation of research reports.

3. The student should develop the habit of summarizing or abstracting research publications that are relevant to his/her counseling style or interests. While the primary concern of practitioners is with the results of research investigations, it is necessary that they pay attention to two other aspects of any study: the subject population(s) and the research setting. The generalizability of results may be severely restricted by either of these parameters.

4. The student should develop the ability to translate research-based knowledge into implications for his/her own counseling style. This particular "ability" can only emerge through intensive and continued practice. Furthermore, since every counselor's style is somewhat unique (although not entirely so), this ability will be manifested in different ways by different students. However, the end-product will always be clearly recognizable — a particular orientation, technique, or behavior that can be adopted by the counselor.

5. The student should develop the habit of incorporating new knowledge and techniques into his/her counseling style. An abundance of evidence suggests that practitioners do not automatically modify their behavior when they become aware of new developments; the behavior change process must be learned through practice. To make possible an educational context in which desirable research usage habits can be developed, it is necessary for research training to become an integrated theme in rehabilitation counselor education programs and an emphasis on research-based knowledge must permeate the curriculum. (Bolton, 1977b, pp. 291–292)

Will a course in rehabilitation research that implements these objectives actually produce rehabilitation practitioners who are research consumers? Two independent lines of evidence lead me to answer in the affirmative. First, a profession that is historically closely related to rehabilitation counseling, social work, has been struggling with the question of the proper role of research training in the curriculum for a number of years and has arrived at conclusions similar to mine, e.g., see Casselman (1972), Kirk, Osmalov, and Fischer (1976), Linn and Greenwald (1974), and Zimbalist (1974). Second, the eminent clinical psychologist Paul Meehl (1971) proposed a nonresearch doctoral program for clinicians in which a research-consuming course would be followed by a continuous "literature seminar" that would involve practice in research-consuming activities. He suggested that the course should "combine a presentation of the major problems in clinical research with primary emphasis on how to spot defective designs and fallacious inferences, and the general principles... would be illustrated by a variety of concrete examples from the research literature" (p. 68). Professor Meehl expressed his confidence in this approach to research training by offering to wager $1,000 that he could train research consumers who would be significantly superior in this function to those who are trained by the usual method of the Ph.D. dissertation!

The final topic that I think merits attention is the research project requirement in the master's degree program. Quoting Meehl (1971): "Isn't it strange to assume, without even discussing the issue, that the best way to train a person to be a good research consumer is to put him through the paces of being a research producer? What evidence is there that this is true?" (p. 67). Two rehabilitation counselor educators (Kauppi & Brummer, 1970) who have thought about the issue echo Meehl's opinion:

> The assumption is usually made that the best way to teach research is to teach people to do it. This may not be a valid assumption for training those who will do research, and it is clearly invalid in training counselors who should use research but whose doing (of research) will be limited. (p. 2)

My position is consistent with these views; there is simply no compelling justification for a *required* research project in rehabilitation counselor education programs. However, students who express an interest in research should be encouraged to take appropriate courses, participate in ongoing projects, and conduct thesis research.

Rehabilitation
Counseling Research

chapter one
Introduction

The beginning student in rehabilitation counseling may well ask: "Why do we do research when we already know what works on the basis of practical experience?" Or, slightly rephrased: "Research only tells us what we already know!" The question (or statement) is important and deserves a documented answer for two reasons. First, the basic attitude of the researcher is one of skepticism and, therefore, the questioning student is (probably unknowingly) adopting an appropriate scientific attitude. Second, a convincing answer will provide some justification for the student spending a considerable portion of his/her valuable time studying this book.

While much research in the social and behavioral sciences does confirm our common-sense expectations, some does not. Practical experience in counseling and rehabilitation provides considerable evidence, *subjectively* interpreted by the practitioner, regarding more effective and less effective service procedures. Most research projects in rehabilitation are simply systematic investigations of practical experience. The primary goal of the research enterprise is the attainment of useful knowledge by *objective,* replicable methods. The following section includes summaries of three investigations that produced results contrary to the investigators' expectations. The obvious point being made is that research does not always tell us what we already know.

THREE REHABILITATION EXAMPLES

The first two studies in this section are concerned with the use of the vocational adjustment workshop, a very important rehabilitation technique. The reader is referred to the recent book by Neff (1978) for a review of the history and theory of the rehabilitative workshop. The third research study evaluates an innovative diagnostic procedure in a state rehabilitation agency office setting.

Psychiatric Rehabilitation

Barbee, Berry, and Micek (1969) reported the results of a study undertaken to investigate the relationship between participation in a work therapy program and measures of treatment duration and rehospitalization for psychiatric patients. The subjects were patients at the Fort Logan (Colorado) Mental Health Center who were randomly assigned to participant (experimental) and nonparticipant (control) groups at the time of their admission. The experimental treatment, work therapy, has been heralded as a highly useful technique for preparing long-term patients for return to independent functioning outside the psychiatric institution. By communicating more realistic expectations of a job, work therapy reduces the patient's fear of leaving the security of the institution and eases his/her transition into the community.

Follow-up interviews with the 100 experimental (work therapy) and 149 control (no work therapy) subjects were conducted 3, 12, and 24 months after each patient's first substantial indication of improvement. The two groups were compared on four dependent variables using statistical significance tests: 1) length of intensive treatment, 2) length of total hospital stay, 3) rate of readmission to any psychiatric facility, and 4) readmission rate to the Fort Logan Mental Health Center.

Which group of subjects (work therapy or control) spent less time hospitalized? Which group had the lower readmission rates? In other words, using the four dependent variables as criteria, did the work therapy program at Fort Logan prove to be successful?

Contrary to the investigators' expectations (referred to as hypotheses), the results indicated that the experimental subjects had significantly longer stays in both intensive treatment and total hospitalization than did the control subjects. Although there was no difference between the groups with respect to readmission to all psychiatric facilities, the work therapy patients had significantly more readmissions to Fort Logan.

What might have accounted for these unanticipated results? The authors suggested that the work therapy program, as it was operated at Fort Logan, may have fostered institutional dependency rather than lessened it. They recommended that work therapy programs be established in the community in order to avoid contributing to hospital dependency. In fact, a longitudinal investigation of the effects of a community-based work therapy program on the rehabilitation of chronic patients at Chicago State Hospital supported this recommendation (Soloff, 1967). This study is reviewed in Chapter 4.

Vocational Development

Shulman (1967) reported the results of an intensive longitudinal study of the vocational development of educable mentally retarded adolescents. Subjects were randomly assigned to an experimental group or to a control group. The 27 experimental subjects received workshop adjustment and counseling services each Saturday during the school year and for 3 weeks during the summer for a 2-year period. The 28 control subjects did not receive rehabilitation services. All 55 subjects participated in three consecutive annual diagnostic sessions of 1 week's duration; at each session a variety of data pertinent to vocational development was collected: 1) workshop data — production and ratings of work behavior, 2) interview data — attitudes, adjustment at home and school, and 3) psychological testing data — standard measures of intelligence, manual dexterity, social development, and self-concept. Thirty-three of the clients were located and interviewed in conjunction with the follow-up study conducted 2 years after the final diagnostic assessment.

Although many important statistical analyses were conducted in this study, the major research question concerned the impact of the experimental treatment: Did the intensive rehabilitation services provided to the experimental subjects enhance their vocational development?

The investigator did not find any statistically significant differences between the experimental and control groups on the many measures that were employed in the diagnostic assessment sessions. He speculated that the negative results may have been due to one of the following possibilities: 1) the particular treatment may not have been potent enough to modify the behaviors comprising the construct "vocational development"; 2) the annual diagnostic assessments were in fact treatments, and therefore the control group received partial treatment; or 3) vocational development is stabilized by age 14 and thus change is not possible. (Regarding the third point, clinical experience with other groups of disabled clients, e.g., young deaf clients, suggests that vocational development can and does occur well beyond age 14.) The follow-up study of 16 experimental and 17 control subjects revealed that 81% of the experimental subjects, versus 65% of the control subjects, had made successful vocational adjustments. The author interpreted this result as indicative of a possible sleeper effect of the treatment. However, the difference is not statistically significant and, therefore, is only suggestive of long-term benefit from the experimental treatment.

Accelerated Diagnostic Services

Usdane (1972) proposed the RIDAC (Rehabilitation Initial Diagnosis and Assessment for Clients) concept as a procedure for enhancing the efficiency of state agency rehabilitation services. The RIDAC unit is a multidisciplinary diagnostic team that typically includes a coordinator, a medical examiner, an interviewer, a psychologist, and a work evaluator. The unit's objective is to accelerate the client service process by reducing delays between referral and movement into active status and by increasing the usefulness of diagnostic information for case planning. In other words, RIDAC should result in faster services and greater effectiveness.

The first large-scale evaluation of a RIDAC unit was carried out by the Texas Rehabilitation Commission (Goldston & Hefley, 1975). The evaluation entailed a research design in which disabled persons who were referred to a local office in Houston were randomly assigned to the experimental RIDAC unit and to traditional diagnostic services (the control group). The research samples, each consisting of more than 700 clients, included all cases that had been closed 1 year after the project terminated.

When RIDAC and traditional samples were compared on various measures of client outcome, no differences were found. For example, the proportions of clients in the major closure statuses (08, 26, 28, and 30) were virtually identical, and the average weekly earnings for the employed clients were the same. Furthermore, analyses of the comparative costs of the two approaches revealed that the average diagnostic cost for RIDAC clients was 2½ times that of the control clients; however, the postdiagnostic services costs were only slightly higher for the RIDAC clients.

Again, we must ask: "Why did such a promising idea receive so little support when put to experimental test?" The "negative results" of the Houston RIDAC project may have been due to the inappropriate use of random assignment. The investigators estimated that approximately 10% of the clients referred to the RIDAC unit may not have been suitable candidates for accelerated diagnosis. In retrospect, it is clear that a more appropriate research design would have incorporated an initial judgment of suitability *before* assignment to the RIDAC and control groups. Fortunately, a more recent evaluation of RIDAC, in which counselors selected clients for referral to the special diagnostic unit, produced more favorable results. This project is reviewed in Chapter 8.

The studies by Barbee and her associates, Shulman, and Goldston and Hefley are important contributions to the advancement of knowledge about rehabilitation services. The results of these investigations suggest that the vocational adjustment workshop must be modified to achieve optimal effectiveness with hospitalized psychiatric patients and educable mentally retarded adolescents, and that rehabilitation clients should receive some preliminary screening before referral to a RIDAC diagnostic unit. In fact, the results of the studies may be unique to the settings (Fort Logan Mental Health Center, Chicago Jewish Vocational Service, and the Houston field office) as well as to the particular disabled populations. Great caution must be exercised in generalizing from the research findings of any given study. No single study ever provides conclusive evidence about anything; knowledge is advanced by the orderly accumulation and synthesis of research results. Rehabilitation practice can only achieve a scientific foundation through the systematic evaluation of current procedures and the flexible adaptation of experimental innovations. Basic to the attainment of an empirical foundation for any applied discipline is the adoption of a set of rules or procedures referred to as the scientific method, which is discussed in the next section.

But first it is necessary to return to the issue that motivated this section, i.e., the contention that research only tells us what we already know from practical experience. Even when research only does confirm the obvious, it still serves an important scientific function. This point was nicely made by Sheehan and Hackett (1978) when they concluded their summary of studies of the relationship between life changes and illness with the following comment:

> Although these findings may only make the obvious explicit, the clarity and the methodological soundness on which they are based are necessary first steps toward increased rigor in investigating psychosomatic illness. (p. 324)

THE SCIENTIFIC METHOD

The scientific method is no more than a refinement of common sense. The primary characteristics of this fundamental approach to answering questions and solving problems are outlined in this section. Two global assumptions underlie the methods of science (Underwood, 1957, pp. 3–6):

1. Determinism: It is assumed that there is *lawfulness* in the events of nature as opposed to random, spontaneous activity. Every natural event is assumed to have a cause. The task of scientific endeavors is to discover the *orderliness* about observed phenomena.
2. Finite causation: It is assumed that every natural event has a discoverable and limited number of conditions that influence it. The task of scientific investigation is to identify the *specific causes* of observed events.

A scientific study begins with the phrasing of a research question. The question may evolve out of a practical problem or may be the logical product of theoretical speculation. An example of the former might be "Does work therapy improve the probability of successful rehabilitation of psychiatric patients?" The latter would be illustrated by "Is work satisfaction a function of the correspondence between an individual's abilities and the ability requirements of the work environment?'' (This is an abbreviated restatement of Proposition II of the Minnesota Theory of Work Adjustment; see Dawis, 1976.) In order for the research question to be amenable to scientific procedures, it must be translated into testable terms. The scientific method requires empirical data that can be evaluated objectively as a basis for addressing the research question. Someone other than the original investigator should be able to repeat the steps of any research study and arrive at the same conclusions. In other words, scientific research studies are subject to verification in accordance with the principle of replicability.

There is no such thing as proof in the realm of empirical research. Theorems are proved in mathematical studies in the sense that they are the logical end products of a series of *deductions* from previous statements, i.e., axioms, postulates, and other theorems. Scientific investigations utilize empirical data, i.e., observable phenomena that are translated by objective procedures into numerical form. Questions are answered tentatively as more evidence is collected; the criterion for assessing the state of knowledge in any given area of research activity is the total weight of the evidence. The logical process is *inductive:* the scientific method rests on arguments from a few cases to a defined universe of phenomena. It is paradoxical that the final decisions regarding the interpretation and meaning of objectively collected and analyzed data are based on subjective judgment. This situation is less true in the physical sciences than in the social and behavioral sciences. It is for this reason, in part, that some philosophers of science have labeled psychology, sociology, and related disciplines ''pseudo-sciences.'' A brief outline of the characteristics of the scientific method is presented in Table 1.

MEASUREMENT AND STATISTICS

Two important subjects that are treated at length in Chapters 2 and 3 were alluded to above. Measurement and statistics merit brief attention at this point because they are the cornerstones of the scientific method as it is applied to behavioral research. First, the translation of the research question into testable terms, or equivalently, the reduction of specified observable phenomena to empirical data, involves the process of measurement. Acceptable measuring instruments possess the characteristics of reliability and validity at a minimal level. Reliable instruments yield similar results when repeated, e.g., a yardstick can provide a fairly reliable assessment of the surface dimensions of a dining room table in that the figures obtained on 3 consecutive days would probably not vary too much. An instrument

Table 1.   Characteristics of the scientific method[a]

Metaphysical Assumptions
1. The assumption of autonomy: The inanimate world is a self-acting, self-perpetuating system in which all changes conform to natural law.
2. The assumption of comprehensibility: There are discoverable relations and forces determining the course of nature.
3. The assumption of uniformity: The laws of nature are invariant; there are no uncaused changes in physical identity.

Historical Characteristics
4. Scientific investigation is progressive: Knowledge acquired by scientific method has increased and continues to increase.
5. Scientific knowledge is efficacious in controlling or altering the course of nature: The result is prediction and control of events.
6. Scientific knowledge presents us with an open universe: The scientific future is not predestined, but, within wide limits may be a selected and novel future.
7. Scientific findings are provisional: The findings of science are provisional and subject to modification or revision as their scope becomes more comprehensive.
8. Scientific laws describe dispositional properties and relations: To describe potentialities and possibilities, science casts its findings in abstract or theoretical form.
9. Scientific inquiry tends to be self-correcting: The requirements of public verifiability, testability, predictability, etc., make scientific inquiry a self-correcting enterprise.

Methodology
10. Empirical: Statements of fact should be based on observation and experiment.
11. Public verifiability: Scientific claims should be open to public verification, examination, and criticism.
12. Testability: Scientific hypotheses should be capable of empirical confirmation or rejection.
13. Definiteness and precision: Concepts are quantified through the application of measurement techniques.
14. Parsimony: The least possible number of assumptions are to be made in the attempt to explain ascertained facts.
15. Comprehensiveness: A science consists of a systematic, coherent, and comprehensive description of observed events.

[a]Adapted from *Notes on Scientific Method* by Professor Solomon Levy, a mimeographed handout in Philosophy 210, University of Kansas City, Spring, 1960.

is valid if it measures what it purports to measure. The yardstick constitutes a valid measuring instrument if the goal is an assessment of the *size* of the table; it may not be a valid measure of the *value* of the table.

The second important operation in the application of the scientific method to behavioral data occurs after the measuring process is complete. Statistical procedures provide an objective device for translating the empirical data into probability statements, which constitute evidence regarding the research question. For example, the result of a statistical significance test might be a statement such as, "The probability of finding a difference as large as that obtained, if treatment A and treatment B are really equally effective, is less than one in a hundred. Therefore, it is concluded that treatment A is more effective than treatment B with chronic, male psychiatric patients." It should be emphasized that the statistical significance test cannot prove treatment A to be more effective. It can only associate a probability value with the empirical data collected by the investigator.

While the vast majority of behavioral researchers do regard quantitative procedures as an essential aspect of the scientific method, there are a substantial minority who do not. The basis of the negative view seems to be a distrust of sterile measurement techniques and aggregate statistical treatment, as the quotes below suggest; however, the minority opinion may reflect a fundamental personality disposition. The first quote is taken from a candid autobiographical statement by Seymour Sarason (1977), a productive and respected clinical/community psychologist:

> In fact, I have gained the least in an intellectual sense, and found the task relatively uninteresting, when I was writing up journal articles based on empirical research. (p. 199)
>   . . . I always felt uncomfortable with and not very competent in statistics and research design. But it went deeper than that. There was and is a fundamental mismatch between what gives me intellectual satisfaction and the requirements of systematic research. (p. 201)

The second quote is from Marrow's (1969) popular biography of the highly influential psychologist Kurt Lewin. The person quoted is Leon Festinger, one of Lewin's many successful students,[1] who was reflecting on Lewin's attitude toward statistics:

> I think his dislike for them was a misconception on his part about what statistics could do for him. He seemed to identify statistics with data that could be collected without systematic theories, and to feel that an individual case would get lost in statistical analysis. Things that don't belong together would be put together, and their meaning obscured. (p. 106)

It would be a mistake to interpret these statements to indicate that quantitative methods are either unnecessary or detrimental to scientific research in the behavioral sciences. Sarason and Lewin would most certainly rec-

---

[1]Among Lewin's students are three psychologists who should be familiar to rehabilitation students: Roger Barker, Tamara Dembo, and Beatrice Wright. In a very real sense, then, Lewin is the father of the somatopsychological school in rehabilitation psychology (see Barker, Wright, Meyerson, and Gonick, 1953; Dembo, Leviton, and Wright, 1956/1975).

ognize the importance of proper statistical analyses of carefully collected data. However, there are a few psychologists who argue that statistical significance tests *are* unnecessary; one prominent individual is quoted at some length in Chapter 2.

OTHER RESEARCH METHODS

Although this book is concerned with methods appropriate for empirical investigation, the reader should be aware of one major nonempirical research method. Synthetic research involves reviewing the research literature available in some defined area of interest and summarizing and integrating the results into tentative conclusions regarding the current state of knowledge. Obviously, the synthetic report is only as strong as the individual studies that provide the basis for it. On the positive side, when several independent research efforts utilizing different samples and varying procedures produce similar results, the appropriate conclusions are greatly strengthened. It should also be clear that the person who prepares a synthetic research report must be familiar with research methodology so that he/she can properly interpret the research literature. In other words, library research that relies on extensive and thorough reviews of research literature should not be regarded as a second-class research activity. In fact, the tremendous volume of empirical studies that are reported in the literature would be virtually incomprehensible if it were not for the integrative surveys that are reported in the *Psychological Bulletin,* the *Review of Educational Research,* the *Rehabilitation Counseling Bulletin,* and other journals that publish synthetic reports on a regular basis. The very important role that "the empirical integrator" plays in scientific psychology was perceived by Underwood (1957) more than 20 years ago:

> If I correctly assess the current situation, it is that we have vast bodies of data even within areas within psychology which desperately need to be brought into some sort of integrative scheme. ... Thus, several hundred research reports may be reduced to a report that can be easily assimilated. ... I furthermore suspect that, at least in certain areas, this work would be far more valuable to our science than the actual research done. ... I guess what I am trying to say is that I do not want to leave the impression that advances in science are made only in the laboratory or in the theoretician's office. The empirical integrator is very much in demand. (pp. 290–291) [Reprinted by permission]

The following examples, all taken from the recent rehabilitation literature, illustrate the flexibility of the synthetic approach and the wide diversity of materials or data to which it is applicable. Anthony, Buell,

Sharatt, and Althoff (1972) reviewed the empirical studies in psychiatric rehabilitation. Three of their conclusions are quoted:

1. Traditional methods of treating hospitalized psychiatric patients, including individual therapy, group therapy, work therapy, and drug therapy, do not affect differentially the discharged patients' community functioning as measured by recidivism and posthospital employment.
2. Aftercare clinics and other forms of moderate community support reduce recidivism. Whether this positive effect is due to the medication administered, the other kinds of services offered, or the type of patient who attends, is not yet clear.
3. Various types of transitional facilities are successful in reducing recidivism but have demonstrated little effect on enabling the patient to function independently in the community as measured by posthospital employment. (p. 454)

A recent update of the research literature pertaining to these three conclusions, by Anthony, Cohen, and Vitalo (1978), generally supported and extended the conclusions.

Roessler and Bolton (1978, pp. 29–40) reviewed and summarized the results of 19 investigations of the personality characteristics of disabled persons that used the Sixteen Personality Factor Questionnaire (16PF; see Chapter 5) and concluded that the following personality manifestations may be observed in disabled persons:

1. A tendency toward introversion (Invia) and self-sufficiency, although some psychiatric disabilities foster an outgoing orientation
2. Increased anxiety, specifically lower ego strength, greater apprehension, and higher ergic tension; with psychiatric disabilities, the possibility of withdrawal and suspicion
3. A tendency to a mood level of frustration and depression (Pathemia), especially with the psychiatrically disabled
4. A tendency to become subdued, with decreased evidence of independent functioning
5. Lowered super-ego strength, especially with psychiatrically disabled persons. (pp. 39–40)

The authors stressed that these conclusions were based on aggregate data. Therefore, while the general trends are highly reliable, the specific conclusions are only suggestive of the possible effects of disablement on the individual. However, these results do provide a comprehensive framework for the counselor who is striving to understand the personality dynamics of the individual client.

Based on a comprehensive review of the literature on self-help groups, Jaques and Patterson (1974) isolated 10 operational assumptions that underlie this important approach to helping; three are given here:

Behavior change is expected by and for each member. Learning a new way of life, presumably more satisfying, is undertaken at the individual's own pace....(p. 53)

The group process consists of actively relating, "owning," and revealing problems, receiving and giving feedback to each other, sharing hope, experiences, encouragement, and criticism in relation to the day-to-day goals of individual behavior change....(p. 53)

Group leadership develops and changes from within the group on the basis of giving and receiving help in keeping with the program's purposes and principles....(p. 54)

Jaques and Patterson emphasized that while the 10 operational assumptions were experientially derived and untested, they are supported pragmatically by the demonstrated help group members receive.

Bolton (1976a) reviewed the results of five demonstration service projects that were designed to rehabilitate (or habilitate) severely handicapped deaf young adults. Seventeen guidelines for rehabilitation practice were derived, for example:

Counseling with deaf clients must be situation specific; language difficulties prevent the meaningful discussion of "philosophical" issues. Information giving is an important dimension of the counseling process.... (p. 147)

Deaf clients will generally require a longer period of time to complete most services and reach a specified level of competence than hearing clients. Rehabilitation programming should take this into account rather than foster unrealistic expectations in deaf clients....(p. 147)

Deaf clients require more intensive instructional supervision in vocational training programs; thus, lower staff-student ratios should be arranged....(p. 148)

In the final example, Roessler and Mack (1975a) examined the literature relevant to the coordination of service delivery programs and drew 12 implications for practice, which included the following:

Service coordination efforts are often perceived as a threat, or as the first step toward a superagency that threatens interagency consensus and equilibrium....(p. 350)

Interorganizational evaluation concerns occur naturally whenever change is suggested or mandated, but do lessen with time as the changes are shown to be effective....(p. 350)

Administering systematic case coordination requires either a lead-agency or a core-staff approach. Aspects of systematic case coordination are central to a formalized coordination model for rehabilitation....(p. 351)

Many other excellent examples of synthetic research are available in the rehabilitation literature, such as Anthony (1973), Bolton (1972c),

Cook (1976), Institute on Rehabilitation Issues (1975), Lindenberg (1977), and Wagner (1977). The interested reader is referred to these papers for additional examples of this important research method.[2] In conclusion, it should be clear that synthetic research plays a vital role in the translation of the results of empirical investigations into implications for rehabilitation practice. Practitioners can have considerable confidence in conclusions based on several studies as opposed to the findings of isolated studies.

EVALUATION OF REHABILITATION RESEARCH

The discipline of rehabilitation research has been in existence for 25 years, having its formal origin in the Amendments to Public Law 565, which was enacted by Congress in 1954. Yet, it is only very recently that a systematic evaluation of the quality and usefulness of this endeavor was undertaken.

With the support of the National Science Foundation, Berkowitz, Englander, Rubin, and Worrall (1975, 1976) conducted a critical review of the methodological adequacy and the policy utility of a sample of 477 research reports that were completed between 1955 and 1973. Berkowitz et al. (1976) defined rehabilitation research projects as those "in which some attempt was made to relate various variables, such as counseling, training, and a host of other services or methods of service delivery, to a change in the status of clients or recipients of the service" (p. 40). Experts rated each of the 477 project reports on a 10-point scale (from poor to excellent) with regard to both methodological adequacy and policy utility.

The results of the evaluation were generally negative. Overall, 44% of the reports were judged to be poor methodologically, 39% were judged in the medium range, and only 17% were rated in the high range. The policy ratings were only slightly better, with 32% in the poor range, 42% in the medium range, and 26% in the high range. The authors concluded that there is a need for improvements in the way that rehabilitation research is funded and conducted, and they offered a number of recommendations for grantors and researchers.[3]

---

[2]Mention should be made of a statistical approach to the integration of research results, known as "meta-analysis," that was devised by Glass (1976, 1978). Smith and Glass (1977) illustrated the procedure by integrating the results of nearly 400 studies of counseling and psychotherapy and concluded that "the average client receiving therapy was better off than 75% of the untreated controls" (p. 754). However, Eysenck (1978) was not impressed with the approach, which he labeled "mega-silliness."

[3]Not surprisingly, the Berkowitz et al. study was not well received by many persons in the rehabilitation research community; six reactions and a reply by Berkowitz et al. are in-

Several individuals have been critical of the state-of-the-art in rehabilitation research. McDaniel (1976) assailed the area of psychological adjustment to disability for its lack of an empirical foundation:

> An overview of the major theoretical foundations of the study of the psychological aspects of physical disability and chronic illness must lead to the conclusion that while we are not devoid of a rationale for our studies, the progress of research and education in rehabilitation fields has definitely been impeded by a relatively weak foundation. In addition, the fact that such an overabundance of largely unfounded opinion and folklore exists in the field makes the job of getting at the facts even more formidable. Nowhere in the literature of any endeavor is there to be found such a great amount of material with such little evidence to support it. But the professions involved in rehabilitation are only now reaching a state of maturity which demands more exacting and precise information. (p. 10)

Interestingly, Dellario (1978) and Murphy (1977) independently criticized rehabilitation researchers for their failure to develop a comprehensive perspective from which to conduct empirical investigations and to integrate research findings. Dellario diagnosed the major problem of rehabilitation research to be a state of "disconnectedness" and proposed *planned change* as a reasonable common perspective with the purpose of rehabilitation research being "to provide understanding of the dynamics of *planned change* in rehabilitation intervention" (p. 39). Murphy suggested that rehabilitation researchers adopt an approach known as ethnomethodology and that they "enter into a sustained, dialectical relationship with handicapped clients" (p. 173).

Two conclusions are warranted regarding the current status of rehabilitation research. First, the field has been subjected to critical examination from external sources as well as from sources within. This openness to evaluation is essential for the ultimate improvement of the discipline. Second, while the judgments have tended toward the negative side, it should be remembered that 25 years is a very short time for research traditions to evolve and for fundamental principles and theories to emerge. Goldenson's (1978) comments on the national research effort in health and medicine can surely be extended to rehabilitation research:

> If we insist on measuring progress in terms of breakthroughs such as polio vaccines, rubella immunization, kidney transplants, and heart surgery, we

cluded in Bolton, B. (Ed.), An evaluation of rehabilitation research. *Rehabilitation Counseling Bulletin,* 1976, *20,* 37–65 (Special Feature). Also, an independent evaluation of the 1974 RSA-sponsored continuation projects by DeGeyndt, Hammond, Ouradnik, and Parkinson (1974) concluded that 69% were average or above average in technical adequacy (see Engstrom, 1975, p. 359, for a summary of this study).

must admit that dramatic advances are few and far between, and we may even begin to wonder what these huge investments of time, talent, and resources are producing. But when we recognize, as we must, that the human organism is infinitely more complex than we ever imagined, we will begin to measure progress in terms of a slow accumulation of knowledge accruing from lengthy, tedious investigations in hundreds of laboratories and research centers. (p. 824)

SUMMARY

While much research in the behavioral sciences serves only to confirm common-sense expectations, some does not. Three examples of investigations that did not support practical experience and clinical intuition were summarized: work therapy did not improve the rehabilitation success rates of psychiatric inpatients, work adjustment services did not stimulate the vocational development of mentally retarded adolescents, and accelerated diagnostic services did not produce more successful rehabilitation outcomes. These results suggest that the vocational workshop must be modified to achieve optimal effectiveness with different disability groups, and that clients must be screened for appropriateness before assignment to an accelerated diagnostic unit.

The primary goal of the research enterprise is the attainment of useful knowledge following a set of procedures known as the scientific method. The scientific method requires empirical data that can be evaluated objectively as a basis for addressing research questions. Two important aspects of the application of the scientific method to behavioral phenomena are the process of measurement and the use of tests of statistical significance. Both topics receive extended treatment in the following chapters. One nonempirical research method, the synthetic review, serves an important role in the integration of studies and the translation of results into implications for counseling practice. Although recent evaluations of the quality and usefulness of rehabilitation research have not been favorable, it is important to realize that the discipline is relatively young and that the subject matter is extremely complex.

chapter two
Statistical Methods

Statistics is the branch of mathematics that provides methods for analyzing numerical data. Statistical methods are usually divided into two sets: 1) descriptive statistics, which include methods of organizing, summarizing, and presenting data, and 2) inferential statistics, which include procedures for reaching tentative conclusions from data based on samples by translating the data into probability statements.

DESCRIPTIVE STATISTICS

Rehabilitation research is concerned with differences among individuals as well as average measures of behavior. Because variability is a universal phenomenon, the study of distributions, the comparisons among distributions, and the relationships among distributions are important topics. In this section basic concepts and tools for studying distributions are described. Readers interested in numerical illustrations and computational exercises should consult one of the several dozen introductory statistical textbooks that are available.

Distributions

A *variable* may be defined as a characteristic that assumes different values. For example, the variable sex assumes the values of male and female, and the variable IQ typically assumes values ranging from 50 to 150, although more extreme scores do occur. The total set of values or scores for any variable is called a *distribution*. All statistical methods require distributions of variables as their preliminary data. Accordingly, the first topic for consideration in descriptive statistics is distributions.

The simplest way of arranging and presenting data is in the form of a *listing*. As the name implies, a listing is a list of the scores for a group of subjects. The first step in organizing a list of scores is to place the scores in order from high to low; the resulting *ordered list* is much easier to examine and summarize. A great improvement in the presentation of a distribution of scores is achieved by constructing a *frequency distribution*. A frequency distribution is prepared by counting the number of times each value of the variable occurs. When the raw frequencies, or counts, are divided by the total number of cases, thus converting to percentages, a *relative frequency distribution* is the result.

Frequency distributions or relative frequency distributions can be presented as *histograms* (bar graphs) to make an easily comprehended graphic summary of the data. The histogram is constructed so that the height of the bar represents the proportion of the total frequency associated with each value of the distribution. Histograms and other modes of graphic presentation of data are extremely useful statistical techniques. A primary goal of descriptive statistical methods is clarity of presentation, and graphic techniques are economical devices for achieving this goal.

A distribution possesses three properties: 1) an average or typical value, 2) variability, and 3) shape or form. These characteristics are discussed in the following sections.

Central Tendency

Two statistics are commonly used to indicate the average score in a distribution. The *mean* is an arithmetical average and, as such, takes into account the absolute magnitude of each of the scores in the distribution. Thus, extremely high or low scores can unduly influence the mean and distort the interpretation of the statistic.

The *median* is the middle score in a distribution. It is calculated by listing the scores for a variable in order of their magnitude and then counting to the middle of the distribution. For example, the median of a distribution containing 30 scores lies between the fifteenth and sixteenth scores so that these two values are just averaged. The median is an appropriate index of central tendency when a distribution contains a few extreme scores because the median does not reflect the magnitude of scores.

Neither the mean nor the median is an adequate summary statistic by itself because neither reflects the variability or the shape of a distribution. It should be obvious that such attributes as sex, race, previous work, and employment can only be summarized by frequency distributions.

Dispersion

Two measures of dispersion are routinely used to describe the extent of variability in a distribution of scores: the range and the standard deviation. The roughest index of variability is the *range,* which is the difference between the highest score and the lowest score. It is calculated by subtracting the lowest score from the highest score. The range by itself is really not adequate for most statistical purposes and should be accompanied by the standard deviation.

The *standard deviation* is an abstract index that has a direct interpretation in terms of the normal distribution, which is discussed in the following section. The standard deviation is the square root of the *variance*, which is the most basic quantity in statistical analysis. The variance is the average squared deviation of a set of scores from the mean of the distribution. Because the standard deviation is virtually the universal index of variability in research, its use is described below.

Shape

The standard deviation is most easily interpreted when a normal distribution of scores can be assumed. The *normal distribution* is the often pictured bell-shaped curve in psychology textbooks. If a frequency distribution has one high point (unimodal) and is fairly symmetrical about that central point, then it is reasonable to use the normal curve interpretation of the standard deviation. The standard deviation tells the percentages of scores that fall in different regions of the normal curve. Figure 1 illustrates that approximately 68% of the scores lie within plus and minus one standard deviation of the mean and that 95% lie within plus and minus two standard deviations. One half of the scores in a normal distribution fall within plus and minus two-thirds of one standard deviation. Any introductory statistics textbook contains a table of the normal curve, which gives the proportion of scores falling between any two points that are measured in standard deviation units.

The preceding paragraph may give the impression that the normal curve was invented to aid in the interpretation of the standard deviation. That is not true. The normal curve is a theoretical relative frequency distribution and, while many physical and psychological traits (e.g., height and intelligence) tend to be normally distributed, no measurable characteristic follows exactly the normal curve. In other words, the normal distribution is not a fact of nature, but rather, it is an idealized mathematical distribution.

However, the normal distribution is at the foundation of theoretical statistics. Almost all tests of statistical significance are normal theory tests. The *assumption* of normally distributed variables is almost universal in applied statistics. Fortunately, most normal theory statistical tests are *robust* under most conditions, i.e., they are not severely influenced by violation of the normality assumption and other assumptions. These topics are discussed further in the section on inferential statistics; they

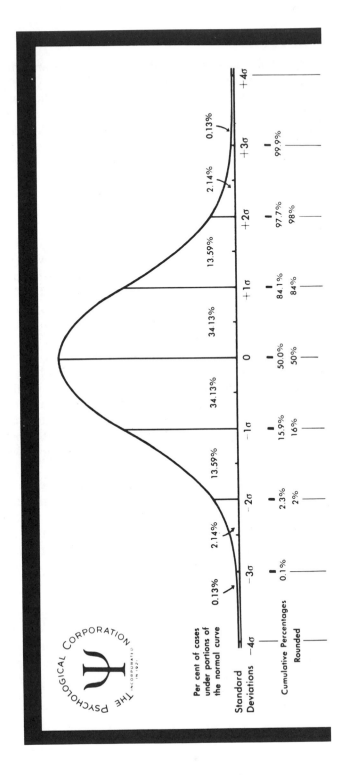

Per cent of cases under portions of the normal curve

0.13% 2.14% 13.59% 34.13% 34.13% 13.59% 2.14% 0.13%

Standard Deviations
−4σ −3σ −2σ −1σ 0 +1σ +2σ +3σ +4σ

Cumulative Percentages
0.1% 2.3% 15.9% 50.0% 84.1% 97.7% 99.9%

Rounded
2% 16% 50% 84% 98%

THE PSYCHOLOGICAL CORPORATION
INCORPORATED IN 1921

18

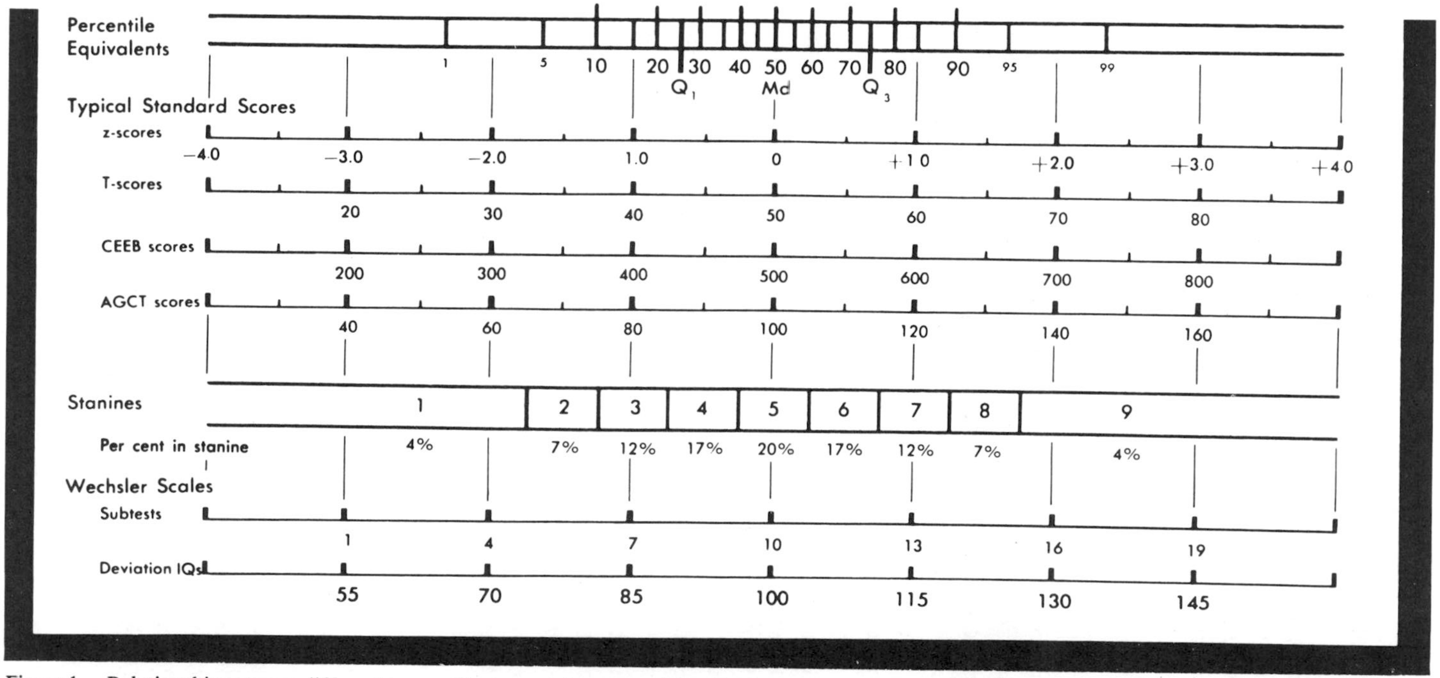
Percentile Equivalents
1
5
10
20
30
40
50
60
70
80
90
95
99
Q1
Md
Q3
Typical Standard Scores
z-scores
−4.0
−3.0
−2.0
1.0
0
+1.0
+2.0
+3.0
+4.0
T-scores
20
30
40
50
60
70
80
CEEB scores
200
300
400
500
600
700
800
AGCT scores
40
60
80
100
120
140
160
Stanines
1
2
3
4
5
6
7
8
9
Per cent in stanine
4%
7%
12%
17%
20%
17%
12%
7%
4%
Wechsler Scales
Subtests
1
4
7
10
13
16
19
Deviation IQs
55
70
85
100
115
130
145

Figure 1. Relationships among different types of test scores in a normal distribution. From Test Service Bulletin No. 48, 1955. Reproduced by permission of the Psychological Corporation.

were briefly mentioned here to stress the importance of the normal distribution.

While distributions can take almost any shape, in practice they are almost always unimodal, and flat (or rectangular) at worst. The most common departure from the normal curve is *skewness*. A skewed distribution is asymmetrical, with one tail truncated. The shape of a distribution may be a useful indicator of some characteristic of the trait measured in the subject sample and can be easily summarized in a histogram.

Correlation

The relationship between two variables is reflected in the degree to which they are correlated. Correlation literally means co-relation or co-variability. Thus, correlation indicates the extent to which persons are ordered in the same way on two different measures. If those persons who score high on one variable also score high on the other variable and the low-scoring persons are likewise consistent, then the two variables would be positively correlated.

The most direct assessment of the correlation between two variables is provided by a *scatterplot*. A scatterplot (or scattergram) is constructed by locating each subject in two-dimensional space using his/her pair of scores on the two variables under consideration. If the set of points tend to fall in a systematic pattern as described above, i.e., high scores on the two variables are associated, as are low scores, then a relationship is present. The information contained in a scatterplot can be quantified in an index that was devised by a statistician, Karl Pearson, some 75 years ago.

The *product-moment correlation coefficient* is a statistic that can take values between + 1.00 and − 1.00. A coefficient of + 1.00 indicates a perfect positive relationship between two variables; a coefficient of − 1.00 indicates a perfect negative relationship. A coefficient of 0.00 indicates no relationship between the two variables. A correlation of + 0.50 summarizes a relationship of exactly the same magnitude as a coefficient of − 0.50; the only difference is the direction of the relationship. If high scores on one variable tend to go with low scores on another variable and vice versa, the relationship is negative.

How is a correlation coefficient of 0.50 (or 0.62 or any other value) interpreted? What does a correlation of 0.50 say about the size of the relationship between two variables? The square of the correlation coefficient is the *coefficient of determination,* and it is the proportion of variance that the two variables have in common. Thus, the correlation of 0.50 indicates that 25% of the variability, or differences among individuals, on one variable is shared with, or overlaps, the variance of the other variable.

Table 2.   Other measures of association

Statistic	Application of statistic
1. Rank order correlation coefficient	A sample of subjects is ranked from high to low on two variables.
2. Point biserial correlation coefficient	A sample of subjects is measured on one continuous variable and one dichotomous variable (e.g., age and sex).
3. Biserial correlation coefficient	A sample of subjects is measured on two continuous variables, one of which is arbitrarily dichotomized (e.g., scores are divided into high and low).
4. Phi coefficient	A sample of subjects is measured on two dichotomous variables (e.g., sex and political affiliation).
5. Tetrachoric correlation coefficient	A sample of subjects is measured on two continuous variables, both of which are arbitrarily dichotomized.
6. Contingency coefficient	A sample of subjects is measured on two categorical variables (e.g., political affiliation and marital status).
7. Correlation ratio	Appropriate when the relationship between two variables is not linear.
8. Coefficient of concordance	A generalized rank order correlation coefficient, e.g., a sample of subjects is ranked by four judges.

One important qualification should be noted; the correlation coefficient is an index of *linear* relationship, i.e., the points in the scatterplot tend to follow a straight line.

Many important data that are collected in rehabilitation research are not appropriately analyzed using the standard correlation coefficient. There are several other measures of association that may be used to quantify the relationships between variables. Eight fairly common procedures are briefly described in Table 2. However, relationships among categorical variables, such as sex, race, previous work, and employment, may not be accurately summarized by a single index. The *contingency table,* which is a form of the scatterplot, is a useful technique for examining and portraying relationships between categorical variables. In fact, the entire statistical presentation in the article on the psychiatric work therapy program by Barbee et al. (1969) that was summarized on pages 1 and 2 of this book is contained in four 2×2 contingency tables! Readers are referred to the original article for examples of contingency tables.

It should be clear that the correlation coefficient can only serve to quantify, or to reduce to a statistical index, the relationships that exist among variables. The correlation coefficient does not tell the reader whether the relationship is strong enough to be useful. The ultimate interpretation of the coefficient depends upon the proposed application. If the purpose of a research study is to confirm a theory, then a correlation in the predicted direction that is *statistically significant,* i.e., greatly exceeds random chance expectation, is sufficient. On the other hand, if the correlation is to be used as a basis for selecting clients for an expensive, long-term rehabilitation program (predictor), then the correlation would have to be of substantial magnitude. The topics of statistical versus practical significance and the use of prediction data in rehabilitation programs are discussed below and in Chapter 6.

INFERENTIAL STATISTICS

Inferential statistical methods consist of a family of techniques for translating empirical data into probability statements that may be used as a basis for reaching decisions about research hypotheses. *Statistical significance tests* associate a probability value with a set of observations made in conjunction with a research investigation. Because a common procedure underlies all statistical tests, it is only necessary for the research consumer to understand the standard model. Accordingly, the major purposes of this section are: 1) to introduce the concept of probability distributions, 2) to overview the logic of statistical hypothesis testing, and 3) to outline the fundamental normal theory test of significance (analysis of variance). The focus of the presentation is on conceptual understanding; again, the reader is referred to an elementary statistics textbook for computational details.

Why are inferential statistical methods necessary? Cannot the researcher or the research consumer simply examine the descriptive statistics (e.g., means, frequency distributions, and scatterplots) that portray the results of an investigation? How does the concept of probability (uncertainty) contribute to the application of the scientific method? Two nonpsychological examples are presented below in order to answer these questions via concrete illustrations.

Probability Theory

All tests of statistical significance are based on theoretical relative frequency distributions, which relate outcome values with probabilities of occurrence. Probability theory had its origins in the practical business of

Table 3.   Probability distribution for the birthday problem[a]

Number of people in the group	Probability of at least two with the same birthday	Approximate odds for a fair bet
5	0.027	
10	0.117	
15	0.253	
20	0.411	70:100
21	0.444	80:100
22	0.476	91:100
23	0.507	103:100
24	0.538	117:100
25	0.569	132:100
30	0.706	242:100
40	0.891	819:100
50	0.970	33:1
60	0.994	169:1
70		1,200:1
80		12,000:1
90		160,000:1
100		3,300,000:1
125		31,000,000,000:1
150		4,500,000,000,000,000:1

[a]John G. Kemeny, J. Laurie Snell, and Gerald L. Thompson, *Introduction to Finite Mathematics,* © 1957, p. 125. Reprinted by permission of Prentice-Hall, Inc., Englewood Cliffs, New Jersey.

games of chance in the seventeenth century. It was sometime later that probability became a subject for scientific study, and eventually, it became the basis for an important branch of applied mathematical science: statistics. The first example that is outlined is the now classic matching birthdays problem.

The Birthday Problem   The birthday problem illustrates the point that intuition does not always provide a reliable analysis of judgmental situations and that probabilistic reasoning can correct intuitive error. The question may be posed: What is the probability that *at least* 2 persons in an unselected group of 50 persons (e.g., shoppers in a supermarket or citizens at a hearing) have exactly the same birthday (i.e., the same day and month of the year)? Or, asking the same question in a slightly different form: How large should the group of persons be in order to make the bet a fair one? Responding to the second question, few people would be willing to bet even money unless there were at least 100 persons in the group. The actual probability figures are presented in Table 3. With a group of 50 persons, the probability of 2 or more persons having the same birthdays is 0.97 (i.e., if the experiment were conducted several thousand times, approximately 97% of the independent samples of 50 persons would contain 2 or more persons with the same birthday). A fair bet situation would exist when the group contained 22 or 23 persons!

Probability theory clearly provides answers to the birthday problem that contradict human intuition. The interested reader is referred to Kemeny, Snell, and Thompson (1957, pp. 124–126) for the formulas and reasoning used to generate the statistics in Table 3.

The Binomial Distribution   The second example of the application of probability theory relies on the popular random device of coin tossing, e.g., the receiving football team is traditionally decided by a flip of the coin immediately preceding the kickoff.

Suppose that a football official of questionable reputation approaches the coach of a college team and claims to be able to influence the outcome of the coin toss. Assume further that the coach is in the middle of his third losing season in as many years and that his contract expires at the end of the current year. However, the coach is somewhat skeptical about the official's claim and he calls the college's statistics department for assistance. The chairman of the department, who is a rabid football fan, agrees to conduct an experimental test to ascertain whether or not the official can, in fact, influence the outcome of the coin toss.

The statistician begins by assuming that the official's claim is unsupportable (the *null hypothesis*). He obtains 100 half dollars from the local bank and meets the official at the football field at 6:00 A.M. the next day. The experimental procedure requires that the official flip each half dollar above head height and let it fall freely to the ground. The statistician instructs the official to produce either a head or a tail before each flip (trial). After each of the 100 trials the statistician records the result as either successful or unsuccessful. After the experiment, the statistician returns to his office to evaluate the data so that he can reach a conclusion regarding the hypothesis and can inform the coach of the results of the experiment.

The official was successful on 66 of the 100 trials. The question that the statistician must address is: Does this result indicate a true ability to influence the outcome of a coin toss, or was the official just lucky in this particular series of 100 tosses? If the experiment were repeated again the next morning would the official do as well, or would he perform around chance level (50 successful outcomes)? Statistical methods enable the statistician to answer these questions in probabilistic terms.

When a *binary* (two possible outcomes) trial is repeated two or more times, and the trials are independent of each other, a *binomial* distribution is generated. When the number of trials is large, the binomial distribution coincides with the normal distribution. Therefore, the statistician uses the normal probability distribution to evaluate the coin tossing experiment. (The statistical procedures are explained in most elementary statistics texts.) Because the probability of the official making 66 successful tosses *purely by chance* is so small (less than one in a thousand), the null hypothesis is rejected, and the statistician immediately calls the coach to tell him the good news and begins placing his bets for the big game on Saturday.

It should be noted that the conclusion is limited to the *statistical* significance of the official's performance (probably a nonchance occurrence); the question of *practical* significance or applicability of the official's ability (the best estimate is that he can determine the outcome of a coin toss approximately two-thirds of the time) must be evaluated in a different context, i.e., the relative importance of winning the right to receive the football first in the game. The topic of statistical versus practical significance of research results is discussed in a later section.

Sampling and Hypothesis Testing

It was concluded that the outcome of the coin tossing experiment exceeded the outcome that would reasonably be expected to occur due to chance fluctuation about a mean of 50 successful trials. However, the result of 66 or more successes will occur approximately one time in one thousand when the null hypothesis is true if the experiment is conducted a large number of times. Therefore, the decision to reject the null hypothesis will be erroneous about 0.1% of the time in the long run. This is referred to as a *type one error* in statistical decision making. By definition, a type one error occurs when a true null hypothesis is rejected. The other kind of error, a *type two error,* occurs when a false null hypothesis is not rejected.

Decision errors occur because inferential statistical methods are applied to samples of data, while the conclusions are *generalized* to the *populations* from which the samples are drawn. Sampling error refers to any discrepancy between the unknown population characteristics *(parameters)* and the measured sample characteristics *(statistics)*. For example, the coin tossing experiment was based on a sample of 100 tosses that was assumed to be representative of the official's coin tossing ability (a hypothetical population that can be thought of as the proportion of successes in one million billion tosses!). The proportion of 0.66 is the statistic that was used to estimate the unknown population parameter, the official's true ability. The point is that whenever a subset of the population of interest is used in a research study, and the purpose of the research is to *infer* something about the population from the sample, some amount of error will be present in the conclusions. Statistical methods allow us to estimate the probabilities and the sizes of errors.

It should be reasonable to assume that at this point the reader can appreciate the importance of statistical significance tests, i.e., the necessity of converting data based on samples into probabilities that can be used to make tentative decisions about hypothesized relationships. Surprisingly, not all social scientists appreciate the role of statistical significance tests in empirical research, and some (a small minority) completely misunderstand the purpose of significance tests. In the preface to the *Handbook for the Strong Vocational Interest Blank,* Campbell (1971, Stanford University Press, pp. ix–x) illustrates this confused point of view:

> A word on statistics. Several thousand statistics are reported in this *Handbook,* mainly means, standard deviations, and correlations. I believe the information has been organized and presented in meaningful ways — showing trends, documenting differences, identifying themes — and I take considerable pride that this has been done without a single test of statistical significance. As I am bound to be faulted for this, I would like to explain my feelings.
>
> I firmly believe that nothing in the history of scientific psychology has retarded progress as much as has the concept of statistical significance. This concept was originally developed to relieve the investigator of deciding what was important and — regrettably — a good many investigators have been willing to have that power taken out of their hands. Indeed, many feel a great deal of discomfort when deprived of the security of a significant, socially acceptable *t*-test.
>
> I have two quarrels with this: first, any researcher who does not know his area well enough to know intuitively — with an intuition that replicates — when he has found a meaningful result can hardly be expected to advance the edge of truth very much. Second, factors whose influence can be detected only when compared with chance are so trivial that they might as well be ignored. Psychological findings established by "different from chance" methods are so chaotic that if laid end to end, they would make a pretty good table of random numbers.
>
> So...no tests of significance in this *Handbook.* Rather the emphasis is on magnitude and replicability of differences, and consistency of trends.

Two points in Campbell's remarks deserve emphasis. First, the birthday problem clearly demonstrates the deficiencies of human intuition — even "an intuition that replicates"! Second, the value of the statistical significance test is that it helps the researcher identify potentially nonchance results. Statistical significance does *not* guarantee meaningfulness (see the last paragraph of the football example), but it does locate meaningless chance results.

In its simplest and most ideal form, an investigation begins with the careful definition of the population of concern. Since most populations are much too large to be studied in their entirety, a representative subset must be selected. The only procedure that ensures representativeness is some type of *random selection,* e.g., select every tenth client admitted during a 3-month period. If the investigation entails the evaluation of a new service procedure, then clients should be *randomly assigned* to the experimental procedure and to the standard service program (control group) by tossing a coin for each successive pair of clients who are selected into the research sample. After the evaluation is completed, inferential statistical methods are used to translate the sample data into statements of probable effectiveness of the new service procedure. The conclusions based on the study of the sample are generalized to the population of clients who are potential candidates for the new program. In the following sections, the prototypical statistical technique (analysis of variance) is used to evaluate the effects of an easily overlooked treatment variable.

MODE OF ADDRESS: AN EXPERIMENT

In medical and paramedical fields, the professional-patient relationship has traditionally been conducted on a formal basis. The patient almost always addresses the practitioner by title and last name, and the practitioner usually addresses the patient in a similar manner. It has been suggested that, in those activities that necessitate a cooperative effort by the practitioner and the patient, maximum progress might better be achieved if the formal tradition were relaxed. Physical and occupational therapy are examples of rehabilitation services that require that the practitioner and the patient work together. Altering the prevailing mode of address may be the easiest way to restructure the practitioner-patient relationship from its traditional expert-dominated form to a cooperative endeavor in which responsibility for recovery is shared equally by both persons. The study outlined below was designed to test one aspect of this hypothesis.

In addition to the standard *reciprocal formal* mode of address, two other less common forms of address may be postulated: the *nonreciprocal* mode, in which the practitioner is addressed formally but addresses the patient by first name, and the *reciprocal informal* mode, in which the practitioner and the patient address each other by first name. These three patterns of address, reciprocal formal, nonreciprocal, and reciprocal informal, constitute the three categories of the experimental *(independent)*

'Adapted from Bolton, B., and Sommer, P., Mode of address and patient satisfaction in rehabilitation: An experimental study. *Journal of Health and Social Behavior,* 1970, *11,* 215–219. The original design, data, and results have been modified for illustrative purposes.

Table 4.   One-way analysis of variance of scores on the participation rating scale

Scores

	Reciprocal formal	Nonreciprocal	Reciprocal informal
	4	6	8
	5	7	9
	7	7	9
	8	8	10
	8	9	10
	8	10	13
	10	10	13
	10	11	16
Mean:	7.5	8.5	11.0

ANOVA Summary Table[a]

Source of variance	Sum of squares	Degrees of freedom	Mean square	F ratio	Probability
Treatment	52.0	2	26.0	5.15	$< .05$
Error	106.0	21	5.05		
Total	158.0	23			

[a]The proportion of variance due to treatments is estimated to be 26%; calculated using a formula presented in Hays (1963, p. 407).

variable. The reciprocal formal treatment may be considered to be a control since it is the conventional pattern of address.

The experiment was conducted in a private, comprehensive rehabilitation hospital for disabled persons. The research sample consisted of 24 recently admitted patients who were assigned to physical and occupational therapy programs. The 24 subjects were *randomly assigned* to the three mode-of-address conditions in blocks of three so that each treatment group contained eight subjects. Because the treatment conditions were applied by physical and occupational therapists, it was also necessary to randomly assign the therapists to the three experimental conditions.

The experiment was carried out over an 8-week period. To assess the effects of the three mode-of-address conditions on the perceived participation of the subjects, a 20-item Participation Rating Scale was developed. Each item of the scale requires a yes/no response and the 20 items are added together to produce a total score. During the eighth week of the study, each subject completed the Participation Rating Scale. Scores on the scale constituted the *dependent* variable of the investigation. The scores for the 24 subjects are listed in Table 4. The question that now must be addressed is: Do the differences among the three sample means reflect real effects of the treatment conditions, or are they due to sampling fluctuation? In other words, would another study of 24 subjects conducted in exactly the same way produce similar results? To answer this question the researcher must turn to inferential statistical procedures.

Analysis of Variance

The appropriate statistical analysis for the data in Table 4 is the one-way analysis of variance (ANOVA). This procedure partitions the variability among the 24 subjects into two major components: 1) systematic variance, and 2) error variance. (The systematic variance may be subdivided into components attributable to several identifiable sources, depending on the complexity of the research design; a two-factor design is outlined in the next section.) The structural model that is the basis for the partitioning of variability in the one-way ANOVA is:

$$\text{Observed Score} = \text{Grand Mean} + \text{Treatment Effect} + \text{Error}$$

Moving the grand mean to the left side of the structural equation makes the calculation of the variance estimates (mean squares) a straightforward task:

$$\text{Observed Score} - \text{Grand Mean} = \text{Treatment Effect} + \text{Error}$$

This equation states that the variability of the observed scores about the grand mean is separated into two parts: variance due to the experimental conditions and error variance. The important point to be made is that the structural model dictates the assumed composition of the dependent variable. In fact, data can be analyzed into treatment variance and into error variance using the structural equation; interested readers are referred to the article by Bolton (1975a) for details. While the *structural assumption* is seldom explicitly stated as such in statistics textbooks, the validity of the conclusions reached from the data analysis are predicated upon it just as much as they are dependent on the distributional assumptions listed below.

The statistical significance test for the ANOVA involves the ratio of two independent variance estimates, one based on the treatment sum of squares and the other based on the error sum of squares. The necessary figures are presented in the ANOVA summary table in Table 4. The reader should note that the F ratio results from dividing 26.0 by 5.05. The F statistic of 5.15 is converted to a probability value using the appropriate theoretical distribution (which is the F distribution). The proper interpretation of the ANOVA is: The probability of the three sample means differing by as much as they do, if the null hypothesis is true, is less than 5 in

100 ($p < 0.05$). Therefore, it is reasonable to conclude that the population means probably are different, with patients under the reciprocal informal mode-of-address condition perceiving their participation as greatest.

This tentative conclusion is contingent on three assumptions:

1. The 24 subjects were *randomly assigned* to the three treatment groups.
2. The dependent variable (scores on the Participation Rating Scale) is *normally distributed* in each of the three treatment populations.
3. The variability of the scores on the dependent variable is the same *(homogeneous variances)* in each of the treatment populations.

The first assumption is absolutely essential to the validity of the statistical test. There is considerable evidence to indicate that most violations of the second and third assumptions have little influence on the validity of the test. (A fourth assumption, that the null hypothesis is true, is expected to be false.) In other words, the normal theory tests are not especially sensitive to violations of the assumptions about distributional properties and are thus *robust* in their application to research data.

The final statistic necessary in order to summarize the results of the mode-of-address experiment is that 26% of the total variability in scores is estimated to be attributable to the differential effects of the treatment conditions. The proportion of variance accounted for gives an index of the *size* of the effect, whereas the inferential statistical test only indicates the probability of a nonchance occurrence.

The Concept of Interaction

The mode-of-address experiment outlined above could be strengthened by adding a second independent variable to the investigation and, thus, possibly accounting for more of the total variability in participation scores. It would be reasonable to hypothesize that male and female patients might respond differently to the three conditions. The experimental design that encompasses the two independent variables simultaneously begins with the random assignment of 12 male patients and 12 female patients to the three mode-of-address conditions. Three hypotheses may be tested in the two-factor design:

1. The three mode-of-address conditions do not differentially affect perceived participation (sex is disregarded).
2. Male and female patients do not respond differently on the Participation Rating Scale (regardless of mode-of-address conditions).
3. The six combinations of sex and mode-of-address conditions do not result in different levels of perceived participation.

Table 5.   Two-way analysis of variance of scores on the participation rating scale

Scores[a]

	Reciprocal formal	Nonreciprocal	Reciprocal informal
Male	4 5 7 8	9 10 10 11	8 9 10 13
Female	8 8 10 10	6 7 7 8	9 10 13 16

Cell Means

	Reciprocal formal	Nonreciprocal	Reciprocal informal	
Male	6.0	10.0	10.0	8.67
Female	9.0	7.0	12.0	9.33
	7.5	8.5	11.0	9.00

ANOVA Summary Table[b]

Source of variance	Sum of squares	Degrees of freedom	Mean square	F ratio	Probability
Treatment	52.00	2	26.00	7.56	< .01
Sex	2.67	1	2.56	0.78	N.S.
Interaction	41.33	2	20.67	6.01	< .01
Error	62.00	18	3.44		
Total	158.00	23			

[a]The 24 scores in Table 4 have been rearranged by separating the males and females under each treatment condition.

[b]The proportion of variance due to treatment is estimated to be 27%, and the variance due to the combination (interaction) of treatments and sex is estimated to be 21%; calculated using formulas presented in Hays (1963, p. 407).

The hypotheses, stated in null form (no difference), refer to population mean values. If the experiment were carried out as outlined above, the Participation Rating Scale scores in Table 5 would represent a possible outcome. (The reader should note that the 24 scores in Table 5 are simply rearranged from Table 4 by separating the male and female patients under each mode-of-address condition.)

As would be expected, the treatment means for the three mode-of-address conditions are exactly the same as in Table 4. The far right hand column indicates that the female patients responded slightly more favorably in perceived participation than did the male patients. With respect to the third hypothesis, the data suggest a possible interaction effect between mode of address and sex. An examination of the six cell means indicates that the males responded least favorably to the reciprocal formal condition, while the females responded least favorably to the nonreciprocal condition. Furthermore, the females responded most favorably to the reciprocal informal mode-of-address condition. It appears that sex may moderate the relationship between mode of address and perceived participation. Are the differences among these sample means due to sampling error, or do they reflect real differences among the population means? This is, of course, the question of statistical significance.

The structural model for the two-way ANOVA design is:

$$\begin{matrix} \text{Observed} \\ \text{Score} \end{matrix} = \begin{matrix} \text{Grand} \\ \text{Mean} \end{matrix} + \begin{matrix} \text{Treatment} \\ \text{Effect} \end{matrix} + \begin{matrix} \text{Sex} \\ \text{Effect} \end{matrix} + \begin{matrix} \text{Interaction} \\ \text{Effect} \end{matrix} + \text{Error}$$

Mean squares and F ratios are calculated to test each of the three hypotheses. The necessary data are presented in the ANOVA summary table in Table 5. (The error mean square is used to calculate each of the F ratios.) The final column on the right indicates that both the mode-of-address effects and the interaction effects are statistically significant beyond the 0.01 level. The sex difference was not significant (N.S.). Furthermore, the magnitudes of the two significant effects are summarized as follows: 27% of the total variance in perceived participation is estimated to be due to differential effects of the mode-of-address conditions, and an additional 21% of the variance is estimated to be accounted for by the unique combination (interaction) of sex and mode of address.

Other Statistical Significance Tests

The ANOVA tests of significance that were considered in detail in the previous sections are typical of most statistical tests of significance in that they 1) establish the probability of a given result, and 2) estimate the proportion of total variability in the dependent variable, which is due to various sources. Table 6 presents a brief summary of 12 of the more common statistical significance tests. The first seven are normal theory or parametric tests, while the last five are nonparametric or distribution-free tests. Several are closely related; for example, the Student's t test is just a special case of the one-way ANOVA. It is not necessary for the research consumer to understand the statistical procedures underlying each of the various tests because the procedures are all based on the same logical foundation of sampling theory and hypothesis testing.

Table 6.   Summary of common statistical significance tests

Statistical procedure	Application of procedure
1. Critical ratio	Comparing two samples
2. Student's *t* test	Comparing two samples
3. Matched *t* test	Comparing two samples when subjects are paired
4. Simple ANOVA	Comparing two or more samples
5. Randomized blocks ANOVA	Comparing two or more samples when subjects are matched
6. Factorial ANOVA	Comparing two or more samples using two or more independent variables simultaneously
7. Repeated measures ANOVA	Assessing changes in subjects at two or more points in time
8. Chi square	Assessing the relationship between two variables of classification in a contingency table
9. Median test	Comparing two or more samples
10. Mann Whitney U test	Comparing two samples
11. Wilcoxon test	Comparing two samples when subjects are paired
12. Kruskal-Wallis H test	Comparing two or more samples

Statistical Versus Practical Significance

Statistical significance refers to the situation where the outcome of an investigation is found to be extremely improbable if the null hypothesis is true; practical significance refers to the actual magnitude of the effect. The two are related in the following way: as the sample size increases, the magnitude of the effect required for statistical significance at a given level decreases. This relationship can be illustrated for the correlation coefficient. With a sample of 20 subjects, a correlation of 0.44 is required for significance at the 0.05 level, while a correlation of 0.22 is significant at the 0.05 level when the sample size is increased to 80 subjects. In general, studies that are based on large samples produce many statistically significant results that may not be very meaningful in terms of practical application.

A good example of the large sample study is the investigation reported by Tinsley and Gaughen (1975). Because their research sample included almost 4,000 former rehabilitation clients, they established the following guidelines for the interpretation of statistically significant results:

Because of the large sample of subjects under study, numerically inconsequential differences having no practical significance may achieve statistical significance. This problem was dealt with in two ways. First, the .01 level of significance was chosen as the critical probability level. Second, omega-squared or Goodman and Kruskal's index of symmetrical predictive association was computed, as appropriate, when statistically significant differences were observed. These indexes provide an indication of the strength of association between the independent variable (group membership) and the dependent variable (work adjustment). (See Hays 1963, pp. 381–384 and 604–606 for a more detailed discussion of these indexes.) Values of .05 or less were interpreted as indicating that the statistically significant difference was of little practical significance. (p. 149)

The other side of the coin is, of course, the research investigation that involves a very small subject sample. Interestingly, a small sample may confer an advantage because differences (or correlations) of greater magnitude are required to achieve statistical significance. Quoting two conclusions from Bakan's (1966) now-classic article:

> Thus, one can be more confident with a small n than a large n. . . . Indeed, rejecting the null hypothesis with a small n is indicative of a strong deviation from null in the population, the mathematics of the test of significance having already taken into account the smallness of the sample. (pp. 429 & 430)

In conclusion, regardless of sample size, the research consumer should always examine the actual differences between means, or should obtain some other indication of the magnitude of the effect (e.g., proportion of variance accounted for by the independent variables) in addition to the traditional index of statistical significance.

The final topic of the chapter is devoted to a clarification of the term *error variance*. In Chapter 3 the total variance for a sample of subjects on a psychological measure is partitioned into true variance and error variance. This (psychometric) error variance component represents the errors of measurement, or *unreliability,* of the instrument. Earlier in this chapter, the basic ANOVA model was described as partitioning the total variability of observed scores into systematic variance and error variance. This (statistical) error variance is comprised of all differences among subjects that cannot be associated with a specific source. Psychometric error variance is distinguished from statistical error variance in that the former is assessed directly using various reliability techniques, while the latter is essentially a "leftover." In most statistical analyses the structural equation could be elaborated conceptually by adding one additional component:

$$\frac{\text{Statistical}}{\text{Error Variance}} = \frac{\text{Unaccounted for}}{\text{Individual Differences}} + \frac{\text{Psychometric}}{\text{Error Variance}}$$

Thus, psychometric error variance (unreliability) is the lower limit for statistical error variance; i.e., if all reliable individual differences were accounted for by the design, statistical error variance would be equivalent to the unreliability of the instrument of measurement for the dependent variable.

Another way of viewing this relationship between the reliability of the dependent variable and the statistical error variance is as follows: the complexity or sophistication of statistical methodology should not exceed the precision (or reliability) of psychometric instruments. This view is well-stated by Lawshe (1969):

> ...very often, the statistical nicety of present methods suggests or implies an order of precision which is not basically inherent in the data. Psychological measurements, at this point in time, are quite unreliable; to suggest otherwise by using unwarranted degrees of statistical precision is for the psychologist to delude others, and perhaps to delude himself. (pp. 122–123)

Not surprisingly, statisticians often see things differently than psychologists do, as the following statement by Wallis (1949, p. 483), quoted in Wainer (1978), indicates:

> So-called "high-powered," "refined," or "elaborate" statistical techniques are generally called for when the data are crude and inadequate — exactly the opposite, if I may be permitted an *obiter dictum,* of what crude and inadequate statisticians usually think. (p. 272)

SUMMARY

Descriptive statistical methods are used to organize, to summarize, and to present data. All statistical methods begin with distributions of variables as their preliminary data. Two statistics are commonly used to indicate the average score in a distribution: the mean, which is the arithmetical average, and the median, which is the middle score. Two measures of dispersion are routinely used to describe the extent of variability in a distribution of scores: the range, which is the difference between the highest and lowest scores, and the standard deviation, which is the square root of the average squared deviation of a set of scores from the mean. The bell-shaped normal distribution is a theoretical distribution that underlies almost all inferential statistical procedures.

The product-moment correlation coefficient is an index of the linear relationship between two variables. The square of the correlation coefficient is the coefficient of determination, and it indicates the proportion of variance that two variables have in common. The interpretation of a correlation coefficient depends upon the proposed application. The contingency table, which is a form of scatterplot, is a useful alternative method for organizing and summarizing categorical data.

All tests of statistical significance are based on theoretical relative frequency distributions, which relate outcome values with probabilities of occurrence. When testing statistical hypotheses, two types of errors may occur: a true null hypothesis may be rejected, or a false null hypothesis may not be rejected. Decision errors occur because inferential statistical methods are applied to samples of data, while the conclusions are generalized to the populations that the samples represent. Random selection and random assignment are the foundations of statistical hypothesis testing.

Statistical methods partition data into two major components: systematic variance and error variance. The structural equation, which reflects the sources of variance and control in the research design, determines exactly how each observation is partitioned. The statistical test of significance involves a comparison of two independent variance estimates. Normal theory tests are generally robust under violations of the two distributional assumptions (normal distributions and homogeneous variances).

Two independent variables are said to interact when the relationship between one of them and the dependent variable is contingent on knowing the level of the second independent variable. Most statistical tests accomplish two objectives: 1) they establish the probability of a given result assuming the null hypothesis is true, and 2) they estimate the proportion of the total variance due to various sources. These two objectives assess the statistical significance and the potential practical significance of research results, respectively. Error variance in the structural equation is comprised of two components: unaccounted for individual differences and psychometric error variance (or unreliability of the dependent variable measure).

chapter three
Fundamentals of Measurement

The scientific method requires that observable phenomena be reduced to empirical data. The measurement process is contained in the set of procedures that translate behavioral events into numerical form. The simplest type of quantification involves assigning numbers to the different subclasses of an attribute, e.g., males receive a score of one and females receive a score of two. More sophisticated measurement procedures utilize the properties of the numerical scale, i.e., order and magnitude. In this chapter, four levels of measurement are described, the development of three measuring instruments is outlined, the important characteristics of reliability and validity are defined and illustrated, and the major sources of information about tests and measures are described.

PURPOSE OF MEASUREMENT

A standard definition of measurement is as follows: Measurement is the assignment of numbers to objects or events according to rules. The rules prescribe the procedures that are followed in assigning numbers to the relevant objects or events. In fact, it can be argued that the procedures or *operations* of measurement define the construct being measured. Thus, intelligence might be defined as the trait that the intelligence test measures. When carried to its logical extreme, *operationalism* prevents the researcher from generalizing beyond the particular instruments of measurement that are employed in any investigation.

A measurement procedure that follows a carefully defined set of rules and that leads to similar results on different occasions under different conditions is said to be *standardized*. Test manuals spell out in detail the steps to be followed in administering and scoring intelligence and aptitude tests to ensure standardization of procedure. Standardization of procedure is the first step toward objectivity in scientific research.

As in the first two chapters, it is again important to acknowledge a dissenting point of view. A number of reputable, scientifically oriented psychologists would take vigorous exception to the first two sentences of this chapter. Wright (1972) has made a particularly insightful critique of extreme operationalism:

> The veritable idolization of quantification in the scientific enterprise has led to a disdain for qualitative description of experience and behavior. Not only is measurement generally seen as necessary in any scientific investigation, but not infrequently it also is regarded as a sufficient condition.
> ...by virtually revering quantification, an enormous scope of psychologically meaningful problems become eclipsed from view, either because they are not felt to be researchable in these terms, or because they become distorted by being shaped to fit the requirements of measurement, or because the quantitative treatment of the data so saps the time and energy of the investigator that he has no reserve left for delving into the fullness of qualitative analysis. To this we can add that even when conceptualization is sufficiently advanced for meaningful quantification, an important place will remain for qualitative descriptions of experience and behavior. Although measurement contributes significantly to scientific advance, it is not fundamental to all scientific advance. (pp. 41–42)

Readers interested in an extended discussion of the dangers of premature quantification and a detailed example of research based on the careful description of problems and concepts in rehabilitation psychology are referred to the classic monograph by Dembo et al. (1956/1975).

MEASUREMENT SCALES

Four levels of measurement can be distinguished: nominal, ordinal, interval, and ratio. Each of these types of measurement is described and illustrated in this section.

Nominal Scale

The weakest level of measurement exists when numbers are used to classify objects, persons, or characteristics. For example, the state/federal rehabilitation program disability coding system constitutes a nominal scale. Clients are classified according to their major disabilities, such as congenital heart disease (640), diabetes (614), and alcoholism (520). The assignment of numbers to the disabling conditions is arbitrary, but clients with different disabilities receive different numerical labels. Nominal data take the form of frequency counts and are not amenable to very powerful statistical analyses.

Ordinal Scale

An ordinal scale exists when the categories of a nominal scale can be ranked from most to least on some dimension. Or, alternatively, a sample of subjects can be rank ordered from most to least. For example, 20 clients could be ranked from most to least difficult in terms of services required or in terms of probability of successful outcome. The numbers assigned to persons or categories that are ranked do *not* reflect magnitude, but only relative position.

Interval Scale

When the distances between any two numbers on a scale are of known size, and the scale points are ordered, an interval scale is achieved. Thus, an interval scale requires a unit of measurement. However, neither the unit of measurement nor the scale points possess absolute magnitude. Intelligence and aptitude tests and some rating scales approach an interval scale of measurement, i.e., the distance between the scores of 47 and 42 is approximately the same as the distance between the scores of 35 and 30. Almost all standard statistical procedures are applicable to interval scale data.

Ratio Scale

A scale that possesses all of the characteristics of an interval scale and, in addition, has a true zero point as its origin is a ratio scale. Few measurement procedures in the social and behavioral sciences yield ratio scales, e.g., zero intelligence cannot be meaningfully defined. Measurement procedures in the social sciences usually assume an arbitrary anchor point, which is generally the mean. Scale values (scores) are then described in terms of distance above or below the mean.

It should be apparent to the reader that the four levels of measurement constitute an ordinal scale with respect to their degree of usefulness. Whenever possible, most researchers assume that their instruments measure at the interval level and apply *parametric* statistical procedures to their data. In fact, most instruments in the social and behavioral sciences generate a scale of measurement that lies somewhere between the ordinal level and the interval level. This does not invalidate the results that are produced because parametric statistical tests are generally robust, i.e., they are insensitive to minor violations of assumptions, such as that of an equal-interval scale of measurement. Interested readers are referred to Hays (1963, pp. 73–76) for a concise discussion of this issue.

SCORES AND NORMS

Instruments of measurement are usually composed of items. An *item* is a simple stimulus, most often a written statement, to which the subject or observer (rater) responds using a predetermined set of alternatives. The items constitute a *sample* of stimuli chosen from a potentially larger number of stimuli that comprise the defined behavioral *domain* of concern, e.g., intelligence, neuroticism, motivation, manual dexterity, and attitudes toward disabled persons. Since the items are presumed to tap one domain, it would follow that the item responses should be added to provide a total score on the major dimension that underlies the domain. The total score is referred to as a *raw* score. For example, if an instrument consists of 20 true-false items, a total raw score could be calculated by adding one point for each true response. Thus, the possible range of raw scores on the instrument would be from 0 to 20 points. Or, alternatively, the 20 items might be divided into two sets of 10 items (which reflect two major underlying dimensions) and a raw score could be calculated for each of the 10-item sets.

Raw scores are seldom meaningful by themselves. Information regarding the performance of a defined sample of subjects is usually needed to interpret or to give meaning to raw scores. The reference group of subjects is called a *norm group* and the set of data that summarizes their performance constitutes the *norms* for the instrument. The norms are thus used to convert raw scores to relative scores, i.e., the scores are relative to the performance of a defined reference group. Several norm groups representing different backgrounds and demographic characteristics are preferable to one large, unselected group, e.g., male college students, army draftees, nurses, and high school teachers. Norms are usually presented as frequency distributions with *percentile* conversions in tabular form. A percentile score indicates the percentage of scores that are lower than any particular score, e.g., a raw score corresponding to a percentile score of 75 exceeds 75% of the scores in the norm group. A more detailed presentation of this topic is available in Bolton, Lawlis, and Brown (1976).

As suggested in a previous paragraph, instruments of measurement are of two general types: *single-score* and *multi-score*. An example of a single-score instrument is described in the next section. The Attitudes Towards Disabled Persons Scale yields a score that reflects the respondent's overall attitude toward disabled persons. In contrast, an instrument developed by Siller, Ferguson, Vann, and Holland (1967), known as the Disability Factor Scales, results in scores on eight components of attitudes toward the disabled, e.g., interaction strain, rejection of intimacy, and imputed functional limitations. Multi-score instruments are generally preferred, on the assumption that most behavioral domains are complex, i.e., human behavior is multiply determined. A statistical technique that is used to develop multi-score instruments is explained and illustrated in Chapters 5 and 7.

In the following sections, the construction and validation of three instruments that have proven useful in rehabilitation research are outlined. The first instrument that is described, the Attitudes Towards Disabled Persons Scale (ATDP), purports to measure just what its title suggests. An attitude is traditionally defined as a predisposition to respond, and thus the ATDP may assess an important antecedent of behavior toward disabled persons. The second instrument, the Scale of Employability, was developed to diagnose deficiencies in the work personality of rehabilitation clients and to assess behavioral change during the vocational adjustment process. The third instrument, the Haptic Intelligence Scale, is a performance IQ test that is used with blind clients. The three instruments illustrate a self-report inventory, an observer-rating scale, and an individually administered clinical test, in that order.

THE ATTITUDES TOWARDS DISABLED PERSONS SCALE

An extensive review of the literature, a summary of the construction of the instruments, and a review of validation studies are presented in the monograph by Yuker, Block, and Younng (1966). The Attitudes Towards Disabled Persons Scale (ATDP) was developed to measure *generalized* attitudes toward disabled persons. In other words, the instrument was devised to assess attitudes toward persons with all types of disabilities, such as blindness, facial disfigurement, and amputation. Two major purposes of the instrument were envisioned: 1) assessment of the attitudes of nondisabled persons toward various groups, and 2) indirect assessment of the motivation and the self-attitudes of disabled persons. The original ATDP contained 20 items and served as a pilot study for the construction of two 30-item scales, known as Form A and Form B. The procedures that were followed in constructing the three scales were similar. Form B is used for illustrative purposes in the following sections.

Item Selection

The first step in the development of the ATDP was a search of the literature to locate statements that describe disabled persons. An initial pool of 300 statements was reduced to 50 tentative items for a preliminary form of the scale by several psychologists using a general criterion of appropriate-

Table 7.   Selected items from the Attitudes Towards Disabled Persons Scale (Form B)[a]

4.	Disabled persons can have a normal social life.
6.	Disabled workers can be as successful as other workers.
8.	Most people feel uncomfortable when they associate with disabled people.
12.	Most disabled persons get married and have children.
17.	Most disabled people expect special treatment.
23.	Most disabled people prefer to work with other disabled people.
27.	It would be best if a disabled person would marry another disabled person.
29.	Disabled persons want sympathy more than other people.

[a]Reproduced by permission of Yuker, H. E., Block, H. R., and Younng, J. H. *The Measurement of Attitudes Towards Disabled Persons*. Albertson, New York: Human Resources Center, 1966.

ness. Each item was expressed as a statement with which the respondent might agree or disagree using a 6-point response format. The preliminary scales were administered to several classes of college students and an *item analysis* was conducted to select 30 items for the final form of the scale. (Item analysis procedures enable the researcher to select the best subset of items from a larger pool. The criterion of goodness of the items is the correlation with the total score. Thus, item analysis maximizes the *internal consistency* of the instrument.) Eight items from Form B of the ATDP are reproduced in Table 7.

Scoring the ATDP

The respondent chooses from six graded alternatives in order to express agreement or disagreement with each item of the ATDP. The six alternatives, with their associated scoring weights, are as follows:

+ 3   I agree very much.
+ 2   I agree pretty much.
+ 1   I agree a little.
− 1   I disagree a little.
− 2   I disagree pretty much.
− 3   I disagree very much.

To obtain a total score for the 30 items, the item scores for the negative statements must first be reversed, e.g., the positive scores to items 8, 17, 23, 27, and 29 are changed to negative and the negative scores are changed to positive. Then all positive scores reflect favorable attitudes toward disabled persons. The scores of the 30 items are then added algebraically (taking signs into account) to produce a total raw score that can range from − 90 to + 90. A constant of 90 is added to the total score to move the range to 0 to 180, eliminating negative scores.

But what does a raw score of 125 mean? Or, what is a score of 85? Do they reflect favorable or unfavorable attitudes toward disabled persons? It is necessary to refer to appropriate norms in order to interpret these scores. The monograph by Yuker et al. (1966) contains a table that converts raw scores to percentile equivalents for four norm groups: disabled and nondisabled males and females. For most instruments of measurement, scores acquire meaning by comparison to appropriate reference (norm) groups. However, a very literal interpretation of ATDP scores can be made using the average of the six response alternatives, e.g., an average item score of + 2 denotes that the respondent agrees pretty much with the 30 statements.

Unfortunately, describing the development of the ATDP does not provide the information needed to support the usefulness of the instrument for research purposes. How can we be sure that the ATDP measures attitudes toward disability? In other words, is the ATDP a *valid* instrument? Does the ATDP provide a *reliable* index of attitudes toward disabled persons (or whatever it measures)? If a person retakes the ATDP a second time after 1 week elapses, does he/she attain a score close to the original score? These very important questions are addressed later in this chapter.

THE SCALE OF EMPLOYABILITY

The construction and validation of the Chicago Jewish Vocational Service (CJVS) Scale of Employability is reported in detail in the monograph by Gellman, Stern, and Soloff (1963). The development of the instrument is summarized in this section and the validation studies are outlined later on in the chapter. The Scale of Employability (SE) was devised for a different purpose than the ATDP; the SE has direct applicability in rehabilitation service programs, especially the vocational adjustment workshop. The SE can serve two primary functions: 1) the assessment of client status as a *diagnostic* basis for program planning, and 2) the assessment of *change* during the rehabilitation program via repeated measurements.

Item Selection

Items for the SE were obtained from two sources: 1) the formal discussions with the service staff of the CJVS, and 2) the examination of previously constructed scales designed to measure work-relevant behavior. Four areas of vocational functioning were considered in selecting and preparing items: 1) the past performance in areas relevant to placement and job maintenance, 2) the stereotypes that enter into employers' hiring practices, 3) the psychological capacities relevant to work behavior, and 4) the current vocational behavior as seen by foremen in rehabilitation workshops.

The 124 final items were grouped into three major scales according to the source of information for the items. The three scales are the *Workshop Scale,* the *Counseling Scale,* and the *Psychology Scale.* In order to simplify this presentation of the SE, only the Workshop Scale is considered. The reader is referred to the original report for information regarding the other two scales.

The Workshop Scale consists of 52 items that are grouped into five subscales. Table 8 contains two representative items from each of the subscales. Each item is completed by the rater (usually a workshop foreman) who selects the most appropriate alternative, i.e., the alternative that most accurately describes the client under consideration.

Scoring the Scale of Employability

Each client for whom the Workshop Scale is completed receives four subscale scores. (The four global items in the fifth group were not combined.) A total score for the first 48 items is also computed. Each item is scored on

Table 8.   Selected items from the Workshop Scale of Employability[a]

I.   Ability to mobilize and direct energy in the work situation
   A.   *Eagerness to work*
     1.   Appropriate: approach is positive and well motivated toward assigned task
     2.   Dutiful: shows no signs of interest but does the assigned task
     3.   Indifferent: will do the assigned task but does not particularly want to
     4.   Rebellious: refuses altogether to do some assigned task
   B.   *Steadiness of work: Nonproduction task*
     1.   Very steady worker during entire daily work period
     2.   Reasonably steady worker during entire daily work period
     3.   Questionable or borderline steadiness
     4.   Inadequate or unsatisfactory steadiness
II. Capacity to tolerate and cope with work pressures, tensions, and demands
   A.   *Punctuality: Morning starting time*
     1.   Never or almost never tardy
     2.   Rather rarely tardy
     3.   Occasionally tardy
     4.   Frequently tardy
   B.   *Fear manifested by client in his dealings with his own foreman*
     1.   Manifests no fear
     2.   Slightly more fearful than is appropriate
     3.   Moderately more fearful than is appropriate
     4.   Considerably more fearful than is appropriate

Table 8 — *continued*

III.   Interpersonal relation with co-workers and foremen
　　A.   *Client's participation in group structures*
　　　　1.　Accepted as a leader: is center of conversation or social activities
　　　　2.　Active participant in social or conversational activities
　　　　3.　Passive participant: essentially a listener, but remains part of the social group
　　　　4.　An isolate from social activities
　　B.   *Intensity of client's resistance to his own foreman's instructions or directions*
　　　　1.　Client displays no resistance
　　　　2.　Client displays mild resistance
　　　　3.　Client displays moderate resistance
　　　　4.　Client displays strong resistance
IV.   Functioning level of ability in work situation
　　A.   *Organization of work method and ability to improve under guidance*
　　　　1.　Follows orderly well-organized work method to accomplish task
　　　　2.　Follows moderately well-ordered work method
　　　　3.　Tends to become moderately slovenly and disorganized, and shows only minimal improvement when corrected
　　　　4.　Tends to become very slovenly and disorganized, and does not improve when corrected
　　B.   *Manual dexterity as related to work requirements*
　　　　1.　No impairment of manual dexterity as related to work requirements
　　　　2.　Slight impairment
　　　　3.　Moderate impairment
　　　　4.　Severe impairment
V.   Overall evaluation: Agency criteria
　　A.   *Predicted placement of client*
　　　　If an appropriately extensive and sustained effort to place the client is made by the agency, the probability that the client can be placed in the regular job market is:
　　　　1.　Average or better
　　　　2.　Slightly to moderately low
　　　　3.　Very low
　　　　4.　Practically none
　　B.   *Predicted work personality of client in job field deemed most feasible by rater*
　　　　In the job field and in the type of employment (regular or sheltered) deemed most feasible by the rater, the client's work personality would probably be:
　　　　1.　Adequate
　　　　2.　Slightly inadequate
　　　　3.　Moderately to considerably inadequate
　　　　4.　Inadequate for performing work duties or for remaining in employment

[a]Reproduced by permission of Gellman, W., Stern, D., and A. Soloff. *A Scale of Employment for Handicapped Persons.* Chicago: Jewish Vocational Service, 1963.

a 4-point scale, and the subscale and the total scores are then the sums of the appropriate item scores.

Norms are not provided for the Workshop Scale or for the other scales of the SE. There are two reasons for this omission. First, local norms and validation studies should be carried out in each setting where the SE is routinely used. Extensive evidence in industrial and educational psychology has demonstrated that predictability is often specific to a particular setting or subject population. Second, the SE probably has its greatest value as a diagnostic instrument, i.e., each item pinpoints possible behavioral deficits, which can receive special attention in the rehabilitation workshop or counseling program.

THE HAPTIC INTELLIGENCE SCALE

The Haptic Intelligence Scale (HIS) is a nonverbal instrument that was developed during the 1950s for use with blind persons (Shurrager, 1961). While the HIS was designed to aid the clinical psychologist in obtaining a more comprehensive intellectual evaluation of blind subjects, the instrument has proven useful in research projects as well. The HIS includes the following six subtests, four of which closely parallel Wechsler Adult Intelligence Scale (WAIS) Performance subtests of similar title:

1. *Digit Symbol*   consists of a plastic plate embossed with simple geometric forms that are identified by the examinee using a numerical key.
2. *Object Assembly*   consists of four dissected objects (block, doll, hand, and ball) that are assembled by the examinee.
3. *Block Design*   consists of four cubes with varied surface texture that are arranged to form patterns.
4. *Object Completion*   consists of 16 familiar objects, each missing some part, that the examinee has to identify.
5. *Pattern Board*   consists of a small pegboard on which the examinee reproduces patterns of pegs.
6. *Bead Arithmetic*   consists of an abacus, which the examinee uses to solve various numerical problems.

The HIS is an individually administered instrument that requires approximately 90 minutes to complete. The primary result of the administration of the HIS is an IQ score that is independent of verbal knowledge and skills. The selection of the normative sample that provides the basis for the calculation of an IQ of an examinee is described below.

Standardization of the Haptic Intelligence Scale

The normative sample that was used to standardize the HIS was selected by matching 700 blind subjects on WAIS Verbal IQs within seven age groups (16–17, 18–19, 20–24, 25–34, 35–44, 45–54, and 55–64) and by sex. The subjects were fairly representative of geographical regions, racial distribution, and rural-urban residential patterns of the United States population (1950 census). The HIS scoring system was constructed by using the 20–34 age group as a reference group and by converting the raw subtest scores to a total scaled score. The total scaled scores were converted to IQ scores (mean of 100 and standard deviation of 15) for each of the seven age groups. Thus, the examining psychologist can determine the IQ equivalent of a total scaled score for an examinee of a given age.

RELIABILITY

All instruments of measurement in the behavioral sciences possess two characteristics to some degree: reliability and validity. The degree to which these properties are present is usually indicated in the form of a correlation coefficient. Both reliability and validity are concerned with the broader issue of *generalizability*. Appropriate coefficients indicate the extent to which a measurement can be generalized to another sample, variable, or point in time. While the two topics are discussed separately, there is an intimate relationship between reliability and validity; this relationship is clarified later in this chapter.

Reliability refers to the *precision* of a measurement. A reliable measurement is one that produces similar results when repeated, i.e., it is a *consistent* procedure in that the objects measured receive the same or similar scores if the procedure is replicated. As random error enters the measurement process, the reliability of the instrument decreases. The major sources of error are: nonrepresentative sampling of instrument content (items), fluctuations in the individual traits over time, poor or inadequate standardization, variation in the test conditions, and subjectivity in the measuring process. An example of subjectivity is when raters are used to translate observed or recorded behavior into scores.

Classical Test Theory

Reliability is a property of instruments of measurement that is estimated by one or more statistical procedures using data from a sample of subjects. Hypothetically, reliability refers to the accuracy of the instrument as it is applied to any given subject. If an individual could be independently measured on 50 consecutive occasions, the variability of the scores about the mean (which would be the estimated true score) would provide a direct assessment of the measurement error. This procedure (repeated testing of one subject) is obviously not feasible with most psychological and sociological measures, and, therefore, a sample of 50 subjects is used to estimate the *average* reliability.

The assumption necessary in using 50 subjects instead of 50 independent testings of one subject is that the variability among individuals provides a reasonable basis for estimating intraindividual variability on a given instrument. It is necessary to postulate a model for a test score in order to arrive at an operational definition of reliability. The standard model in classical psychometric theory states that an observed (raw) score is composed of two components: a true component and an error component. In equation form:

$$\text{Observed Score} = \text{True Score} + \text{Error}$$

For example, an observed score of 6 may reflect a true score of 5 and an error of $+1$. If it were possible to know the true scores for a sample of 50 subjects, and then to administer an instrument to measure the variable under consideration, each of the subjects' observed scores could be partitioned according to the model; for example:

$$6 = 5 + (+1)$$
$$8 = 9 + (-1)$$
$$4 = 6 + (-2)$$
$$6 = 7 + (-1)$$
$$4 = 4 + (\ \ 0)$$
$$3 = 6 + (-3)$$

Then, if the correlation between the observed scores and the true scores were calculated, and the correlation coefficient were squared (coefficient of determination), it would indicate the proportion of variance in true scores that was accounted for by the observed scores. This is the psychometric definition of reliability: the proportion of the total variance of an instrument that is true variance.

Obviously, the reliability coefficient cannot be calculated in this way because true scores are not known before the test is administered (and can only be estimated afterward). Thus, an indirect procedure is needed. If some reasonable assumptions are made (e.g., that errors of measurement are independent of true scores), then it can be demonstrated that the total observed variability in scores for a sample of subjects can be divided into two parts consistent with the model postulated above: true variance and error variance. In equation form:

$$\text{Total Variance} = \text{True Variance} + \text{Error Variance}$$

Then, reliability, which was defined above as the proportion of the total variance that is true variance, can be summarized as:

$$\text{Reliability} = \frac{\text{True Variance}}{\text{Total Variance}} = \frac{\text{Total Variance} - \text{Error Variance}}{\text{Total Variance}}$$

It is clear from the last equation that reliability involves the direct estimation of errors of measurement. In the following two sections the standard methods of estimating test reliability are outlined and illustrated.

Methods of Estimating Reliability

Test/Retest   The most common procedure used to estimate the reliability of an instrument is to readminister the test to a sample after a 1- to 2-week interval. Then the scores on the first administration are correlated with the scores from the second administration, and the correlation coefficient is a test/retest reliability coefficient. The correct interpretation of an obtained reliability coefficient of $r = .82$ is that 82% of the variance in observed scores on the instrument is due to true differences among individuals, while 18% reflects the various types of measurement error.

The reader may wonder why the reliability coefficient is not squared in order to be interpreted as a coefficient of determination. It will be recalled that the reliability coefficient is the square of the (hypothetical) correlation between the scores on either the first or the second administration of the test and the true scores of the subjects in the sample. Thus, the reliability coefficient can be interpreted directly as a percentage of variance.

Alternate (Parallel) Form   The outstanding weakness of the test/retest method is that it does not take into account random errors due to sampling of content. The purpose of the reliability estimate, then, is not to give the highest possible coefficient, but rather to provide an accurate estimate of the extent to which a measurement is generalizable. Whenever possible, the reliability of an instrument should be improved by such methods as increasing the representativeness of the item sampling procedure or improving the standardization. However, the reliability coefficient should only reflect the actual dependability of the measurement process.

All things considered, the use of two or more parallel forms, each administered to the same subjects with a 1- to 2-week interval between administrations, provides the best estimate of the reliability of an instrument. This method is not employed nearly as frequently as the test/retest method, or as the two methods outlined below, because of the additional effort that is necessary to construct a second form of an instrument that is a mirror image of the original form. (Ideally, the alternative forms are constructed simultaneously.) In general, the other procedures tend to overestimate the functional reliability of most instruments.

Split-Half   This procedure is often used as a substitute for the alternate form method of reliability estimation. The items within a test are arbitrarily assigned to two forms, e.g., odd-numbered items may comprise one set and even-numbered items may comprise the other set. Then, each subject in the sample receives two scores on the instrument, i.e., a score on the odd-numbered items and a score on the even-numbered items. In other words, the single instrument is scored as two separate tests. Then, the two sets of scores are intercorrelated and the correlation is "stepped up" using the *Spearman-Brown prophecy formula* to estimate the reliability of the instrument of double length (the original test was divided into halves). Since both halves are administered at the same time, individual fluctuations over time do not enter into the reliability estimate, which is, therefore, probably inflated.

Internal Consistency   Reliability estimates based on item homogeneity indices (e.g., Coefficient Alpha and Kuder Richardson Formula 20) are the ultimate logical extension of the split-half method. The intercorrelations among the items that comprise the instrument are stepped up to estimate the reliability of the total score, which is, of course, the sum of the item scores. Internal consistency estimates can be shown to be the average of all possible split-half coefficients that can be calculated for a given test. It is obvious, then, that internal consistency reliability estimates suffer from the same defect as the split-half method, i.e., they do not take into account individual fluctuations in the trait that is measured. Thorndike (1976) provides an in-depth discussion of the topics summarized in this section.

THREE REHABILITATION EXAMPLES

Attitudes Towards Disabled Persons Scale

Extensive reliability data for the ATDP are provided in the manual by Yuker et al. (1966). The reliability estimates for Form B are summarized:

Test/retest   Two studies are reported. Twenty-eight nondisabled subjects were retested after 4 months ($r = 0.71$) and 81 nondisabled subjects were retested after 5 weeks ($r = 0.83$).

Alternate forms   Forms A and B of the ATDP were administered simultaneously to three samples ranging in size from 57 to 154. The reliabilities ranged from 0.60 to 0.83. Forms A and B were administered
to the three samples with an interval from 6 weeks to 5 months between testings. The sample sizes ranged from 31 to 58 and the reliabilities were 0.41, 0.73, and 0.76.

Split-half   Seven studies are reported, six using nondisabled subjects.
Sample sizes ranged from 42 to 194 and the reliability coefficients
ranged from 0.72 to 0.87.

Several points regarding the reliability of the ATDP are in order.
First, a large number of reliability studies using different methods are reported. They provide the potential user with considerable data regarding
an important psychometric characteristic of the instrument. In general,
the reliabilities run in the 0.70s and the 0.80s. These are satisfactory coefficients for a relatively brief instrument.

Scale of Employability

Two reliability studies are reported by Gellman et al. (1963) for the Workshop Scale. In the first study, 50 clients were rated and rerated at the end
of the sixth and seventh weeks in the workshop by two different foremen.
The reliability coefficients for the four subscales and the total score were
0.39, 0.56, 0.63, 0.30, and 0.52, respectively. This design would be analogous to the alternate forms of reliability with a 1-week interval between
administrations (the two raters constitute different forms).

Because there was some question about the possibility of differential
client change during the week between ratings, which would have attenu-
ated the reliability estimates, a second study was undertaken. Foremen
were assigned in pairs to observe each of 44 clients during the second week
in the workshop. Their independent ratings were intercorrelated, resulting in reliabilities of 0.58, 0.13, 0.47, 0.64, and 0.52 for the four subscale
scores and the total score.

The only reasonable conclusion that could be drawn from these two
studies is that the reliability of the Workshop SE is rather modest when reliability is operationalized as interrater agreement. However, it should be
noted that the reliability of an instrument can be increased by lengthening
it. This can be accomplished with a rating instrument simply by averaging
the scores assigned by independent raters. For example, if the total scores
assigned by the two raters using the SE in the second study summarized
above were averaged, that combined score would have an estimated reliability of 0.68. If three raters' total scores were averaged, the reliability of
the combined score would be estimated to be 0.76. These estimates were

calculated using the generalized Spearman-Brown prophecy formula, which is explained by Nunnally (1967).

Haptic Intelligence Scale

Two types of reliability data are reported in the manual for the HIS (Shurrager, 1961):

Test/retest   The HIS was readministered to 136 subjects after a minimum of 6 months had elapsed since the first testing. The average reliability for each of the subtests was 0.76. The retest reliability of the total score based on five of the subtests was 0.91. (Bead Arithmetic was excluded because few subjects had completed both testings.)

Split-half   Odd-even reliability coefficients for the subjects in the 20–34 age range were calculated. The average stepped-up reliability coefficient for five subtests was 0.87. (Digit Symbol is a speeded test and a split-half coefficient would be spuriously inflated.) The split-half reliability coefficient for the total sample was 0.95.

The HIS clearly provides an estimate of nonverbal intellectual functioning that is reliable enough for individual diagnosis, as well as for any conceivable research purpose. In general, subjects tend to perform consistently on the instrument.

VALIDITY

An instrument is valid if it measures what it purports to measure. A test may be valid for some purposes and not for others. For example, a test may be a valid measure of aptitude for a particular skill training program, but may have no validity for predicting response to psychotherapy. Thus, validity is not a global property of instruments of measurement. The validity of any test must be established for each intended purpose. Like reliability, validity is an empirically determined property of tests. Furthermore, validity is not an all-or-none characteristic; the extent of validity is usually summarized as a correlation coefficient or a related statistic. The three major types of validity (content, criterion-related, and construct) are briefly reviewed below and illustrated in the following section.

Methods of Assessing Validity

Content Validity   The adequacy of the sample of items from the domain of interest is the primary criterion by which content validity is judged. Scholastic achievement tests and job proficiency tests, which are used extensively in educational and vocational training programs, are usually evaluated according to their content validity. The content of attainment tests must reflect the important knowledge and skills that constitute mastery of a subject if the instrument is to be considered valid. Content validity is clearly a matter of professional opinion to a great extent. It cannot be tested directly; however, it can be evaluated more accurately if the test is constructed following a plan that outlines the broad areas of competencies to be achieved.

Criterion-Related Validity   If an instrument is constructed for the purpose of estimating some other behavior, referred to as the *criterion,* then either *concurrent* or *predictive* validity strategies are used to determine if the instrument is successful. Examples of criteria that are relevant to the goals of the rehabilitation process are improved personal adjustment, completion of a training program, placement in employment, and independent living. Criterion-related validity is assessed by correlating scores on the test with scores on the criterion for a sample of subjects. Predictive validity refers to the situation where the criterion scores are obtained at some future time, while the concurrent validity strategy refers to the simultaneous collection of test scores and criterion data. Criterion-related validity is most applicable to instruments of measurement used in clinical work, i.e., tests used in making decisions on diagnosis, selection, and classification. Often, the measurement of the criterion presents more difficulties than the development of the instrument. The so-called criterion problem is discussed further in Chapter 5. Criterion-related validity coefficients are limited by the reliability of the instrument and the criterion; reliability is a necessary but not a sufficient condition for validity. An unreliable instrument cannot be a valid measure of anything, but a reliable instrument has the potential to be a valid measure.

Construct Validity   Construct validation is the all-encompassing set of procedures that are concerned with determining the underlying trait that an instrument measures, e.g., intelligence, attitudes, motivation, and anxiety. Instruments that possess construct validity are required in the confirmation of theories of behavior. Theories are concerned with the relationships among variables, and the instrumentation must validly measure the specified variables in order to support or disconfirm the theories. All types of evidence are accumulated in an effort to clarify just what the test measures, e.g., content representativeness, correlations with various criteria, comparison of older and younger subjects, and effects of experimental treatments on scores. Obviously, there is no global index of construct validity. Furthermore, construct validity is never finally established; it is always in process because judgmental integration of the total empirical evidence available regarding the instrument constitutes its construct validity. The reader is referred to the chapter by Betz and Weiss (1976) for an extended discussion of test validity.

THREE REHABILITATION EXAMPLES

None of the three instruments that are being used for illustrative purposes in this chapter could be appropriately evaluated in terms of content validity (although item sampling procedures were used in constructing the ATDP and the Scale of Employability). The interested reader can find numerous examples of content validity studies in the manuals for academic achievement tests. The Workshop Scale of Employability is considered first because its validity requirements are rather straightforward.

Scale of Employability

As its name suggests, the SE was developed to provide an estimate of the workshop client's probability of employment. While it could be argued that the SE was proposed as a measure of the construct "employability," it is clear from the monograph by Gellman et al. (1963) that the purposes for which the instrument was designed are primarily clinical applications. Thus, the assessment of the validity of the Workshop Scale of Employability involved correlating scores with selected criteria of successful employment. Three criteria were chosen: 1) placement within 3 months after leaving the workshop, 2) placement within 12 months after leaving the workshop, and 3) maintenance of employment. The validity studies were conducted in two workshops in different cities. It is worth repeating that an instrument may be a valid predictor in one situation and have no relationship with similar criteria in another setting. Thus, the use of two different workshops provided evidence regarding the generalizability of the results.

The validity coefficients for the Workshop Scale total score for 500 clients of the Chicago workshop were 0.23, 0.23, and 0.26 for the three criteria of early placement, long-term placement, and maintenance. The corresponding validity coefficients for a sample of 100 clients of the Indianapolis Goodwill Workshop were 0.43, 0.43, and 0.31. The validity coefficients for the four subscales were generally of the same magnitude as the total scale validities.

Placement in employment was clearly more predictable using the Workshop Scale in Indianapolis than in Chicago. What factors may have accounted for this difference? First, the Chicago client sample may have been composed of subsamples that were differentially predictable, e.g., placement for males may have been more difficult than for females, or white clients may have been more predictable than nonwhites. Second, the criteria may have reflected economic conditions prevailing in Chicago, as well as other circumstances that would tend to attenuate the validity coefficients. Other issues and problems that occur with prediction studies are discussed in Chapter 6.

A final question to be raised concerning predictive validity is: How good is a coefficient of 0.43? The answer must be qualified further by asking: For what purpose? For predicting employment of an individual client? For selecting clients for long-term training programs? As evidence supporting the (construct) validity of the instrument? While these questions are addressed in Chapter 6, it can be stated here that a validity coefficient of 0.43 is about average. Seldom do coefficients exceed 0.60. It should be noted that subsequent research has supported the validity of the Scale of Employability. A review of 10 research projects by Bolton and Soloff (1973) led to the conclusion that "In almost every project, the Scale proved to be a significant predictor of outcome, and in several cases, it was the only promising instrument in a battery" (p. 77).

Attitudes Towards Disabled Persons Scale

Establishing the validity of the ATDP required that all types of evidence be ascertained regarding the variable that was measured. The primary strategy that was followed was to correlate ATDP scores with other variables that would logically be expected to assess a similar trait. Correlations with actual behavior toward disabled persons would constitute the strongest evidence (an attitude is defined as a predisposition to action), but few behavioral studies have been conducted. Yuker et al. (1966) summarized a large number of relevant empirical studies in three chapters that cover the personality correlates, the attitudinal correlates, the experiential correlates, and the behavioral correlates of the ATDP. The evidence taken as a whole is consistent with expectations derived from personality and attitude theory, and thus supports the construct validity of the ATDP.

For example, it might be hypothesized that aggression and hostility would be correlated with negative attitudes toward disabled persons. Three of the seven studies that investigated this hypothesis with nondisabled adolescent and adult samples produced statistically significant correlations that supported the hypothesis, while the other four (nonsignificant) correlations were in the predicted direction. The authors carefully evaluated the evidence and concluded that aggressive and hostile feelings were related to negative or nonaccepting attitudes toward disabled persons as measured by the ATDP.

In the experiential domain, it could be reasonably hypothesized that nondisabled persons who have been in contact with disabled persons would tend to be more accepting of them than persons who have not had any contact with the disabled. (This is just a special case of the more general hypothesis that states that interpersonal interaction results in increased positive attitudes.) The authors reviewed more than two dozen studies and concluded that "There is clear evidence that the closer the social and personal contact with the disabled, the greater the acceptance of disabled persons in general" (Yuker et al., 1966, p. 87).

Is the ATDP a valid measure of attitudes toward disabled persons? A variety of studies indicate that it is, and, therefore, that a generalized measure of attitudes toward disabled persons is meaningful and potentially useful. As always, additional studies will further define the construct measured by the ATDP.

Haptic Intelligence Scale

To a great extent, the validity of the HIS depends on the fact that it parallels a well-known measure of intelligence (the Wechsler Adult Intelligence Scale). This, of course, does not establish that the HIS is a valid measure of intelligence. New intelligence tests are traditionally correlated with older tests to provide initial validity evidence. The HIS scores were correlated with WAIS Verbal IQ scores for the group of subjects 20 to 34 years old in the original research sample. The resulting correlation of 0.65 indicates that the two tests do measure some common elements. The correlation is difficult to interpret because too high a correlation would mean that the HIS was essentially redundant with the WAIS Verbal IQ, while too low a correlation would pose the question of whether both tests were assessing general intellectual functioning. Since validity refers to a specific purpose, the practical usefulness of the HIS will eventually be determined by studies that relate IQ scores to measures of educational and vocational success.

SOURCES OF INFORMATION

Tests in Print II (Buros, 1974) lists about 2,500 commercially available psychological tests. *Measures for Psychological Assessment* (Chun, Cobb & French, 1975) contains annotated references for more than 3,000 measures used in articles that were published in 26 psychological and sociological journals during the period from 1960 through 1970. *A Sourcebook for Mental Health Measures* (Comrey, Backer & Glaser, 1973) contains abstracts describing more than 1,100 unpublished or lesser-known instruments. And, *Sociological Measurement* (Bonjean, Hill & McLemore, 1967) lists more than 2,000 measures that were located by a survey of four leading sociological journals for the 12-year period from 1954 through 1965.

While there is some overlap among these four sourcebooks, it is obvious that the number of measurement instruments developed by social scientists is astronomical. This view is reinforced when it is realized that many of the more than two dozen compendia of measures that are available today are focused on highly specialized areas, e.g., child development, self-concept, political attitudes, alcoholism, drug abuse, vocational development, and reading tests. (The specialized reference volumes are cited in the four sourcebooks above and some are described later in this section.) A conservative estimate of the population of measurement instruments in psychology, sociology, and related fields would be 10,000 different scales and inventories.

Regardless of the precision of this estimate, it is apparent that rehabilitation practitioners and researchers have potential access to an enormous number and variety of measurement instruments and assessment devices. The following sections describe the most useful reference volumes currently available.

The Institute of Mental Measurements

The late Oscar Buros devoted his professional career to the development and publication of a set of reference volumes that have organized and evaluated the literature of psychological and educational testing for the last half century. The backbone of Buros' project is the series of *Mental Measurements Yearbooks* (MMYs), of which eight have been published since 1938. The *Eighth MMY* was published in the fall of 1978, just six months after Dr. Buros' death.

The *MMYs* include thorough descriptions of all commercially available tests, one or more "frankly critical" reviews of most instruments that were written by measurement and subject specialists, and bibliographies of all published references on the applications and validity of the tests. In addition to the *MMYs,* two comprehensive volumes of *Tests in Print* (Buros, 1961, 1974) have been published, as well as specialized monographs that contain selected material from the *MMYs* and *Tests in Print* covering the following types of tests: English, foreign languages, intelligence, mathematics, reading, science, social studies, and vocational.

Perhaps the most interesting and ironic piece of historical information surrounding the development of the *MMYs* is that Professor Buros' initial goal was to establish a test user's research organization. He attempted repeatedly over a period of 25 years to obtain funding for this project, but he was never successful (Buros, 1968). The test-reviewing service was only an afterthought. It is interesting to speculate about whether there would be a reference series comparable to the *MMYs* today if Professor Buros' skills in grantsmanship had been more effective back in the

1930s. Still, Oscar Buros probably would have made a notable contribution, regardless of any particular turn of events, because his view was future oriented and he (obviously) possessed the capacity for hard work.

The well-deserved praise that the *MMY* series has received should not be allowed to obscure an important point: The professional test reviews are unstandardized, are of uneven quality, and often reach contradictory conclusions. Who is the unsophisticated test user to believe when experts disagree? There is simply no substitute for educated test users who can evaluate the test manual and available research studies in light of their own purposes and needs.[5]

The Institute for Social Research

In the early 1970s, the Institute for Social Research (ISR) at the University of Michigan initiated a project to develop a National Repository of Social Science Measures. *Measures for Psychological Assessment* (Chun et al., 1975) was the first product of this ambitious project. This reference volume consists of computer printouts from the Repository, which was assembled from a systematic search of 22 psychological and 4 sociological journals for the period from 1960 through 1970. Two major sections, "Primary References" and "Applications," and two indices comprise the volume. The section on Primary References lists the original sources in which some 3,000 measures were first described. The Applications section provides information on about 6,600 instances in which the measures have been used.

Each of the 3,000 Primary Reference entries contains a reference to the original source, the title of the measure, some keywords descriptive of the content of the measure, and a list of all known applications of the measure. Each entry in the Applications section includes the original reference, a set of terms indicating the types of information available in the article, and a list of the measures used in the article.

Despite the broad title, the range of instruments indexed in *Measures for Psychological Assessment* is fairly limited. In addition to those measures obviously related to mental health, the following are included: 1) measures of individual moods, traits, behaviors, and some attitudes; 2) measures of interpersonal relationships or behavior; and 3) measures of characteristics of organizations, cultures, or social groups. Measures of

---

[5]This paragraph originally appeared in slightly different form in my review of *Personality Tests and Reviews II* (*Personnel Psychology*, 1976, *29*, 131–134). The concluding sentence (which is omitted above) was "I am confident that Professor Buros would concur with this statement" (p. 133). In a letter to me dated April 19, 1976 Professor Buros wrote "I fully concur with your comment that 'there is simply no substitute...' Unfortunately, there are few such persons. Your statement bears repeating over and over." It is hoped that this book will contribute to the education of test users in rehabilitation counseling.

intelligence, measures of aptitude, and most attitudinal measures were omitted because they have been covered extensively in other reference volumes.

Unfortunately, the Repository is not being updated because neither of ISR's proposals — a long-range plan of incorporating the system into the *Psychological Abstracts* and an interim plan of continuously updating the system — was funded. Unless some constructive steps are taken in the near future, psychological research and practice will be overwhelmed by the population explosion of measures.

Other Relevant Sources

Of the more than two dozen compendia of measures currently available, several merit brief mention. *A Sourcebook for Mental Health Measures* (Comrey et al., 1973) consists of abstracts of more than 1,100 unpublished tests and inventories covering 45 subject areas. *Measuring Human Behavior* (Lake, Miles & Earle, 1973) contains fairly detailed evaluative reviews of 84 carefully selected instruments that were designed to measure various aspects of "social functioning" and also includes reviews of 20 other sourcebooks of instruments. The two volumes of the *Directory of Unpublished Experimental Mental Measures* (Goldman & Saunders, 1974; Goldman & Busch, 1978) that have been published so far include descriptions of approximately 600 tests that are not commercially available. The instruments are arranged in a 22-category system, grouped according to function and content, and note purpose, source, and related research. The Educational Testing Service of Princeton, N.J., has developed the "ETS Test Collection," which is an extensive library of unpublished standardized tests, inventories, and assessment devices. Copies of the tests may be purchased by qualified users. New acquisitions to the library are listed in a bimonthly periodical, the *Test Collection Bulletin,* which has been published since 1968. A useful reference guide to other compendia, sourcebooks, and test services is available (see Backer, 1972).

Measures in Rehabilitation

The most comprehensive reference guide to tests and instruments in rehabilitation is the *Handbook of Measurement and Evaluation in Rehabilitation* (Bolton, 1976b). Included in this multi-authored volume are selective reviews of tests and measures in the following areas: intelligence, aptitude and achievement, personality, vocational interests, vocational abilities, blindness, deafness, mental retardation, client outcome, and counselor performance. *Program Evaluation: A Resource Handbook for Vocational Rehabilitation* (Bennett & Weisinger, 1974) contains a compendium of 146 measures and indexes that were located in 75 studies and articles concerned with the evaluation of vocational rehabilitation programs. The recent monograph by Backer (1977) contains capsule descriptions of selected instruments designed to assess the success of rehabilitation clients' outcomes. Additional measurement instruments and questionnaires are described in Chapter 5 and the Appendix at the end of this chapter.

SUMMARY

Measurement is defined as the assignment of numbers to objects or events according to rules. A measurement procedure that follows a carefully prescribed set of rules is said to be standardized. Four levels of measurement can be distinguished: 1) a nominal scale — numbers are used to classify objects, 2) an ordinal scale — objects are ranked in order from high to low, 3) an interval scale — requires a unit of measurement, and 4) a ratio scale — requires a true zero point as the origin. Most instruments in the social and behavioral sciences generate a scale of measurement that lies somewhere between the ordinal level and the interval level.

Instruments of measurement are usually composed of items that are added to produce a total raw score. Raw scores are interpreted by comparison to the performance of a reference group of subjects called the norm group. Multi-score instruments are generally preferred to single-score instruments on the assumption that most behavioral domains are complex. Three instruments, the Attitudes Towards Disabled Persons Scale, the Scale of Employability, and the Haptic Intelligence Scale, illustrate the procedures of item selection, item scoring, and item standardization.

Reliability and validity are two important characteristics possessed to some degree by all instruments of measurement in the social sciences. Reliability refers to the precision of a measurement. As random error enters the measurement process, the reliability of the instrument decreases. The psychometric definition of reliability is the ratio of true variance among subjects to their total variance in scores. Four methods are used to estimate reliability: 1) the test/retest — the instrument is readministered after a short interval, 2) the alternate form — two forms of the instrument are administered to the same sample with a short interval between testings, 3) the split-half — an instrument is randomly divided into two tests, and 4) the internal consistency — the intercorrelations among the test items are the basis for an estimate of the reliability of the instrument.

An instrument is valid if it measures what it purports to measure. Validity is not a global property of instruments; validity must be established for each intended purpose. There are three major types of validity. Content validity is reflected in the extent to which the sample of test items is representative of the domain of interest. Criterion-related validity (predictive or concurrent) is assessed by correlating scores on the test with scores on a criterion for a sample of subjects. Construct validity is concerned with determining the underlying trait that an instrument measures using a variety of research strategies. The three instruments described previously were used to illustrate the various methods of evaluating the reliability and the validity of measurements.

A conservative estimate of the number of measurement instruments in the social sciences is 10,000 different scales and inventories. Sources of relevant information include the *Mental Measurement Yearbooks, Tests in Print, Measures for Psychological Assessment, A Sourcebook for Mental Health Measures, Measuring Human Behavior, Directory of Unpublished Experimental Mental Measures, Handbook of Measurement and Evaluation in Rehabilitation,* and *Program Evaluation: A Resource Handbook for Vocational Rehabilitation.* (Appendix 1, page 62, contains descriptions of nine tests and inventories that were developed for the assessment of the rehabilitation client's and counselor's characteristics and behavior.)

appendix one
Selected
Rehabilitation Instruments

The three instruments used in this chapter for illustrative purposes, the Attitudes Towards Disabled Persons Scale, the Scale of Employability, and the Haptic Intelligence Scale, were selected from several dozen measurement instruments that have been constructed for use in rehabilitation counseling and research. In this appendix, nine additional tests and inventories are briefly overviewed to provide a more representative picture of the instruments that have been developed for the assessment of the rehabilitation client's and counselor's characteristics and behavior.

ACCEPTANCE OF DISABILITY SCALE

Linkowski (1971) developed an Acceptance of Disability (AD) Scale based on Dembo, Leviton, and Wright's (1956) concept of loss, which postulates the occurrence of four value changes in physically disabled persons who have accepted their loss: 1) the enlargement of scope of values, 2) the subordination of physique, 3) the containment of disability effects, and 4) the transformation from comparative values to asset values. The AD Scale consists of 50 statements that reflect attitudes and values within the four areas of acceptance of loss. The respondent indicates the extent of his/her agreement or disagreement with the 50 items using the same 6-point response continuum as the ATDP. The AD Scale is scored by summing the responses to all 50 items: the unidimensional structure was supported by the results of two principal components analyses.

The reliability of the AD Scale is indicated by a split-half coefficient (stepped-up) of 0.93 obtained for 46 clients at a rehabilitation center. Evidence for the validity of the AD scale is generally supportive. First, a sample of 55 physically disabled college students scored significantly higher than the clients at the rehabilitation center, a difference that is consistent with the logical expectation that college students would be more mature and thus more accepting of their disabilities. Second, the AD Scale correlated highly ($r = 0.81$) with the ATDP for the 46 rehabilitation clients, a reasonable finding since the ATDP, when administered to disabled persons, is an indirect measure of self-attitudes. Finally, Linkowski and Dunn (1974) correlated the AD Scale with measures of self-esteem and satisfaction with social relationships for the sample of 55 disabled college students; the resulting correlations were 0.52 and 0.34, respectively. The authors concluded that the acceptance of disability is an aspect of the general self-concept, relating to both self-esteem and satisfaction with social relationships (p. 31).

HANDICAP PROBLEMS INVENTORY

Wright and Remmers (1960) constructed The Handicap Problems Inventory (HPI) to quantify the impact of disability as it is perceived by the disabled individual. The HPI is a checklist of 280 problems attributable to physical disability. By marking those problems that are perceived to be caused or aggravated by the handicapping condition, the disabled person reveals the significance that he/she attaches to the impairment. The HPI items are categorized into four life areas or subscales: personal, family, social, and vocational.

The HPI norms are based on a sample of more than 1,000 persons who were determined, by thorough medical examinations, to have substantial and permanent physical disabilities. Internal consistency reliability coefficients for the four subscales were uniformly high, ranging from 0.91 to 0.95. Although there have been no systematic validation studies reported, a variety of evidence suggests that the HPI possesses some validity, e.g., respondents in the normative sample with secondary disabilities reported more problems associated with their disabilities (Wright & Remmers, 1960, p. 6), and physically disabled patients who were rated as improved by their physiatrists reported fewer problems early in their hospitalization (Rosillo & Fogel, 1970, pp. 195–196). The HPI can be used clinically as an inventory of disability-related problems that require attention and as a research instrument in the study of adjustment to disability, e.g., see Mathews' (1966) investigation, which is summarized in Appendix 6 (page 183). Lasky and Salomone (1971) modified the HPI by changing the response format to a 6-point scale and by reducing the number of items to 140.

HISKEY-NEBRASKA TEST OF LEARNING ABILITY

The Hiskey-Nebraska Test of Learning Ability (H-NTLA) is the only individually administered intelligence test designed for use with deaf subjects that has been standardized separately on deaf and hearing samples (Hiskey, 1966). The H-NTLA is a performance scale that can be administered entirely via pantomimed instructions; hence, it may be used with mentally retarded, speech handicapped, bilingual, and other subject populations that are penalized by verbal intelligence tests. The scale consists of a series of performance tasks that are organized in ascending order of difficulty within 12 subscales. Eight of the subscales are administered to subjects in the age range from 3 to 10 years, and seven subscales are administered to subjects 11 to 17 years of age. While the tasks are untimed, the total administration time required is usually less than one hour.

The standardization samples used in the H-NTLA are sufficiently large and broadly representative of the respective populations to provide reasonable confidence in the derived scores. Both the deaf and hearing samples contain more than 1,000 youngsters 3 to 17 years of age. Split-half reliability estimates for the younger and older subsamples of deaf and hearing subjects all exceed 0.90. The issue of the validity of the H-NTLA has probably been unnecessarily complicated by the use of the term *Learning Age* to summarize test performance. In fact, correlational data suggest that *Learning Age* and *Mental Age* are identical constructs. Correlations between the H-NTLA (or its predecessor) and the Stanford-Binet, WISC, Leiter, and other scales for various samples of deaf, mentally retarded, and bilingual children typically range from the 0.70s to the 0.90s (Hiskey, 1956, 1966; Lewis, 1969; Mira, 1962; Shutt & Hannon, 1974; and Willis, Wright & Wolfe, 1972). Furthermore, correlations between the H-NTLA and standard achievement test scores for deaf subjects parallel the relationship between IQ and achievement test scores typically found with hearing subjects (Giangreco, 1966). Readers interested in a more detailed appraisal of the instrument are referred to the *Eighth Mental Measurements Yearbook* review by Bolton (1978b).

MINNESOTA IMPORTANCE QUESTIONNAIRE

The Minnesota Theory of Work Adjustment originated in a program of research on the vocational placement of rehabilitation clients that began in the late 1950s at the University of Minnesota (Dawis, 1976). The two major constructs in the theory are needs and reinforcers. Specifically, the vocational needs, which are learned through previous reinforcement experiences, are defined as classes of preferences for reinforcers. The Minnesota Theory postulates that work satisfaction is enhanced when the correspondence between an individual's needs and the reinforcers available in the work environment is maximized. Twenty dimensions of vocational need were formulated, e.g., ability utilization, authority, creativity, security, and social service.

The Minnesota Importance Questionnaire (MIQ) is a 210-item pair-comparison instrument that generates a profile of a person's vocational needs (Gay, Weiss, Hendel, Dawis & Lofquist, 1971). An MIQ profile may be interpreted in terms of the relative importance to the individual of the 20 work reinforcers or in terms of the degree of correspondence with the need reinforcer patterns for 148 diverse occupations that represent 12 occupational groups. The median internal consistency coefficients for the 20 MIQ scales average about 0.80, retest reliabilities (2 weeks or less) average in the low 0.80s, and stability coefficients (4 to 10 months) are typically in the 0.50 to 0.60 range. Retest reliability coefficients for the entire MIQ profile average around 0.90, with stability coefficients in the 0.70 to 0.80 range (Gay et al., 1971, pp. 37–40). A variety of concurrent validity studies based on hypotheses derived from the Theory of Work Adjustment have supported the validity of the MIQ.

REHABILITATION COUNSELOR JUDGMENT SCALE

Moran, Winter, and Newman (1972) devised the Rehabilitation Counselor Judgment Scale (RCJS) to measure rehabilitation counselors' inclinations to take risks in the decision-making tasks that characterize their daily work. The RCJS consists of 12 items that portray difficult referral situations. Each item describes a disabled person, a rehabilitation plan requiring appropriate services, and an alternative to the requested plan. The situational ingredients that contribute to the difficulty of the cases include severity of disability, stigmatized disabilities, and employment histories. Respondents estimate the probability of success of each of the 12 rehabilitation plans and indicate their agreement with the decision to accept the client for services using a 5-point scale. The risk-taking index is derived from the discrepancies between the probability estimates and the level of acceptance for each of the 12 items.

The reliability of the RCJS is indicated by retest coefficients of 0.51 for 28 students (Moran et al., 1972, p. 217) and 0.68 for 38 students (Moran, 1971, p. 11) and by split-half coefficients (stepped-up) of 0.73 and 0.75, using larger samples comprised of students and counselors. The opinions of practitioners, administrators, and rehabilitation educators suggest that the 12 items of the RCJS possess content validity, i.e., they represent realistic rehabilitation referrals and service plans. A study by Moran (1971) found that university-trained counselors were significantly more risk-oriented than agency-trained counselors. Winter (1976) used the RCJS in an investigation of rehabilitation team decision-making and concluded that group decisions may be more risk-oriented than individual decisions.

REHABILITATION TASK PERFORMANCE EVALUATION SCALE

Wright and Fraser (1975) constructed the Rehabilitation Job Task Inventory (RJTI) for the purpose of assisting VR agency officials in personnel decision-making, i.e., the selection, classification, utilization, and evaluation of rehabilitation personnel. A comprehensive analysis of the rehabilitation counselor's role produced an extensive task bank of more than 500 items that were reduced to a final set of 294 tasks in the RJTI. The tasks represent 12 functional areas: administration/supervision, evaluation, consultation, professional and agency development, client counseling and planning, client assessment, job placement, referral and community relations, case management and special services, intake and eligibility determination, recording and reporting, and incidental client assistance and clerical work. Each of the tasks was rated by rehabilitation administrators, clinical practicum supervisors, and rehabilitation educators on three variables: educational requirement, experiential requirement, and impact on client. The data were used to establish civil service classifications of rehabilitation jobs.

The Rehabilitation Task Performance Evaluation Scale (RTPES) is a modification of the RJTI that contains the same 294 tasks, but uses a self-report format with a 5-point response (superior, above average, average, below average, inferior) to evaluate the quality of task performance. Respondents are also asked to provide estimates of the time spent on each task. The RTPES clearly has numerous potential applications in rehabilitation personnel utilization, as well as in research on the rehabilitation counseling process. A brief discussion of some of the personnel management uses of the RTPES is available in Fraser and Wright (1977).

SCALE OF CLIENT SATISFACTION

Reagles, Wright, and Thomas (1972a) developed the Scale of Client Satisfaction (SCS) to assess client satisfaction with the intervention services provided by rehabilitation counselors during the vocational rehabilitation process. The SCS consists of 14 items that were completed by 483 rehabilitated clients as part of a follow-up survey that was administered (by personal interview and mail) 6 months after the termination of services. The responses to the 14 items were weighted by a scaling technique known as reciprocal averaging, which resulted in a procedure for calculating a total score with an estimated internal consistency of 0.83. Although the SCS items sample client satisfaction with a relatively wide range of rehabilitation activities, they tend to emphasize direct interaction with the rehabilitation counselor.

In a parallel investigation, Reagles, Wright, and Thomas (1972b) examined the relationship between client satisfaction, as measured by the SCS, and 18 interventive counselor and agency process variables for a subsample of 232 rehabilitated clients. Twelve of the 18 rehabilitation process variables were significantly correlated with client satisfaction. In every instance, the greater the number of counselor contacts or the amount of time or agency monies expended, the higher the level of client satisfaction expressed. These results suggest that increased counselor intervention may be a determinant of enhanced client satisfaction, and, at the same time, support the construct validity of the SCS.

SUBROLE RATING SCALE

Richardson and Rubin (1973) developed the Subrole Rating Scale (SRS) for the analysis of the rehabilitation counselor's verbal interview behavior. They defined the primary unit of analysis, the subrole, as follows: "(a) counselor response behavior which the counselor introduces at a particular point in the interview to bring about desired relationships or to elicit an immediate client response, the goal of which is to facilitate the client's problem solving behavior" (1973, p. 48). An extensive review of content analysis schemes in counseling research and an examination of typescripts of interviews from practicing rehabilitation counselors produced 20 counseling process categories, which were later collapsed to 12 subroles: information seeking — specific; information giving — administrative; communication of values, opinion, and advice; listening — client expression; information giving — educational and occupational; information seeking — exploratory; clarification, reflection, and restatement; supportive; information giving — client-based; information giving — structuring; friendly discussion and rapport building; and confrontation.

Because the SRS is a rating instrument, data concerning its reliability are crucial. In the original investigation Richardson and Rubin (1973) reported an interrater agreement between 64% and 70% and a rerating agreement with a 1- to 2-week interval of 85% to 89%. However, in a subsequent analysis when ratings were aggregated across interviews to generate composite profiles for individual counselors, the estimated reliability coefficients for the 12 major subroles ranged from 0.89 to 0.99 with a median of 0.94 (Rubin, Bolton, Krauft, Richardson & Bozarth, 1974, pp. 12–14). Several of the conclusions of the nationwide Counselor-Client Interaction Project, which is summarized in Chapter 4, are derived from Subrole Rating Scale data. Also, the three verbal interaction styles research (see Appendix 6 following Chapter 7) used subrole rating data.

WORK ADJUSTMENT RATING FORM

Bitter and Bolanovich (1970) constructed the Work Adjustment Rating Form (WARF) to measure the work readiness of rehabilitation clients. The instrument was designed primarily for use by counselors and workshop foremen working with the mentally retarded in workshops to assess the potential for training and workshop adjustment progress. The WARF contains 8 subscales, each having 5 items, for a total of 40 items. The five items for each subscale describe five different levels of performance from low to high and require a simple yes/no judgment by the rater. The eight subscales are: Amount of Supervision Required, Realism of Job Goals, Teamwork, Acceptance of Rules/Authority, Work Tolerance, Perseverance in Work, Extent Client Seeks Assistance, and Importance Attached to Job Training.

The reliability of the WARF was evaluated by having three counselors and a workshop foreman rate the same sample of clients; the interrater correlations ranged from 0.67 to 0.98 for all pairs of raters, indicating fairly high interrater agreement. The predictive validity of the WARF was assessed by correlating the ratings by four counselors and one foreman with the employment obtained two years after the clients left the workshop program. The median biserial correlation was 0.72, suggesting that the WARF is a potentially useful prognostic instrument (Bitter & Bolanovich, 1970, p. 617). A subsequent investigation by Bitter (1970) concluded that rater bias can significantly influence the predictive validity of the WARF for individual raters, but that the average reliability and validity estimates are not significantly affected.

chapter four
Research Design

Some basic principles of research design were introduced in the brief research examples in Chapter 1 and in the mode-of-address study that was outlined in Chapter 2, e.g., randomization, treatment and control groups, independent and dependent variables, research hypotheses, and statistical significance. The purposes of this chapter are: 1) to delineate the fundamental principles of research design, 2) to illustrate those principles with a variety of examples from the rehabilitation counseling literature, and 3) to alert the reader to the limitations of several common designs.

The following research designs are discussed and illustrated: descriptive, or survey; one-group pretest-posttest; pretest-posttest control group; posttest-only control group; ex post facto, or nonexperimental; correlational; and behavior modification investigations. Two special types of correlational studies, predictive and factor analytic studies, as well as longitudinal investigations and program evaluation studies, are considered in detail in subsequent chapters. It should be understood that these designs are not mutually exclusive and that in some cases the overlap is considerable. But for instructional purposes the designs serve as useful, organizing categories.

DESCRIPTIVE STUDIES

The most basic research design is the descriptive study, or survey, of a particular group of subjects. The sample that is studied is usually assumed to be representative of a population of interest, and often is a random sample from a carefully defined population. One or more instruments are administered to the subjects for the purpose of ascertaining information about the relevant characteristics of the population. The data are then presented in the form of simple descriptive statistics, e.g., percentages, frequency distributions, means, and crosstabulations, hence the name descriptive studies. Two examples are given to illustrate this important type of research design.[6]

A Survey of Counselor Perceptions

Wright, Smits, Butler, and Thoreson (1968) conducted a comprehensive survey for the purpose of assessing rehabilitation counselors' perceptions of the problems encountered in the delivery of services to clients. The research sample in this investigation consisted of 280 rehabilitation counselors who were employed by the general rehabilitation agencies and the rehabilitation agencies for the blind in five states — Illinois, Indiana, Michigan, Ohio, and Wisconsin.

The instrument that was developed for this investigation, the Rehabilitation Counselor Survey (RCS), contained 66 major items that addressed problem areas within every category of counselor function, e.g., case finding, eligibility determination, counseling, and service provision. Consistent with good instrument construction procedures, two preliminary versions of the RCS were tried out in pilot interviews, and revisions were made.

The final version of the RCS was administered to each of the 280 counselors in the sample by professional interviewers from the University of Wisconsin Survey Research Laboratory. Because the questions were of the open-ended, or free response, variety, a tremendous volume of data was generated. The counselors' perceptions of problems were coded, organized, and summarized in a form that was useful to administrators, inservice trainers, counselor educators, and rehabilitation researchers. While it is clearly impossible to present the results of the survey here, some of the major perceived problems are worth noting. The counselors viewed their clients' lack of motivation for rehabilitation (44%) and unrealistic attitudes toward seeking employment (29%) as primary impediments to successful rehabilitation. Interestingly, the counselors were equally willing to blame themselves for their own lack of knowledge or skill in one of their areas of function or responsibility (44%). The counselors also felt that their work was impaired by: the large caseloads (27%), the excessive clerical work (23%), the other procedures of the agency (28%), a lack of understanding or cooperation on the part of other professional groups within the community (44%), and a lack of diagnostic, training, and/or medical facilities within the community (36%).

---

[6]The examples that are used in this chapter to illustrate the various designs were selected to represent a variety of topics relevant to rehabilitation counseling. Obviously, many other excellent studies could have served equally well. Readers seeking additional examples are referred to the recent volumes edited by Bolton, B., & Jaques, M. E. *Rehabilitation counseling: Theory and practice* and *The rehabilitation client*. Baltimore: University Park Press, 1978 and 1979.

Of what specific value is this kind of information? Obviously, it indicates the presence of problems that are thought by counselors to contribute to the inefficiency in the vocational rehabilitation process. Some of the problems are amenable to administrative modifications, and others may require educational campaigns and the construction of facilities. Other problems suggest that counselors may need more psychological training, and some indicate the areas for future research on the rehabilitation counseling process.

Personality Characteristics of COPE Patients

DeCencio, Leshner, and Leshner (1968) studied the personality characteristics of hospitalized patients with the diagnosis of chronic obstructive pulmonary emphysema (COPE). The research was undertaken to provide a better understanding of the effects of COPE on personality functioning and to establish a more realistic basis for the evaluation of rehabilitative approaches directed toward COPE patients.

The 43 male subjects were hospitalized with a primary diagnosis of COPE. Upon admission to the pulmonary unit, each patient was evaluated by a multidisciplinary team. The psychological evaluation included the administration of the Minnesota Multiphasic Personality Inventory (MMPI). In comparison to the MMPI norm group, the COPE sample scored significantly higher on the three scales that constitute the neurotic triad — hysteria, depression, and hypochondriasis. However, when the COPE sample was compared to three other groups of disabled subjects (multiple sclerosis, rheumatoid arthritis, and spinal cord injury), the COPE patients scored consistently lower, or were better adjusted.

The authors concluded that the study provided support for the hypothesis that COPE patients, as a group, differ from nondisabled persons with regard to certain personality characteristics. The important point to understand concerning this conclusion is that it does *not* logically imply that COPE *caused* the observed differences in personality functioning, although this may be true. An association between two variables (the presence of disability and the higher scores on the MMPI) does not mean that one variable caused the other. Simply stated, correlation does not imply causation. Shontz (1975, pp. 30–37) discusses in some detail the interpretative problems in research on the relationship between physical disability and behavior.

Literally hundreds of investigations have been reported in the rehabilitation and psychology literature dealing with the personality characteristics of various disability groups. The interested reader is referred to the review by Shontz (1971) and to the classic compendium by Barker, Wright, Meyerson, and Gonick (1953).

ONE-GROUP PRETEST-POSTTEST STUDIES

Descriptive studies are important steps in the development of a body of knowledge about rehabilitation clients and the rehabilitation process. But descriptive investigations must be followed by experimental studies in order to establish cause-effect relationships and thus to generate a truly scientific basis for rehabilitation practice. The remainder of this chapter is concerned with the characteristics and limitations of various standard research designs, with particular emphasis on the type of conclusions that are warranted. The study summarized next illustrates a fairly common research design, the *one-group pretest-posttest design,* which, unfortunately, is methodologically very weak. The specific weaknesses are discussed in the following section.

Survival Camping: A Rehabilitation Treatment

Collingwood (1972) reported the development, implementation, and evaluation of "Camp Challenge," a 3-week camping program designed as a demonstration and service project for male problem youths in Arkansas. The program was developed on the premise that the survival camping process provides a context in which effective interpersonal behaviors can be learned and self-discipline and self-respect can be enhanced. The program was viewed as an initial therapeutic client service to prepare the young men for the vocational rehabilitation process in terms of more appropriate behavior and attitudes.

The total camp program (experimental treatment) lasted approximately 3 weeks. There were four basic stages to the program: basic training, backpacking expedition, counseling, and follow-up. The participants spent the first 8 days at a resident camp learning to work together as a team, becoming proficient in the basic camping and survival skills, and getting into physical shape. Following basic training, the group, which consisted of 5 leaders and 21 delinquency-prone male adolescents, went on a 9-day backpacking expedition through the Ozark mountains. Toward the end of the 9 days, pairs of boys went on 24-hour survival details, where they had to secure their own shelter, food, and fire. After returning to the resident camp, the boys spent 2 days participating in group counseling, individual consultation with the leaders, recreational activities, and equipment cleanup. After leaving the program, the boys reported to their rehabilitation counselors. A concrete rehabilitation plan was then developed with the aid of the camp staff reports and personal consultations.

Twenty-one boys between the ages of 15 and 18 began the program; 19 boys successfully completed it. Of the boys who completed the program, 3 were from one of the training schools in Arkansas, 10 were from the Arkansas Rehabilitation Service First Offender Program, and 6 were from a large rehabilitation facility.

The effect of the camping program on the participants was assessed through a variety of measures. The hypothesis that guided the design of the program and the selection of the research instruments was that successful completion of the program would result in an increase in physical fitness. Physical fitness would facilitate an increase in a positive body attitude, which in turn would increase the participant's general self-concept and feeling of internal control in his life. The specific measures that were administered before and after the program included: four basic fitness tests, the Body Attitude Scale, the Index of Adjustment and Values (self-concept), an Internal-External Control Scale, and the Jesness Personality Inventory; the Behavioral Rating Inventory and the Behavioral Problem Checklist were completed by parents and counselors.

The results of the statistical analyses clearly supported the research hypothesis. Furthermore, the behavioral ratings by parents and counselors were consistent with the program objective and the self-reported measures: parents and counselors noted an increase in the frequency of positive behaviors and a decrease in the frequency of negative behaviors. The rehabilitation counselors indicated that the program had a definite positive effect upon the boys, especially in terms of increasing their rehabilitation potential. A follow-up contact 4 months after the program terminated revealed that almost all of the participants in the program were engaged in positive activities, such as vocational training, school, and employment. The involvement in positive activities was in direct contrast to the participants' status prior to the program.

Collingwood (1972) concluded that "in summary, all the data and measurements obtained point out that the camp program made a substantial impact upon the participants and facilitated relevant behavioral and attitudinal changes" (p. 31). Is this a reasonable conclusion? Does the research design allow us to accept the proposition that a survival camping experience can facilitate (cause) positive changes in attitudes and behavior in delinquency-prone youth? To answer this question, it is necessary to consider in detail some possible sources of weakness or invalidity in the design.

Inadequacy of the One-Group Pretest-Posttest Design[7]

An important distinction exists between the *internal* validity and the *external* validity of research designs. Internal validity is concerned with the

---

[7]This section relies to a great extent on the survey by Campbell, D. T., & Stanley, J. C. *Experimental and Quasi-experimental Designs for Research.* Chicago: Rand-McNally, 1963.

question of whether or not it was the experimental treatment that *caused* the measured effect. External validity refers to the extent to which the obtained results can be *generalized* to other settings, treatments, or populations. Both types of validity are required if any research investigation is to add to the reliable extension of knowledge. However, internal validity is the first requirement because it would be meaningless to generalize an unspecifiable effect. In practice, the two classes of validity often appear to be competing, therefore it may be difficult to have both classes; i.e., the tighter a research study becomes (it utilizes more laboratory controls), the less realistic it is, and thus the less representative (generalizable) are the results; on the other hand, the more the investigation approaches a field study (and becomes realistic and therefore generalizable), the more difficult it is to ensure the controls that are necessary to achieve internal validity.

The study by Collingwood must be viewed critically and the results must be labeled tentative at best. The lack of a *control* (untreated) group of subjects who received the same pretest and posttest measures precludes the unequivocal conclusion that survival camping effected the positive changes that were recorded for the experimental group. In the absence of a control group it is impossible to know which changes, if any, could be attributed to the experimental treatment, and which changes were due to other factors.

The one-group pretest-posttest design is relatively weak because several sources of improvement, in addition to the experimental treatment, may be plausible. The major rival hypotheses are:

1. *History* Specific events, in addition to the experimental variable, that occur between the pretest and posttest measurements could influence the outcome of the posttest scores, e.g., the announcement that the head team leader was appointed to the President's Council on Physical Fitness could have served to positively influence subjects (a hypothetical example).
2. *Maturation* Processes within the subjects operating as a function of the passage of time per se, e.g., adolescent boys grow in spurts, with amazing developmental changes often occurring during the summer months. Furthermore, in remedial situations, a process of spontaneous remission, which is analogous to wound healing, may be mistaken for the specific effect of the treatment.
3. *Testing* Taking a pretest has an effect on the score of a second testing (referred to as *reactive effects*). The process of measurement may even change the method by which the outcome is being measured (due to cues, practice, etc.). For example, the pretest physical fitness eval-

uation may have merely provided the subjects with an opportunity to learn and practice the evaluation tests.

4. *Instrumentation*   Changes in the observers or in the knowledge of the experiment on the part of raters may produce changes in the obtained measurements. For example, the parents and rehabilitation counselors who completed the behavioral ratings of the participants may have been influenced by their own knowledge of the program.

5. *Statistical Regression*   Apparent improvement from pretest to posttest occurs because the subjects were selected for their extreme scores on the related measures. Regression effects are not suspect when the group is selected for independent reasons; thus, statistical regression does not seem to be a legitimate criticism of the survival camping study.

The five sources of error that were summarized and illustrated above may jeopardize the internal validity of the one-group pretest-posttest design. The external validity of the design may be limited by a reactive effect:

6. *Reactive Effect of Pretesting*   The pretest might increase or decrease the subject's sensitivity or responsiveness to the experimental variable and thus make the results obtained for a pretested population unrepresentative of the effects of the experimental treatment for the unpretested population. Therefore, the appropriate conclusion may be that the pretest-treatment combination produced the measured effect, i.e., the pretest becomes an integral part of the treatment. (But the generalizability of the study must still be qualified by the question regarding internal validity.)

PRETEST-POSTTEST CONTROL GROUP DESIGN

Collingwood's study of the effects of survival camping on delinquency-prone youth would have been greatly strengthened by the use of a control group.[8] The improved design would have consisted of a sample of 40 participants who were *randomly assigned* to two groups of 20 subjects each. One group would have been arbitrarily (randomly) selected to participate in the survival camping program. All subjects would take the pretest/posttest series of measures, and their parents and counselors would com-

---

[8]Because of the ethical problem involved in withholding needed services from clients for research purposes, the use of control groups in rehabilitation settings is often precluded. However, Reagles and O'Neill (1977) have recently proposed three design strategies that may have applicability where control groups are not feasible. The interested reader should consult their article.

plete the behavioral ratings *without* knowing who was assigned to the experimental group and who was assigned to the control group. The five threats to internal validity listed above would be neutralized by the *pretest-posttest control group design,* which is illustrated next.

The Benefits of Group Counseling

Roessler, Cook, and Lillard (1977) conducted an investigation of the effects of a systematic group counseling program on rehabilitation clients at the Hot Springs Rehabilitation Center. The group counseling program, known as Personal Achievement Skills (PAS), is a self-modification procedure that is conducted in a group setting. Clients learn communication techniques, problem-solving techniques, and behavioral self-control techniques through a series of structured exercises and activities. (See Roessler and Bolton, 1978, for a detailed description.) The authors hypothesized that PAS training would increase clients' optimism, maturity, and motivation and would lead to better rehabilitation outcomes.

The experimental (PAS) group included 23 clients who completed the PAS training program, which consisted of daily 2-hour sessions for a 5-week period. The control group of 20 clients, who met for 5 hours a week for a 5-week period, participated in a group discussion that focused on personal hygiene. It should be stressed that the control group did in fact receive a "treatment" that was selected to rule out (or control for) possible explanatory variables, such as special recognition and grouping.

To assess the benefits of the PAS training program, three self-report instruments were administered on a pretest-posttest basis, i.e., instruments were administered before the study began and administered again after the training programs were completed. Cantril's Self-Anchoring Striving Scale, The Facility Outcome Measure, and goal attainment scaling were used to measure life perspective, vocational and interpersonal maturity, and goal achievement, respectively. Chi square and analysis of covariance tests were calculated to determine whether the PAS group or the personal hygiene group had made significantly greater gains from pretest to posttest.

The results of the statistical analyses supported the authors' hypotheses: 1) an improvement in life perspective was much more likely to occur in the PAS group, 2) the PAS training contributed to significantly higher client perceptions of vocational and interpersonal maturity, and 3) the PAS participants reported much greater movement toward their stated goals. The authors concluded that systematic group counseling programs, like the PAS training, that stress goal-setting and communication skills have the potential to enhance clients' optimism about life and their perceptions of work-related behaviors and skills.

Of the six design weaknesses that were outlined for the one-group pretest-posttest design, only the reactive effect of pretesting threatens the external validity of the pretest-posttest control group design. In other words, the generalizability of the PAS training program results may be restricted to those situations in which pretest assessments are made. This source of invalidity seems especially plausible for those instruments on which subjects know, or are told, their initial status. In other words, if the pretest measures are an integral part of the treatment program, the effects of the training per se cannot be separated from the influence of being measured. Before moving on to the strongest of the research designs, some elaboration on the concept of control is appropriate.

The Concept of Control

It should be clear to the reader at this point that the goal of research design is to establish the basis for an unambiguous interpretation of the treatment effect. That is, the research objective is to specify those aspects of the experimental treatment that caused identifiable changes in the subjects.

Some kind of comparison is included in most research studies. For example, in the investigation of COPE patients, the MMPI norm group, as well as three other samples of disabled subjects, were used for comparative purposes, i.e., they were used to put the results of the COPE sample into a meaningful perspective. In the remainder of this section, several types of control procedures are briefly discussed and some examples are reviewed. But first, a broad definition of *control* must be given: control procedures, or techniques, serve the purpose of eliminating or holding constant irrelevant differences, or competing explanations, that confuse the interpretation of the treatment effect. Also, it should be emphasized that *randomization* is the most fundamental control procedure. However, random assignment is not possible in many investigations, and, consequently, the interpretation of results is limited. The term *control group* has been used several times in this chapter and in previous chapters. It generally refers to a group of subjects who do not receive the experimental treatment that is being investigated. The control group either receives no treatment or receives an irrelevant treatment in order to provide a baseline with which to compare the results of the experimental group.

Seldom does a control group receive no type of treatment, because a lack of treatment is usually not the only feasible alternative to the experimental treatment group. Furthermore, we assume that any treatment program worthy of investigation is better than no treatment program at all. Hence, most control groups are really "control treatment" groups, i.e., the control group receives a treatment that is irrelevant to the purpose of the study, and that lacks the essential elements believed to be critical in effecting client change on the dependent variables. For example, in the evaluation of PAS training, the control group participated in a group discussion on personal hygiene. In selecting this particular control treatment, the authors reasoned that the important factors of attention and grouping would be provided for the control subjects, but that the personal hygiene training would *not* affect clients' optimism, maturity, and goal achievement that is measured by the dependent variables. (The results supported their conjecture.)

When investigating complex phenomena, it is not unusual for researchers to employ two or more control groups. An outstanding study by Evans (1976) illustrates the use of two control groups. Evans evaluated an attitude change strategy, based on Lewin's theory, in which a disabled person interacted in a prescribed manner with the subjects in the experimental group. The mode of interaction was designed to provide the non-disabled subjects with a degree of structure and security that would in turn lead to the formation of positive attitudes. In the first control group, subjects who were interviewed by a disabled person served as the control variable of contact with a disabled person. In the second control group, subjects who were interviewed by a nondisabled person provided the control variable of contact, or attention, with a nondisabled person, which was unrelated to the purpose of the study. Although the results of Evans' study supported the efficacy of the experimental treatment in modifying attitudes toward disabled persons, the investigation suffers from the same weakness as the PAS training study. Because the attitude measure was administered to all subjects in the three groups on a pretest/posttest basis, the generalizability of the results is threatened by the reactive effect of pretesting. However, as with the PAS study, it is valid to conclude that the structured social interaction with a disabled person, when preceded by the completion of the attitude questionnaire, will produce positive attitude change.

To control for the reactive effect of pretesting, Evans could have added a second experimental group that was not pretested. If the posttest scores of this group were comparable to those of the pretested experimental group, then the reactive effect of pretesting could be ruled out as an explanation for the observed attitude change. A variation on this type of control is illustrated in an experimental evaluation of the Employment-Seeking Preparation and Activity (ESPA) program conducted by Keith, Engelkes, and Winborn (1977).

Another control group procedure that is fairly common in counseling research is the naturally occurring comparison group. This form of control group is easily identified, because random assignment is not involved. Rather, appropriate comparison groups are selected from already existing groups. Of course, the comparison subjects are selected because they differ systematically from the "experimental" subjects on the independent variable; the important point is that the comparison subjects may differ in other unspecified ways from the experimental subjects. Anthony and Carkhuff (1970) used graduate students in philosophy for comparative purposes in their evaluation of the effects of graduate training on students in rehabilitation counseling. Fourth-semester rehabilitation counselor trainees scored higher on several relevant measures than fourth-semester philosophy students (and first-semester rehabilitation students), leading the authors to conclude that "specific training in rehabilitation counseling has effects independent of graduate training in general" (p. 340).

An additional control technique that is often used with naturally occurring comparison groups is matching. The experimental and comparison groups may be matched on those variables that are known or believed in advance to be potential explanatory variables. Matching is accomplished by pairing subjects in the groups on the specified variable(s) and by deleting all unmatched subjects from the analyses. With randomized control groups, matching may be used to increase the precision of the comparison between the experimental and the control groups; however, matching is not a substitute for randomization because all relevant competing explanatory variables cannot be known in advance.

The final approach to control relies on statistical methods. Three of the investigations mentioned in this chapter (Evans, 1976; Keith et al., 1977; Roessler et al., 1977) employed analysis of covariance procedures to increase the precision of the comparisons between experimental groups and control groups. Two cautions are in order concerning a statistical approach to control. First, like matching, analysis of covariance is not an effective substitute for randomization. Second, it requires either pretesting of subjects or some kind of relevant preexisting information. If the pretest has the potential to be reactive, then the increase in precision may be offset by the loss of generalizability.

POSTTEST-ONLY CONTROL GROUP STUDIES

Contrary to popular opinion, pretesting is *not* essential to an adequate experimental design. The random assignment of subjects to groups ensures that the groups are similar (within the limits of statistical sampling) on all possible subject characteristics. Again, matching is *not* an appropriate procedure for the purpose of equating groups; however, it may be a useful adjunct technique for reducing statistical error variance, as illustrated in the next study. The strongest experimental design, then, is the *posttest-only control group design*. An outstanding example of this design is summarized next.

A Work Therapy Research Center

Soloff (1967) described a study, conducted by the Chicago Jewish Vocational Service, of the influence of an extramural rehabilitation workshop program on the potential for rehabilitation of hospitalized, chronically ill mental patients. To test the hypothesis that the workshop service, which was located 3 miles from the state hospital, improved the patients' prospects for rehabilitation, the effects of two alternative rehabilitation services were studied: 1) the standard hospital services routinely offered to all inpatients at the Chicago State Hospital, and 2) a daily recreational therapy program located outside of the hospital at the Chicago Mental Health Center.

Subjects entered the project from selected wards of the state hospital. They were matched in groups of three, according to age, sex, ward of residence, length of hospitalization, and marital status, and were randomly assigned to one of the three service programs. One hundred forty-nine subjects participated over a 5-year period: 55 subjects were in the workshop sample, 57 subjects were in the state hospital sample, and 37 subjects were in the recreational therapy sample, because the latter program operated for only 3 years.

The workshop program was a simulated work situation in which, for a period of 9 months, clients worked 6 hours a day, after an initial stage of shorter hours. At first, clients traveled to and from the workshop on a bus that was provided by the hospital; within 3 months, most had stopped using the hospital's bus and began to travel by public transportation. Besides the workshop, services included individual counseling, job placement, follow-up counseling, and, where necessary, family counseling.

The program was evaluated by comparing results for the three groups on seven major criteria. These criteria were: 1) the proportion of subjects who were "successful," that is, subjects who met one or more of the following conditions: discharged from the hospital, worked in competitive employment, or participated in an ongoing, prevocational or activity program in the community; 2) the proportion of subjects discharged from the state hospital within 1 year of the completion of their programs; 3) the proportion of subjects so discharged who were in the community 6 months or more without rehospitalization; 4) the proportion of discharged subjects continuously in the community for at least 1 year following discharge; 5) the average number of weeks in the community for those subjects who were discharged; 6) the proportion of subjects who obtained competitive employment; and 7) the proportion of working subjects who retained employment for at least 6 months.

An analysis of the comparative results for the three programs according to the seven criteria supported the hypothesis that the workshop program, which was located off the hospital grounds, added a significant dimension to the prospects for success of chronically ill state hospital patients. The proportion of workshop subjects who achieved success exceeded the proportion of successful subjects in both of the other programs on six of the seven criteria. The recreational therapy program had more positive results than the state hospital program on the same six criteria.

When subjected to tests of statistical significance, the differences in results among the three programs on the seven criteria fell into three groups. First, on the overall success criterion, workshop program results were significantly superior to those of the state hospital program (57% versus 30%, $p < 0.01$). Results for the recreational therapy program (43%) fell between the results of the other two programs and were not significantly different from either program. Second, on the criteria of discharge from the state hospital, of securing employment, and of maintaining employment, workshop program results were superior to those of the state hospital program at a somewhat significant level ($p < 0.10$). Results for the recreational therapy program again fell in the middle and were not significantly different from either of the other two programs. Third, on the other four criteria, none of the program differences were statistically significant.

These results suggest a pattern. The workshop program results were more superior to the results of the regular state hospital program on those criteria where the staff exerted the most direct influence on subjects. Once the subjects were in the community or were employed, their contacts with staff diminished or stopped, and the influence of the staff in helping to maintain gains was minimized. An analysis of staff ratings of community adjustment for those clients who had been discharged supports the results of the above pattern in that no statistically significant differences were found by program.

Three of the major conclusions derived from the study were:

1. It is possible to improve the chances for rehabilitation of chronically ill state mental hospital patients through the use of a rehabilitation

workshop program located off the hospital grounds. It may be possible to succeed at rehabilitation by using a recreational therapy program, but the results of the program do not indicate that recreational therapy is the best therapy.

2. The superiority of the workshop program results is most evident when the staff's direct influence is the greatest — just after program completion. Once clients are in the community, and this is, of course, relevant only for those clients who get there, differences in adjustment among the program groups tend to disappear.

3. While the results of the workshop program in securing competitive employment are clearly superior, the percentage of people getting jobs (25% of the total workshop sample) was small. The percentage maintaining employment over 6 months was even smaller. The success of the program is much more striking in promoting discharge than in promoting employment.

EX POST FACTO STUDIES

The *ex post facto* (or retrospective) design is fairly common in field studies. It is not a true experimental design because the independent (treatment) variable is *not manipulated* by the investigator. Rather, subjects are *selected* because they have or have not been exposed to the experimental variable. In other words, subjects are assigned to treatment groups by procedures beyond the control of the researcher. The ex post facto design is appropriate when random assignment of subjects to groups is difficult or impossible.

A well-known example from medical sociology concerns the alleged relationship between smoking and lung cancer. In the simplest analysis, the observed statistical correlation cannot be interpreted as "smoking causes lung cancer" because smokers select themselves (i.e., they are not randomly assigned) into the experimental group; smokers and nonsmokers differ in many other ways and any of these other differences (singly or in combination) might predispose smokers to lung cancer. The important point is that observed differences cannot be attributed (causally) to the subject difference, which was the basis for classification into the comparison groups. Many ex post facto studies include an attempt to match the natural groups on relevant variables in order to rule out alternative causes, e.g., smokers and nonsmokers may be matched on age and marital status.

A slightly different version of the retrospective design is illustrated in a study by Ingwell, Thoreson, and Smits (1967). They compared the accuracy of social perception of 12 disabled and 12 nondisabled female college students (matched on age, race, and grade point average). The subjects were obviously assigned to the comparison groups by circumstances beyond the control of both the researchers and the subjects themselves. So, while the assignment process may be considered to be random, it occurred at a point in time well before the study was conducted, and, thus, the only defensible conclusions that can be stated regard currently existing differences between the two groups. The differences obtained in social perception could have been caused by anything except differences in age, race, and scholastic achievement.

The results of ex post facto studies can never be statements of cause and effect similar to the results of true experiments. But the ex post facto investigation does serve as a useful hypothesis-generating procedure; its tentative conclusions are *suggestive* of causal relationships, which can be evaluated in carefully controlled experimental studies. The strength of the ex post facto design is that it describes the situation as it exists without experimental tampering. Thus, external validity, from a descriptive point of view, is excellent. The retrospective design is illustrated by two nationwide investigations conducted in state rehabilitation agencies. The first was concerned with the rehabilitation counseling process and the second examined supervisory practices in district offices.

Rehabilitation Counselor Behavior and Client Outcomes

The Counselor-Client Interaction Project (Bozarth, Rubin, Krauft, Richardson & Bolton, 1974) was a 5-year nationwide field study that addressed the question: "What kinds of counselors are effective with what kinds of clients in producing specific types of rehabilitation outcomes?" This question assumes that all counselors are not equally effective with all clients and, therefore, that an *interaction* exists between the styles of the rehabilitation counselor and the different types of clients. Another way of stating the interaction is to say that client variables *moderate* the relationship between counselor styles and the outcome measures (see Bolton & Rubin, 1974, for a detailed presentation of the interaction model).

Eleven state agencies and two agencies for the blind, each with 10 counselors who served 10 clients, comprised the study sample. Due to the many problems that occur in conducting field studies, the final sample for the longitudinal data analyses (initial intake through follow-up 6 months after closure) contained less than 250 clients. However, each of the clients completed a battery of psychological tests (Tennessee Self-Concept Scale, Sixteen Personality Factor Questionnaire, and Mini-Mult) at intake, 4 months after intake, and 12 months after intake. In addition to routinely collected demographic data, the Rehabilitation Gain Scale was completed at the three time periods noted above. Six months after closure the Minnesota Survey of Employment Experiences was mailed to the client. The Counselor-Client Interaction Project was clearly designed to focus on changes in client functioning in the areas of vocational adjustment and self-reported personality adjustment.

The independent variables of primary concern were counselor affective qualities and verbal behaviors, which were quantified via ratings from tape recordings of the actual counseling interviews. Each counselor in the study who mailed in one or more tapes for at least two clients received rating scores on the 3 interpersonal skill dimensions of empathy, respect, and genuineness, and on 12 behavioral subroles, e.g., information seeking — specific; information giving — administrative; communication of values, opinions, and advice; and listening/client talk. (The Subrole Rating Scale is described in Appendix 1, p. 93.) Demographic data reported by the counselor were also collected.

Some of the major conclusions that were derived from the extensive data analyses are:

1. Rehabilitation counselors are not a homogeneous group performing in a unitary manner. Three interaction styles were identified: Information Providers, Therapeutic Counselors, and Information Exchangers.
2. Rehabilitation counselors spend the majority of their job roles engaged in information-seeking behaviors, information-giving behaviors, and advice-giving behaviors.
3. Higher levels of interpersonal skills tended to be related to higher vocational gain at closure, higher monthly earnings at follow-up, positive psychological change 10 months or more following intake, and greater job satisfaction at follow-up.
4. Lower levels of empathy and respect were associated with less vocational gain and a lower proportion of successful closures for psychologically disabled clients.
5. Vocational adjustment and client-reported psychological adjustment emerged as independent dimensions of client change during the rehabilitation process.

The final step in the interpretation of the results of the Counselor Client Interaction Project was the translation of the data-based conclusions into implications for rehabilitation counseling practice. The following general implications were drawn:

1. Allow the rehabilitation counselor's work role to be more flexible; consider the revision of work emphases and rewards.
2. Include more interpersonal skill training for rehabilitation counselors — it pays off.
3. Begin to move toward the differential assignment of rehabilitation clients to counselors.
4. Consider psychological adjustment as a possible rehabilitation goal in itself.

From the design perspective, the important point to be noted about this investigation is that it is an ex post facto investigation. The independent variables (counselor interpersonal skills and subrole behaviors) were only measured; they were *not* manipulated. Counselors assigned themselves to the high, medium, and low subrole conditions and interpersonal skill levels by virtue of their counseling behavior. The counselors in the three groups probably differed on many other relevant behavioral dimensions. Therefore, the conclusions that were stated above indicate that various kinds of counselor behaviors are *associated* with certain kinds of changes in client adjustment, but should *not* be interpreted as *causal* factors in the absence of additional, confirming evidence. An experimental design that could test the tentative conclusions from the Counselor-Client Interaction Project would require that counselors be randomly assigned to subrole usage conditions or interpersonal skill levels and then instructed or trained to function in a manner consistent with their group assignment. The criterion variables could be measured and, if differences were obtained, appropriate causal inferences could be made. Despite its weaknesses, the retrospective investigation is an important research strategy, but the results and conclusions that emerge are generally not a sufficient basis for the revision of rehabilitation counseling practice.

Management Practices in District Offices

Viaille, Hills, and Ledgerwood (1973) conducted an investigation of management practices in vocational rehabilitation (VR) district offices. Their study involved comparisons on a wide variety of measures between five "effective" offices and five less effective offices that were geographically representative of VR offices in the United States.

The criteria of effectiveness were actually provided by the state directors in the five states who were first asked to identify two offices for the study, one in the upper 20% and one in the lower 20% in effectiveness.

Then, each director listed the criteria that he used in making the designations. Three major criteria of effectiveness emerged from the five lists: production, administrative practices, and community relations.

Each of the 10 district offices in the study was visited for 1 week by a researcher who interviewed one supervisor and four counselors, administered various questionnaires and standardized instruments, and completed case reviews for a random sample of client case records. The instruments that were used included a background questionnaire, the Profile of Organizational Characteristics, Marvin's Management Matrix, the Personal Contact Checklist, the Minnesota Satisfaction Questionnaire, and the Case Review Schedule. The statistical comparisons were based on 25 supervisors (13 from the more effective offices and 12 from the less effective offices), 115 counselors (53 and 62), and 559 clients (289 and 270).

Among the many differences that were found between the more effective and the less effective VR district offices, the following differences are of especial interest. Both counselors and supervisors in the more effective offices perceived their offices as being more participative organizations. Supervisors in the more effective offices rated themselves higher on three action patterns: working through others, producing worthwhile results, and generating usable ideas. More effective supervisors spent more time on public relations, felt that the performance standards were more realistic, and believed that their pay was based on performance. Supervisors, as well as counselors, in the more effective offices tended to be better satisfied with their work. Finally, the comparisons among the client caseloads established rather clearly that the less effective offices were serving more difficult clients, i.e., more publicly referred, emotionally and mentally disabled, younger, black, single persons with less education, and persons more likely to be unemployed and receiving assistance at the time of acceptance.

How are these results to be interpreted? What do they tell us about the antecedents of VR office "effectiveness"? First, the results are consistent with the criteria used by the state directors to identify the more effective and less effective offices. Second, they suggest that certain kinds of supervisory practices *may* enhance agency effectiveness, e.g., emphasis on participative organizational structure and community relations. Third, it is virtually impossible to disentangle the influence of uncontrolled differences, such as more difficult caseloads in the less effective offices, on management practices and overall effectiveness. Still, the study provides valuable preliminary information about the characteristics of more effective and less effective district offices.

CORRELATIONAL STUDIES

Correlational studies are very similar to ex post facto investigations in that the independent variables in both designs are not manipulated by the researcher, but are only measured. The main difference between correlational and ex post facto studies is that the hypothesized independent variables in the latter design are usually *potentially* amenable to manipulation by the researcher, e.g., counselors' interpersonal skills can be enhanced by training, and attitudes toward disabled persons are modifiable, while the independent variables, such as intelligence, severity of disability, and age, in correlational studies may not be susceptible to modification, except by the selection of subject samples. A difference that is more apparent than real concerns statistical procedures; the results of correlational studies are typically reported in the form of correlation coefficients, while ex post facto results are usually presented as mean differences. This is a minor distinction because correlation coefficients are routinely tested for statistical significance and almost all tests of significance have correlational, or strength of association, analogues.

Time Spent on Placement

Zadny and James (1977a) investigated the relationship between the rehabilitation counselors' reports of time and effort devoted to job placement and the rehabilitation outcomes of their clients. The 208 counselors in the study were a random sample of practitioners in seven western states.

The counselors estimated their total travel, placement-related travel, and the number of hours per week that they normally devoted to nine activities, including job placement and job development. Caseload statistics for each counselor were collected from the state agencies. The variables included the number of total rehabilitations (status 26 closures), the number of rehabilitated severely disabled clients, the average earnings of rehabilitated clients at closure, the proportion of clients placed in competitive employment, and the proportion of cases closed as not rehabilitated after planned services had been delivered (status 28 closures).

Correlations were calculated between the travel and the time estimates, which were presumed to be the independent, or causal, variables, and the client service outcome measures, which were hypothesized to be influenced by the counselor's activities. Although the coefficients were of modest size, several were statistically significant and were in the anticipated direction, suggesting that greater placement efforts produce more successful rehabilitations. Specifically, counselors' estimates of time spent on both placement and job development, miles traveled per week, and amount of travel devoted to making placement, were all *negatively* correlated with the proportion of cases closed not rehabilitated.

The authors' conclusions merit quotation, because they place the results of their study in perspective and at the same time stress the limitations of correlational studies:

> While net time and travel are relatively crude measures, the pattern of correlations is consistent with the contention that counselor commitment to job development and to placement is one way to place clients. As time spent on activities having a direct bearing on placement increased, total rehabilitations increased and cases closed not rehabilitated decreased. The level of effort devoted to other activities, with the exception of planning, failed to yield comparable patterns. The limitations of correlational data preclude a causal interpretation, but the results do suggest that attention to placement can be time well spent. (Zadny and James, 1977a, pp. 34–35)

Analysis of the State-Federal System

Kunce, Miller, and Cope (1974) analyzed the relationships among 12 critical rehabilitation variables using data on almost 700,000 clients in 54 state rehabilitation programs for 1968 and 1969. The objective of their investigation, which they designated as "macro data analysis" because the state program was the unit of analysis, was to assess the relationships of rehabilitation program characteristics to client outcome variables.

The 12 program variables represented one of three distinct categories. The *input* variables were: caseload feasibility, state per capita expenditure, and cases per 100,000 population. The *process* variables included: months in active caseload, cost of case services, percent funds for workshops, percent funds for maintenance, percent funds for training, and percent funds for counseling and placement. The *output* variables were: cost per rehabilitation, rehabilitation rate per 100,000, and rehabilitant's salary. Caseload feasibility was quantified using a procedure developed by Kunce and Miller (1972), which is explained in Appendix 5 (page 163).

The statistical analysis of the data was straightforward: each of the 12 variables was correlated with every other variable and the coefficients were arranged in a convenient matrix. After discussing the results, Kunce, Miller, and Cope summarized their findings and conclusions as follows:

1. Rehabilitation rate and rehabilitant's salary represent two distinctly different measures of program outcome and are inversely related to each other.
2. Agencies are more likely to achieve higher rehabilitation rates if they serve larger numbers of cases, have sufficient financial resources,

spend proportionally more money on workshops and less money on training and maintenance, and keep clients in active service status for a shorter time.

3. Agencies are more likely to place clients in higher paying jobs if they work with fewer, but more select, clients; have limited resources in terms of state money; and tend to spend more of their money on training than on workshops.

4. Indications of caseload feasibility can be obtained from those client characteristics that relate to general employer hiring practices (e.g., previous education and prior employment).

5. Agencies in the southeastern United States have higher rehabilitation rates but lower rehabilitant's salary in contrast to those in western states.

6. The percentage of money spent for training significantly increases rehabilitant's salary regardless of the agency's caseload difficulty. The use of training, however, tends to reduce client turnover and may result in a lower rehabilitation rate.

7. The percentage of monies allotted for counseling and training tend to favorably influence final salary.

8. In the evaluation of program effectiveness, consideration should be given to several output measures because programs may be unfairly evaluated using a single criterion.

The important point to emphasize about correlational studies, as was true with ex post facto investigations, is that the significant correlations only indicate that the variables are associated. It could be that a causal relationship is reflected in a significant correlation, but this is not necessarily so. For example, the seventh conclusion reached by Kunce et al. *implies* that spending more money for counseling and training will lead to higher salaries for rehabilitants. While this may be true, it should be obvious that a more controlled research design is required in order to substantiate that conclusion. All that the results of the Kunce et al. study really can say is that the rehabilitants in states that spend a higher proportion of money on counseling and training receive higher average weekly salaries at closure.

However, it should be equally obvious from the conclusions listed above that correlational studies generate much potentially useful information and suggest numerous hypotheses for future research. Finally, Flynn (1975) reanalyzed the Kunce et al. data set using a sophisticated multivariate procedure called *path analysis* and reached conclusions that were similar to those based on the straightforward examination of the intercorrelation matrix. Readers interested in a comprehensive statistical evaluation of the state-federal rehabilitation system are referred to the recent dissertation by Flynn (1978).

BEHAVIOR MODIFICATION STUDIES

Included in this category of studies are a wide variety of designs and procedures ranging from those that focus on a single variable to treatment programs that incorporate many component procedures. The single variable investigations typically address clinical problems that are amenable to intensive operant conditioning techniques. The behavioral therapy literature contains numerous examples of these procedures (see Craighead, Kazdin & Mahoney, 1976; Kazdin & Wilson, 1978; O'Leary & Wilson, 1975).

At the other end of the continuum is the research approach advocated by Azrin (1977). His use of behavioral methodology emphasizes the development of multi-component treatment programs that are based on an analysis of the specific elements of complex personal-social problems. This general strategy for applied behavioral research is described by Azrin (1977) and is illustrated by his highly successful job-finding club.

The Job-Finding Club

Azrin, Flores, and Kaplan (1977) devised and experimentally evaluated the effectiveness of an innovative job counseling program known as the job-finding club. Job finding was conceptualized as behavior requiring a number of complex skills, which should be learned best in a structured learning situation, that stressed such factors as motivation, maintenance of behavior, feedback, imitation, and practice. Accordingly, a comprehensive program was developed for assisting the job seeker in every area that was believed to be influential in obtaining a job.

The job-finding club met daily and the clients were encouraged to attend the sessions each day until they obtained jobs. The group meeting format allowed the use of a buddy system for assistance, advice, encouragement, mutual auto transportation to employers, role playing, supervision of telephone inquiries, mutual review of resumes, and sharing job leads. In addition, the following areas received emphasis: family support, full-time job search, expansion of the range of positions that are considered, dress and grooming, and personal attributes. The specific procedures for obtaining and pursuing job leads included: job leads from other job seekers, friends and relatives, former employers, telephone contact, personal referral, resume development, interview instruction and role playing, call back, and job-finding materials and aids.

Participants in the evaluation of the job-finding club were recruited through a variety of sources, e.g., state employment service, newspaper advertisement, and industrial personnel departments. The only criteria for selection were that the individual desired full-time employment and was not currently employed fulltime. Clients were matched on an overall measure of probable employability and were randomly assigned to the job-finding club and a no-treatment control group. (Subjects in the control group were simply left alone to use their own resources in searching for a job.) Two months after the clients entered the counseling program, 90% had obtained jobs in contrast to just 55% of the matched control subjects. Furthermore, the mean starting salary for the jobs obtained by the counseled clients was significantly higher than that of the noncounseled job seekers. Also indicating the effectiveness of the job-finding club was the high negative correlation ($r = -0.80$) between the proportion of sessions attended and the number of days unemployed for the counseled clients; in other words, regular attendance increased the probability of locating a job quickly.

The authors concluded that these results provided the first controlled demonstration that a job counseling program is more effective than the usual unstructured job seeking. A subsequent replication study by Azrin and Phillip(1979)extended the initial positive findings to handicapped clients. Furthermore, the control group in this second investigation received an alternate method of job counseling that consisted of lecture, discussion, and interview rehearsal components. Still, the results were even more impressive with handicapped clients: after 2 months 89% of the job-finding club clients had obtained jobs in comparison to only 19% of the control subjects. Readers interested in additional job placement programs applicable to disabled clients are referred to the special issue of the *Rehabilitation Counseling Bulletin* (Salomone, 1977).

OTHER DESIGNS

Two additional types of research studies deserve brief mention due to their prevalence in the rehabilitation literature. Case studies of single subjects have long been recognized as an important source of hypotheses for experimental research. When carefully prepared they provide insights into the dynamics of the adjustment to disablement and the process of counseling with disabled clients that are not available in less intensive research studies. The reader is referred to Shontz (1965) for an excellent discussion of the strengths and limitations of case studies.

Other research approaches that employ single subject strategies have emerged from the behavioral therapy literature (see Hensen & Barlow,

1976), and from the psychometric tradition (see Cattell, 1963; Holtzman, 1963). Another approach that may be classified as single subject research is the autobiography. In fact, one of the classic works in rehabilitation psychology is Wright's (1960) derivation of general principles of adjustment to disability (e.g., coping, succumbing, and "as if" behavior) that were abstracted primarily from autobiographical accounts and case histories. Two recent autobiographical accounts that provide insights into the rehabilitation process are those of Caywood (1974) and Goldiamond (1976).

The second research design that is fairly common in rehabilitation is the demonstration study. As the name suggests, this type of investigation is used to demonstrate the applicability of an innovative service procedure to a particularly difficult-to-serve group of clients. The purpose of the demonstration study is not to evaluate the effectiveness of the treatment program, but only to assess its feasibility as a service procedure. Controlled evaluations often proceed from demonstration studies. But the initial concern is not with whether or not the new program is more effective than some other treatment approach, but is simply with establishing that a particular group of clients can be served. Demonstration studies, then, are often used to initiate rehabilitation services for a group of clients that heretofore had been underserved or neglected.

Multiply handicapped deaf clients have traditionally been difficult to rehabilitate. Bolton (1974a) described a comprehensive program that was implemented at the Hot Springs Rehabilitation Center expressly to enhance services to deaf clients. The program included case management and counseling services, personal-social preparatory services (personal adjustment training, supervised living, recreational activities, and group counseling), and vocational preparatory services (vocational evaluation and adjustment, skill training, and job placement). One-half of all ex-clients achieved competitive employment, while two-thirds of those who graduated from vocational training programs did so. Another example of a demonstration study is the Cooperative Living project sponsored by the Texas Institute of Rehabilitation and Research (Stock & Cole, 1975). Because some severely disabled persons cannot live effectively in traditional housing environments, this project developed the concept of "adaptive housing," which refers to special living arrangements that include attendant care, food services, and transportation on a shared basis. A tabulation of the activities of 39 severely disabled persons before and after entering the project demonstrated that adaptive housing can help these individuals lead productive lives. The Arkansas Spinal Cord Injury project, which is described in Chapter 9, provides a third example of the demonstration study.

SUMMARY

Descriptive research studies are important steps in the development of a body of knowledge about rehabilitation clients and the rehabilitation process, but they must be followed by experimental studies in order to establish cause-effect relationships and thus generate a truly scientific basis for rehabilitation practice. A common experimental design, which is methodologically very weak, is the one-group pretest-posttest design. The lack of a control group of subjects precludes the conclusion that the experimental treatment caused any of the measured changes. Other possible sources of improvement fall within the categories of history, maturation, testing, instrumentation, and statistical regression.

When subjects are randomly assigned to experimental and control groups, a stronger design is achieved (referred to as the pretest-posttest control group design). However, the external validity of this design is still potentially threatened by the reactive effect of pretesting. Contrary to popular opinion, pretesting is not essential to an adequate experimental design. The random assignment of subjects to groups ensures that the groups are similar on all possible subject characteristics. Thus, the strongest experimental design is the posttest-only control group design.

Control procedures serve the purpose of eliminating or holding constant irrelevant differences or competing explanations that confuse the interpretation of the treatment effect. Standard control techniques include the use of randomization, control treatments, naturally occurring comparison groups, matching, and statistical adjustment.

The ex post facto design is fairly common in field studies. It is not a true experimental design because the independent variable is not manipulated by the investigator. Subjects are selected because they have or have not been exposed to the experimental variable. The results of ex post facto studies can never be statements of cause and effect, but their tentative conclusions are suggestive of causal relationships, which can be evaluated in true experimental studies. Correlational studies possess the same limitations as ex post facto investigations.

An important type of behavior modification study emphasizes the development of multi-component treatment programs that are based on a behavioral analysis of complex psychosocial problems. The chapter concludes with references to various single subject approaches and brief descriptions of demonstration service projects in rehabilitation.

chapter five
Assessment of Outcomes

The traditional measure of successful outcome in vocational rehabilitation counseling has been placement in gainful employment, or more generally the achievement of a 26 closure status, which includes noncompetitive employment and nonremunerative employment categories in addition to competitive employment. In recent years there has been increasing dissatisfaction with the so-called 26 closure system (see Haakmeester, 1975; Hawryluk, 1972; Thomas, Henke & Pool, 1976). The two main criticisms of the narrow emphasis on vocational adjustment are that important aspects of clients' psychosocial adjustment are neglected and that employment goals may be unrealistic for the most severely disabled clients.

ISSUES IN THE ASSESSMENT OF OUTCOMES

The assumption underlying the vocational rehabilitation philosophy is that successful vocational adjustment will lead to satisfactory adjustment in other areas of living. Discussing this topic more than 20 years ago, Super (1957) hypothesized that "assisting a client to use his assets in order to make a better vocational adjustment will result in his being able to make a better adjustment in other areas of living" (p. 301). Why this is a reasonable hypothesis is evident in a statement by Menninger (1964, pp. xiii–xvii) which is paraphrased here:

> In American life, work is an essential activity of the mentally healthy person; work provides the opportunity to participate, to contribute, and to be productive; work provides the opportunity to win the approval of others, and thus, self-approval; work provides the opportunity to develop satisfying social relationships, a sense of belonging, and an identification with "the working group" in the larger sense of the phrase.[9]

---

[9]The role of work should also be viewed in context. Kasl (1978, pp. 5–6) summarized a variety of survey evidence to demonstrate that work is not as important to Americans as a number of authors have suggested, i.e., work is not the central life activity or concern for most people — health, family, and community are regarded as more important.

Crites (1969, pp. 346–354) reviewed the research literature in vocational psychology pertaining to the relationship between vocational adjustment and general psychological adjustment and concluded that they are moderately related. (Relevant studies in rehabilitation counseling are examined later in this chapter.)

The issues in the measurement of rehabilitation outcomes that are discussed below can best be introduced by posing a series of questions:

1. How should we measure the success of a rehabilitation program?
2. Is vocational adjustment the primary goal of rehabilitation, or should psychosocial functioning be considered?
3. Is the counselor's opinion the most important index of status or improvement, or do we value the client's self-assessment of his/her level of functioning?
4. Are vocational and personal adjustment interdependent processes, or can one occur without the other?
5. In general, what are the major dimensions underlying client status and rehabilitation outcome?

While rehabilitationists do not disagree with the notion that vocational adjustment provides a foundation for successful life adjustment, many believe that other aspects of client functioning should be considered in assessing rehabilitation success (see Athelstan, Crewe & Meadows, 1973; Clowers & Belcher, 1978; Neff, 1971, pp. 111–113). Four basic issues can be delineated that are relevant to the "criterion problem" in rehabilitation counseling.

Economic Versus Noneconomic Measures

Because rehabilitation legislation defines both the handicap and the potential for rehabilitation in vocational terms, economic criteria, such as job placement, occupational level, and salary, have remained the dominant measures of individual accomplishment and program effectiveness. Only recently have measures of the quality of the job placement (satisfaction and satisfactoriness) been developed for use in rehabilitation counseling (Dawis, 1976). In addition, a number of instruments have been proposed to assess nonvocational or psychosocial dimensions of rehabilitation outcome; several instruments are reviewed in this chapter.

Self-Report Versus Observer Rating Measures

Available criterion instruments in rehabilitation rely on a variety of data sources, e.g., demographic information, questionnaire responses, case service and closure data, counselor ratings, and follow-up interviews. Several investigations in rehabilitation counseling and psychotherapy indicate that criteria may be source-specific. For example, Berzins, Bednar, and Severy (1975) analyzed psychological change in psychotherapy clients by using pretest and posttest data based on the clients' self-reports and on the ratings by therapists and psychometrists. They concluded that "the development of consensual measures of outcome is imperative for the systematic evaluation of the effects of diverse therapeutic interventions" (p. 10). The statement certainly applies with equal force to rehabilitation counseling. The issue of client and counselor perspectives is considered in depth in the next section.

Unidimensional Versus Multidimensional Measures

The basic theoretical issue here is whether success in rehabilitation counseling is a global construct that can be measured on a *single* continuum or whether success actually consists of several relatively independent components that should be quantified as a *profile* of separate measures. While instrumentation has been developed proceeding from both orientations (or assumptions), the standard procedure has been simply to enumerate a variety of relevant criteria for which instruments exist. This *multiple* criteria approach should be distinguished from a *multidimensional* approach to the assessment of rehabilitation outcome, because the latter entails a systematic research design and the application of appropriate psychometric procedures. This important issue of dimensionality of rehabilitation outcome is also treated in depth in this chapter.

Relative Versus Absolute Measures

Most rehabilitation counselors and supervisors would agree that the degree of success that any client achieves can only be evaluated in terms of his/her initial status. A severely retarded client earning $20 per week in a sheltered workshop may represent a much greater success than an upper extremity amputee earning $100 per week in competitive employment. Nevertheless, absolute measures continue to predominate in research projects and service programs. One reason for the infrequent use of relative measures is that they introduce technical problems associated with the quantification of change from pretest and posttest scores. This topic is discussed in conjunction with the dimensionality issue and again in Appendix 7 (page 192).

CLIENT AND COUNSELOR PERSPECTIVES

The issue of client and counselor perspectives in the assessment of client psychological and vocational adjustment has important implications for the provision and the evaluation of rehabilitation services. Now that the client is recognized as an equal-status participant in the rehabilitation counseling relationship (Arkansas Rehabilitation Research and Training Center, 1975; Randolph, 1975), his/her viewpoint is considered to be just as valid as the counselor's opinion. One of the first areas of mutual concern for the client and the counselor who work together is that of assessing the extent of the client's rehabilitation needs or the level of functional adjustment. This assessment is critical for two reasons: 1) it indicates the magnitude of services that are required to restore the client to optimal functioning, and 2) it provides an index of client "difficulty," which serves as a baseline for the evaluation of client benefit, and by implication, counselor effectiveness (see Chapter 9). When a second assessment is made at the time of case closure, the pretest/posttest differences are used to indicate the extent and the type of changes in client functioning that have occurred as a result of the provision of rehabilitation services.

The Fundamental Issue

The fundamental issue that is being addressed in this section can be stated simply: Are the major psychosocial and vocational dimensions in rehabilitation client assessment perspective-specific? In other words, do we have to specify the measurement viewpoint when we conceptualize and assess client adjustment? Or more concretely, should we conclude, for example, that family support as viewed by clients, and family support as assessed from the counselor perspective, are different constructs? While this question, variously phrased, cannot be answered with any degree of finality at this time, it should be realized that the generic problem of method variance has been debated extensively in the recent psychometric literature (see Fiske, 1973, 1976; Golding, 1977; Huba & Hamilton, 1976; Jackson, 1977). The particular aspect of method variance that arises from differences in measurement perspectives has been treated in considerable detail by two prominent psychometricians: Fiske (1971b) has argued that observations from different perspectives are measuring different constructs; the contrasting point of view is advocated by Cattell (1973) who maintains that underlying constructs can be isolated by using the convergence of several methods of measurement. These two opposing positions are summarized next.

Historical Background

In a now classic paper Campbell and Fiske (1959) outlined a research paradigm for assessing the convergent and discriminant validity of psychological measures; introduced the notion of a trait-method unit, which suggests that psychological construct and measurement method may be inseparable; and documented the pervasiveness of method variance in psychological measurement. While most research psychologists have accepted the validity of the Campbell-Fiske analysis and conclusions, which most subsequent research has supported, at least one prominent psychometric personologist has resisted the conclusion that method variance extensively confounds trait measurement. Cattell (1973) has refined his perturbation theory over a period of several decades. The principle of "indifference of the medium" and the concept of "instrument-free trait patterns" postulate that, while traits cannot be measured without some contamination by the method of observation, a source trait that can be isolated by using the convergence of several methods of measurement does exist (p. 232).

In direct contrast to Cattell, Fiske (1971b) has emphasized "the fact that observations from different perspectives are so different in quality and so independent empirically that they should be treated as relevant to separate constructs or subconstructs" (p. 59). Fiske defines a perspective as a viewpoint from which personality phenomena can be observed (e.g., subject, peer, and psychologist) and notes that research findings indicate that the more dissimilar the viewpoints from which observations are made, the lower the relationship between them. In summary, Fiske's position maintains that personality traits are perspective-specific.

Psychiatric Studies

Nine studies in the literature have directly addressed the issue of convergence of perspectives in the domain of psychopathology. Ellsworth, Foster, Childers, Arthur, and Kroeker (1968) conducted a large-scale investigation of the behavioral adjustment of 178 male schizophrenics. They found modest correlations (few were above 0.30) between patients' self-reported psychopathological symptoms on a 17-item scale and a variety of behavioral ratings completed at several points in time by the hospital staff and the patients' relatives. Park, Uhlenhuth, Lipman, Rickels, and Fisher (1965) compared ratings of distress level and improvement during drug treatment by 138 neurotic patients and their psychiatrists. The median correlation for a 64-item modification of the Hopkins Symptom Checklist Discomfort Scale was 0.51.

Four relevant studies used the Hamilton Rating Scale for Depression. Prusoff, Klerman, and Paykel (1972) found correlations of 0.36 and 0.81, during the acute episode and at recovery, respectively, between total severity scores derived from the Hamilton Scale and a self-report inventory completed by 147 depressed patients. Carroll, Fielding, and Blashki (1973) reported a correlation of 0.41 between the Hamilton Scale and the

Zung Self-Rating Depression Scale for 67 depressed patients. Schwab, Bialow, and Holzer (1967) reported a correlation of 0.75 between the Hamilton Scale and the Beck Depression Inventory for 153 medical patients, and Williams, Barlow, and Agras (1972) found that the same instruments correlated 0.82 for a sample of 10 depressed psychotic patients.

Three pertinent MMPI studies have been published. May and Tuma (1964) found low correlations (a range from 0.13–0.37) between three MMPI scales (Pa, Pt, and Sc) and various psychiatric rating scales completed by nurses, physicians, and psychiatrists for 100 schizophrenic patients. Spitzer, Fleiss, Endicott, and Cohen (1967) reported correlations between a priori selected MMPI scales and the 13 symptom scales of the Mental Status Schedule for 60 female schizophrenics: the coefficients ranged from 0.08 to 0.70. Lorr and Gilberstadt (1972) compared two diagnostic typologies, one was based on the Inpatient Multidimensional Psychiatric Scale and the other was based on MMPI profiles, for 335 hospitalized psychotics. The degree of overlap between the self-report and the interview-based typologies was slight.

These investigations can be summarized as follows: all investigations were carried out in psychiatric settings and used hospitalized patients as subjects; a variety of instruments of the self-report and rating scale formats were employed; the obtained correlations ranged from nonsignificant to high; and higher correlations resulted when the samples were heterogeneous in composition, the variation in behavioral symtomatology was extensive, and the item content and format of the measurement instruments that were employed were similar.

Rehabilitation Studies

In conjunction with a nationwide study of the rehabilitation counseling process (Bozarth, Rubin, Krauft, Richardson & Bolton, 1974), 108 applicants for services with psychiatric disabilities completed the Mini-Mult (a short form of the MMPI) and were interviewed by private psychologists who completed the Psychiatric Status Schedule (PSS) for each applicant. The Mini-Mult summarized the clients' subjective views of their emotional status while the PSS provided an "objective" assessment from the psychologists' perspectives. Statistical analyses of the resulting multivariable-multimethod matrix revealed a substantial convergence of client and psychologist perspectives. The assessment of depression was the symptom area in which the greatest agreement occurred ($r = 0.60$), while the canonical analysis that used all Mini-Mult and PSS scales produced a correlation of 0.75, which approaches the theoretical maximum when unreliability of the scales is considered. Details regarding this investigation are available in the article by Bolton (1977c).

Another study by Bolton (1978c) was designed to empirically evaluate the issue of perspectives within the rehabilitation counseling relationship. The sample consisted of 103 rehabilitation clients who were accepted for services by 10 counselors in the Little Rock office of the Arkansas Rehabilitation Service. Each client completed the Human Service Scale (HSS) and was evaluated by his/her counselor using the Client Outcome Measure (COM) at the time of acceptance. The results of the study were that: 1) clients and counselors were seldom in close agreement in their independent judgments, e.g., the highest interperspective correlation $(r = 0.42)$ occurred between the parallel economic scales that included relatively "objective" items, such as work status, weekly salary, and the source of support, and 2) the discrepancies between client and counselor responses to these "objective" items suggest a possible ceiling on the degree of interperspective convergence that can be achieved. Regardless, three conclusions from this investigation deserve emphasis. First, it is important to reaffirm the basic axiom of client involvement: the opinions of service receiver and service provider should both be regarded as legitimate and equally valid perspectives. Second, both client and counselor judgments of client adjustment should be routinely collected and systematically recorded. Third, procedures should be devised for integrating the client's and the counselor's judgments of client adjustment into the rehabilitation planning process, as well as into the agency program evaluation scheme. The critical aspect of this procedure would, of course, refer to the situation where the client and the counselor disagree (Bolton, 1978c, pp. 287–288).

Tseng (1972a) examined the convergence of the self-evaluations of 117 clients who were enrolled in vocational training programs at a comprehensive rehabilitation center and the ratings completed by their vocational instructors. Clients and instructors, using 5-point scales, independently completed identical rating instruments that included 11 personal attributes (e.g., punctuality, cooperativeness, appearance, and courtesy) and 6 work proficiency attributes (e.g., work skill, quality of work, and observance of safety practices). Seven of the 17 interperspective correlations were statistically significant, but moderate in magnitude; the three highest correlations were 0.42 for work skill, 0.37 for quality of work, and 0.33 for punctuality.

Three investigations of the dimensionality of rehabilitation outcome include the measures of client change during the rehabilitation process from the perspectives of clients and practitioners (see Albrecht & Higgins, 1977; Bolton 1974b, 1978d). The extent of interperspective convergence in the assessment of client change is similar to the assessment that occurred in the studies of the client's initial status or functioning during vocational training that were discussed above. These data suggest that clients often view their situations as either more or less favorable than do the rehabilitation professionals who are working with them. The implication for researchers and consumers of rehabilitation research is that the judgment of success or lack of success is often a function of the point of view of the observer.

(Although they do not deal with outcome measurement, three additional investigations have addressed the topic of client and counselor perspectives. Hill (1978) contrasted the perceptions of patients and personnel in a physical medicine setting, Leviton (1973) compared professional and client viewpoints on seven critical issues in rehabilitation, and Walls and Masson (1978) examined differences between clients and members of their families regarding disability-related problems.)

DIMENSIONALITY OF REHABILITATION OUTCOME

The study of the interrelationships among measures of vocational, psychosocial, and physical functioning of rehabilitation clients is central to the resolution of the "criterion problem" in rehabilitation counseling. In this section, three topics are overviewed: 1) the delineation of the issue of dimensionality, i.e., can rehabilitation success be reduced to composite scores on a single continuum, or are there two or more relatively independent aspects of client adjustment? 2) the review of correlational and dimensional investigations of rehabilitation clients' adjustment in various areas of functioning, and 3) the discussion of the conceptual and statistical problems that occur in the quantification of client change during the rehabilitation process.

The Fundamental Issue

The recognition of the importance of dimensional problems in rehabilitation research can be traced back to the early developmental stages of the Minnesota Studies in Vocational Rehabilitation; Scott, Dawis, England, and Lofquist (1958) concluded that

> the study of interrelationships among criteria is probably the most neglected aspect of research in this field. The potential rewards of such study are very attractive when it is considered that it might be possible to determine a minimum number of criterion variables that would account for most of the variability in work adjustment. (pp. 58–59)

Some 15 years later, Conley (1973) reviewed the conceptual, measurement, and statistical issues in constructing a weighting system for the evaluation of case closures and asked a question concerning the difficulty of combining (or weighting) client change variables: "How does one combine vocational benefits with nonvocational benefits when the latter are not measured in monetary terms?" (pp. 32–33). A more fundamental question is, of course, *should* vocational and nonvocational measures of client adjustment be combined?

The basic issue, unrecognized in most weighting schemes, is that of dimensionality. If the vocational and nonvocational domains overlap substantially (i.e., vocational and nonvocational measures are highly correlated), then combining them into a composite index may be a reasonable procedure. But, if vocational change is relatively independent of nonvocational change, combining them into a weighted score would be entirely unjustified. Thus, the assessment of dimensionality is logically the first priority in addressing the criterion problem in rehabilitation counseling. (The problem of dimensionality is not unique to applied research. Both Skinner (1961) and Underwood (1957) have recognized the salience of the dimensionality issue in traditional experimental psychological studies; see Chapter 7.)

Correlational and Dimensional Studies

Several investigations have addressed the question of dimensionality of rehabilitation outcome. Some have relied on data collected at case closure only, while others have used change scores; the results of most studies have been reported as correlations between various types of measures, yet some investigations have used factor analytic procedures to summarize a matrix of intercorrelations. The studies reviewed below are generally ordered from the less sophisticated to those that are more statistically complex.

Three investigations have found relationships between self-esteem and subsequent employment. MacGuffie, Jansen, Samuelson, and McPhee (1969) reported that, among applicants for state rehabilitation services, those clients with higher self-concepts were more likely to have been closed in employment. Favorable attitudes toward self were correlated with return to work for a sample of physically disabled clients (Barry, Dunteman & Webb, 1968). And self-acceptance was related to employment for a sample of clients with epilepsy (Schwartz, Dennerll & Lin, 1968). While the results of these studies indicate that clients who evidence better psychological adjustment do have a higher probability of achieving employment, the results do *not* warrant the conclusion that psychosocial and vocational measures should be combined into a single index of rehabilitation success. In other words, just because two (or more) measures overlap to some degree, it does not follow that they are reflecting the same underlying construct. Factor analytic studies are more appropriate for addressing this question. Before moving to the factorial studies of rehabilitation outcome, an investigation of the relationship between physical functioning and psychosocial adjustment is summarized.

Albrecht and Higgins (1977) examined the interrelationships among changes in physical functioning, as rated by physical therapists, and the changes on self-reported indicators of social functioning for a sample of 122 patients in two physical rehabilitation centers. The majority of the subjects suffered from spinal cord injuries and cerebrovascular accidents. In each setting, two physical therapists, using scales that measure various aspects of self-care and mobility, rated each patient twice (at the times of entrance to and departure from the centers). The therapists also directly evaluated patients' changes in motivation and attitudes toward self, others, and disabled persons that were observed during the center stay. Also on a pretest/posttest basis, each subject completed instruments that measure attitudes toward self, others, and disabled persons, as well as the Rotter Internal-External Locus of Control Scale. Finally, ratings of the patients' cooperation in, and the completion of, treatment activities were derived from content analyses of the minutes of staff meetings. The following results were observed in the (partial) correlation matrix of change scores: 1) the changes in various types of physical functioning (self-care and mobility) were highly interrelated, 2) the changes in physical functioning and self-reported social functioning (attitudes and perceived control) were virtually unrelated, 3) the changes in physical functioning were moderately correlated with the judges' ratings of change in social functioning, 4) the changes in self-reported social functioning were uncorrelated with the judges' ratings in the same areas (i.e., there was no evidence of interperspective convergence), and 5) the cooperation and completion of services was minimally related to improvement in both physical functioning and social functioning. The conclusions of Albrecht and Higgins (1977) are well-stated:

> Although the two conceptual criteria of rehabilitation success, physical and social functioning, are recognized and in common use within the institutions studied, the operational measures of each do not intercorrelate to such a degree that improvement in one would necessarily imply improvement in another. As a consequence, assessments of physical functioning and attitudes must be considered as independent measures of rehabilitation success. These two sets of indices measure different aspects of the rehabilitation process which are not necessarily related.... In conclusion, our study indicated that successful modification in physical function does not necessarily imply im-

provement in social function in a rehabilitation setting. However, a caution should be noted. The effects of people-changing organizations do not necessarily end with the termination of institutionalization. Therefore, while functioning on different criteria may not be highly related in the short-term, future research is needed to examine these relationships during an extended time period after institutionalization. (pp. 43 & 44)

The results of three-dimensional investigations of rehabilitation outcome for state agency clients have reached essentially the same conclusion as the Albrecht and Higgins (1977) study; however, the two broad domains of concern in the state agency studies were vocational functioning and psychosocial functioning. In the first investigation (Bolton, 1974b), two self-report inventories, the Mini-Mult and the Tennessee Self-Concept Scale, were administered to 70 rehabilitation clients shortly after referral and again at closure. In addition to the 12 psychological change scores obtained from the questionnaires, three vocational change variables were constructed using referral and closure information from agency records. The correlation matrix of 15 (residual) change scores was factor analyzed using an oblique rotation (see Chapter 7); three factors resulted: 1) improved vocational functioning, 2) improved self-concept, and 3) reduced anxiety. The first factor was uncorrelated with the other two factors, leading to the *tentative* conclusion that vocational success and psychosocial adjustment are independent dimensions of client change during the rehabilitation process. The conclusion was regarded as tentative because perspectives and domains were confounded, i.e., vocational functioning was assessed only from the agency point of view and psychosocial adjustment was only measured from the clients' perspectives.

Because the results of the initial study could not be considered to be conclusive, a replication of the study was carried out (Bolton, 1978d). In the second investigation, vocational and psychosocial indices of client change were obtained from the independent reports of clients and their counselors, thus eliminating the design problem that was present in the first study. Thirty-one clients completed the Human Service Scale and were rated by their counselors on the Client Outcome Measure at the time of acceptance for rehabilitation services and again at closure. The results of a factor analysis of the correlation matrix of (residual) change scores, in conjunction with an examination of the interperspective correlation matrix, supported the conclusions that "psychosocial adjustment and vocational adjustment are distinguishable yet related dimensions of client improvement during the rehabilitation counseling process" (Bolton, 1978d, p. 13). A recent study by Growick (1979) produced results that were generally consistent with this conclusion.

Measurement of Change

The measurement of changes in clients' functioning from the time of acceptance for rehabilitation services to closure or to follow-up is a critical concern, because the objective of rehabilitation is the enhancement of clients' psychosocial and vocational adjustment. Thus, it is unfortunate that the quantification of change is a major unresolved psychometric problem. There are two basic approaches for constructing change scores from pretest and posttest measures: 1) raw difference scores and 2) residual gain scores (which are sometimes called base-free or adjusted posttest scores).

Raw differences scores are the simplest to calculate (the pretest scores are subtracted from the posttest scores), but they have the undesirable property of being negatively correlated with initial status, i.e., subjects who are low at pretest can only stay low or improve, while initially high-scoring subjects can only remain high or deteriorate. Consequently, raw difference scores have limited applications in investigations of client change.

In contrast, residual gain scores (which are calculated by subtracting the predicted posttest scores from the actual posttest scores)[10] are uncorrelated with initial status. However, the measurement of improvement or deterioration is relative to the initial score level, i.e., the magnitude of any subject's change can only be interpreted by comparison to other subjects who shared the same initial score level.

Both the raw and residual approaches to the quantification of change are plagued by the unreliability/invalidity dilemma (Bereiter, 1963). The essence of this dilemma is that the higher the correlation between pretest and posttest administrations of an instrument (which reflects the temporal stability of the variable and suggests that the same construct is being measured), the lower is the reliability of the change scores. Conversely, when the temporal stability is low, implying that the same construct is not being measured at the pretest and posttest administrations ("invalidity"), the reliability of the change scores is higher. Of course, the reliability of the instrument sets an upper limit on the reliability of the change scores.

A third approach to the analysis of pretest/posttest data, which is closely related to the residual gain procedure and is applicable to treatment group situations, is partial correlation, or analysis of covariance. Two studies that were reviewed previously illustrate the use of these procedures in rehabilitation research: Albrecht and Higgins (1977, p. 40) employed partial correlations, and Roessler, Cook, and Lillard (1977), using

---

[10]The residual score is the part of the posttest score that remains after the part that is predictable (via linear regression) from pretest status is removed.

analysis of covariance, analyzed pretest/posttest data in an experimental/control group design.

A fourth approach to the measurement of change does not require pretest and posttest administrations because clients' changes are rated directly after a period of observation. For example, Albrecht and Higgins (1977, p. 39) asked judges to rate changes in patients' motivation and attitudes after an extended period of observation.

Although more sophisticated variants of the residual gain/partial correlation approach have been proposed (see Cronbach & Furby, 1970; O'Connor, 1972), it is sometimes difficult to see how algebraic manipulations can resolve what appears to be a more fundamental measurement problem. In fact, Carver (1974) has outlined a complete reformulation of the measurement process for the quantification of change. However, his proposal was not very well received by traditional psychometricians (see Cronbach, 1975).

For practical purposes there are two types of research situations in which the analysis of clients' changes are of interest: 1) studies of the effectiveness of a particular treatment on a sample of clients (analysis of group change data), and 2) studies of individuals' differential responses to treatments (analysis of individual change scores). Investigations of the former type usually involve partial correlation or covariance analysis, while the latter situation typically requires some form of residualized scores. The reader desiring a straightforward review of the problems in measuring change, accompanied by several numerical examples that parallel the situations described above, should consult the document by Hummel-Rossi and Weinberg (1975).

MEASURES OF REHABILITATION OUTCOME

Several scales and instruments that have been developed or adopted for use in rehabilitation counseling research are reviewed. First, those instruments that *assume* that rehabilitation success is a unidimensional construct are described. The remaining scales and inventories are based on a multidimensional conception of client functioning.

Unidimensional Measures

In conjunction with a large-scale study of a state rehabilitation agency (see Chapter 7), Eber (1966) developed two composite criterion measures based on clients' closure and follow-up data. Scores on the first dimension, Vocational Adequacy at Closure, are calculated as a weighted combination of four variables: work status at closure, DOT job code at closure, weekly earnings at closure, and successful closure code. Scores on the second dimension, Vocational Adequacy at Follow-up, are defined as a weighted composite of four additional variables: employment at follow-up, work status improvement from closure, job satisfaction, and counselor estimate of success. Vocational Adequacy at Closure is almost a pure measure of economic/vocational success, while the parallel dimension at follow-up is slightly less so. Eber (1966) provided a theoretical justification for these composite dimensions:

> While any one variable, representing for example, earnings or job status, is subject to the consideration that this variable may not be the most meaningful measure, the factor underlying a number of these variables, as it emerges from the analysis, is a broader concept and a more inclusive one. (p. 43)

In a recent chapter, Eber (1975), emphasizing the two outcome variables of short-range and long-range success, summarized his earlier research.

Stein, Bradley, and Buegel (1970) reported the construction of an 11-step composite criterion of employment experience. Postcounseling employment information was obtained from a 2-year follow-up questionnaire administered to 1,020 Veterans Administration rehabilitation clients. Three variables (current job status, length of time on longest job since discharge from hospital, and number of jobs held since discharge) were combined to form 11 brief descriptions of work adjustment that were ranked according to their economic value to society by 10 experienced counselors. The result was an 11-point scale of vocational success.

In contrast to the two composite measures described above, the Rehabilitation Gain Scale (RGS) developed by Reagles, Wright, and Butler (1970a, 1971, 1972) contains items that tap psychosocial adjustment as well as vocational functioning. The RGS consists of 20 items that reflect vocational success (e.g., earnings, hours worked each week, work status, primary income source, whether the client was having trouble finding a job, the client's expressed chances of getting a desired job, and prediction of future employment) and personal and social adjustment (e.g., client's assessments of physical and mental health; amount of public assistance received; and the extent of the client's participation in activities where he/she worked, with his/her family, with others in the community, and with formal clubs and organizations). Selected items are reproduced in Table 9. The instrument is completed by the client prior to, and following the provision of, rehabilitation services. Statistical procedures were utilized to develop two sets of weights that are applied to the pretest/posttest questionnaire responses and that result in three composite scores: status prior to rehabilitation, status following rehabilitation, and difference or

Table 9.   Selected items from the Rehabilitation Gain Scale[a]

---

1. How is your general physical health? Aside from any disability that you might have, how would you describe your physical health?
    (1) excellent; (2) good; (3) fair; (4) poor; (5) don't know

3. Are you having trouble finding a job at this time?
    (1) no; (2) not looking; (3) yes

8. Which of the following activities do you take part in along with other members of your family?
    (a) social activities such as visiting other people, going to parties or club meetings, etc.
    (b) family games
    (c) family discussions
    (d) attending church with family
    (e) outdoor or sports activities with family: picnics, hikes, etc.
    (f) other family projects (describe) _____

9. What is the total number of hours you spend each week on the activities you circled in list above?____hours per week

18. Weekly earnings at acceptance versus weekly earnings at closure? $____ at acceptance; $____ at closure (nearest dollar)

19. Work status at acceptance versus work status at closure?
    (a) wage-earning or salaried worker (competitive labor market)
    (b) wage-earning or salaried worker (sheltered workshop)
    (c) self-employed (except BEP)
    (d) business enterprise managed by a state agency (BEP)
    (e) homemaker
    (f) unpaid family worker
    (g) not working-student
    (h) not working-other

20. Amount of assistance at acceptance versus amount of public assistance at closure $____at acceptance; $____at closure

---

[a]Reproduced by permission of Reagles, K. W., Wright, G. N., and Butler, A. J. A scale of rehabilitation gain for clients of an expanded vocational rehabilitation program. *Wisconsin Studies in Vocational Rehabilitation*, No. 13. Madison: University of Wisconsin, Regional Rehabilitation Research Institute, 1970, pp. 69–74.

gain score. It is important to note that the authors (inappropriately) evaluated the assumption of unidimensionality using internal consistency reliability procedures; they should have employed factor analysis or some other dimensional technique (see Chapter 7).

Hawryluk (1974) also developed a rehabilitation gain scale that was patterned after the RGS. His instrument included five components: hours per week gainfully employed, weekly earnings, work status, economic dependency, and psychological well-being. Unlike the RGS, items concerning social and recreational activities were excluded. Using pretest (referral) data and follow-up data, relative change scores are calculated for each of the five components; the component scores are then summed to produce a composite index of rehabilitation gain.

The four unidimensional measures of client outcome possess the advantages of comprehensiveness (for the particular domain of interest) and adequate reliability. Their common weakness is that they may be averaging several meaningful independent criteria into a combination score that has no specific interpretation, i.e., Can vocational success and personal-social adjustment be meaningfully added together and labeled as gain? Is it possible for clients to succeed vocationally and to adjust poorly in other areas, and vice versa? If so, what does their gain score represent? The measurement instruments that are discussed below illustrate a different approach to the criterion problem.

Multidimensional Measures

The Human Service Scale (Kravetz, 1973) was designed to provide a multidimensional assessment of rehabilitation needs from the client's perspective. The seven subscales, which are closely related to Maslow's basic need categories (see Bolton, 1979a) are: Physiological, Emotional Security, Economic Security, Family, Social, Economic Self-Esteem, and Vocational Self-Actualization. Item analysis, factor analysis, and other psychometric procedures were used to reduce an original item pool of 158 items to 80 items that are scored on the seven subscales. Illustrative items are reproduced in Table 10. The internal consistency reliability coefficients for the subscales range from 0.69 to 0.97 with a median of 0.86. Preliminary analyses of the subscale intercorrelations did not support Maslow's hierarchical ordering of needs (Kravetz, 1973), but the results of recent studies have provided evidence for the validity of the Human Service Scale (Bolton, 1977d; Growick, Butler & Sather, 1979). Reagles and Butler (1976) have discussed the possible uses of the Human Service Scale in assessing clients' service needs.

The Client Outcome Measure is a counselor-rating instrument that was shortened from a longer scale developed by the Oklahoma Rehabilitation Agency (Westerheide, Lenhart & Miller, 1974, 1975). The employment orientation of vocational rehabilitation counseling provided the general framework for the instrument. The items emphasize the clients' functional ability in relation to employment. The Client Outcome Measure consists of five subscales: Vocational Functioning, Physical Functioning, Economic/Vocational Status, Family Relationships, and Work Tolerance. The subscales consist of two to five items. Each item requires a counselor's judgment using 5-point anchored continuua. Examples are given in Table 11. Interrater reliabilities for the original Oklahoma sub-

Table 10.   Selected items from the Human Service Scale[a]

I. *Physiological:* The extent to which the client experiences symptoms, aches and pains, health problems, and the effects of these complaints on his/her normal daily activity.

    10. How often are you bothered by shortness of breath when not exercising?

        a. very often   b. often   c. as often as not
        d. sometimes   e. hardly ever

    52. How often do you worry about your health?

        a. very often   b. often   c. as often as not
        d. sometimes   e. hardly ever

II. *Emotional Security:* The extent and frequency of feeling on the part of the client of uncertainty, indecisiveness, worry, depression, discouragement, restlessness, anger, helplessness, and other unpleasant emotional states.

    12. How often do you feel down or discouraged because your major problems cause you to waste time?

        a. very often   b. often   c. as often as not
        d. sometimes   e. hardly ever

    34. How often have you consulted a doctor, psychiatrist, psychologist, or anyone else about a nervous problem?

        a. very often   b. often   c. as often as not
        d. sometimes   e. hardly ever

III. *Economic Security:* The extent to which the client is worried about financial problems.

    48. How often do you worry about not having enough money?

        a. very often   b. often   c. as often as not
        d. sometimes   e. hardly ever

    60. Which of the following statements best describes your present financial situation?

        a. very good   b. good   c. average
        d. poor   e. very poor

IV. *Family:* The extent to which the client reveals problems in communication with family members, receiving help from the family, spending time with the family, problems in family life, and relationships in general.

    9. How often do you have trouble showing your feelings to your family?

        a. very often   b. often   c. as often as not
        d. sometimes   e. hardly ever

    42. About how much time a week do you spend doing things together with your family?

        a. 5 hours or less   b. 6 to 11 hours   c. 12 to 17 hours
        d. 18 to 23 hours   e. 24 hours or more

V. *Social:* The nature and extent of the client's involvement in social activities, contacts with friends and acquaintances as opposed to social withdrawal, isolation, and inactivity.

    55. How many hours each week do you spend on activities with other people in your community?

        a. 1 hour or less   b. 2 to 7 hours   c. 8 to 13 hours
        d. 14 to 19 hours   e. 20 hours or more

— *continued*

Table 10 — *continued*

---

58. How many people do you know with whom you feel free to talk about personal things and problems?
    a. very many   b. many   c. some
    d. a few   e. none

VI. *Economic Self-Esteem:* The extent to which the client's economic and employment status reflects economic dependency, unemployment, or underemployment.

1. What is your *main* source of support?
    a. your own earnings (wages, workshop payments, income from your own business)
    b. savings, property, or other investments
    c. earnings of someone else in the family
    d. Social Security, pension payments, or Unemployment Compensation payments
    e. Public Assistance or welfare payments

78. How steady is your present job or the work you do?
    a. very steady   b. steady   c. reasonably steady
    d. unsteady   e. very unsteady

VII. *Vocational Self-Actualization:* The extent to which the client feels stimulated and challenged in his/her job and the extent to which he/she derives personal, social, and vocational satisfaction from the job.

64. How often does your *present* work let you make decisions on your own?
    a. very often   b. often   c. as often as not
    d. sometimes   e. hardly ever

76. How often are you told in your *present* work that you have done a good job?
    a. very often   b. often   c. as often as not
    d. sometimes   e. hardly ever

---

[a]Reproduced by permission of Reagles, K. W., Wright, G. N., and Butler, A. J. *Human Service Scale.* Madison: University of Wisconsin, Regional Rehabilitation Research Institute, 1973.

scales averaged in the 0.80s (Westerheide & Lenhart, 1973); however, the reduction in the number of items and their rearrangement using the results of factor analytic studies should be noted. A preliminary factor analysis of the 15 items comprising the COM supported all the subscales except Work Tolerance (Bolton, 1978c).

THREE APPROACHES TO INVENTORY CONSTRUCTION

Goldberg (1972) defined a strategy of (multi-scale) inventory construction as "a systematic procedure for grouping and keying items to form a set of scales from the same item pool" (p. 12). There are three main strategies

Table 11.   Selected items from the Client Outcome Measure[a]

I.   *Vocational Functioning*
    B.   Decision-Making Ability
        1.   Will neither help make decisions nor take action if others help; counselor must arrange other professional assistance before client can proceed toward rehabilitation.
        2.   Others make decisions for him and manage his personal affairs.
        3.   Prefers others to make decisions but will take some part in decision-making process.
        4.   Slow, but eventually makes own decisions.
        5.   Takes strong active role in decision making.
II.   *Physical Functioning*
    B.   Physical Independence for Tasks other than Mobility
        1.   Constant need for attendant services.
        2.   Dependent for several major tasks.
        3.   Dependent for one major or several minor tasks.
        4.   Minimal assistance required.
        5.   Totally independent.
III.   *Economic/Vocational Status*
    C.   Work Status
        1.   Not working other.
        2.   Trainee or worker (non-competitive labor market).
        3.   Homemaker, unpaid family worker, not working student.
        4.   Wage or salaried worker (sheltered workshop), state agency managed business enterprise (BEP).
        5.   Wage or salaried worker (competitive labor market) or self-employed (except BEP).
IV.   *Family Relationships*
    A.   Role in Family
        1.   Conscious effort to disrupt family.
        2.   Refuses to assume appropriate role.
        3.   Participates in familial affairs but evidence of underlying ambivalence toward family.
        4.   Assumes appropriate role but some counselor reservation.
        5.   Assumes appropriate role.
V.   *Work Tolerance*
    A.   Physical Stamina
        1.   Current disability status precludes employment.
        2.   Unable to work full-time because of physical condition.
        3.   Sedentary work, low stress, or close supervision required but able to work full-time.
        4.   Occupations limited to light physical activity but able to work full-time.
        5.   Minimal restrictions to type of work client can do.

[a]Reproduced by permission from the *Client Outcome Measure,* Arkansas Rehabilitation Service, Little Rock, Ark.

for constructing multi-scale questionnaires: 1) the rational (or theoretical) approach relies on expert judgments to allocate items to scales that have been defined a priori using a theoretical scheme (such as Maslow's basic need categories), 2) the factor analytic (or internal) strategy uses the correlational structure of the initial item pool as a basis for clustering items into relatively independent and homogeneous subscales, and 3) the empirical (or external) procedure uses criterion groups formed on the basis of data external to the item pool to assign items to subscales that discriminate among the various groups. Each of these strategies for developing multi-scale inventories is illustrated in this section with an instrument that has been employed in rehabilitation counseling research.

An obvious question that has occurred to test developers and measurement specialists is: Which of the three strategies produces the best (most valid) instruments? Two comprehensive investigations have addressed this question. Using the item pool from the California Personality Inventory, Goldberg (1972) constructed a number of 11-scale inventories using the three main strategies, as well as other procedures for comparative purposes. The ability of the inventories to predict a variety of criteria (derived from peer ratings and behavioral indices) was assessed for different kinds of predictor functions (see Chapter 6). Three results are noteworthy: 1) the average cross-validities for the three strategies were quite similar, 2) there was a sizeable criteria-by-strategies interaction effect, i.e., selected criteria were more predictable for one strategy than for the others, and 3) a set of short rational scales provided the most efficient predictions. In a recent study, Burisch (1978) replicated Goldberg's finding of little difference in validity among the three main strategies. Burisch emphasized that, all other things being equal, the rational approach to inventory construction would seem to be the best choice because it is simpler, less expensive, and achieves acceptable results with shorter scales.

The Rational Approach

The Tennessee Self-Concept Scale (TSCS; Fitts, 1965) is one of the most popular instruments developed during the last 15 years. It ranked fourteenth in total number of references for personality tests during the 1969–1971 triennium and was one of only nine tests to improve in rank order by 30 points or more from *Personality Tests and Reviews I* to *Personality Tests and Reviews II* (Buros, 1975, pp. xxv–xxvii). The TSCS has been used in several studies of disabled populations (see Roessler and Bolton, 1978, pp. 24–26).

The TSCS consists of 90 self-descriptive statements to which the examinee responds on a 5-point Likert scale. (Ten additional items are scored on a separate Self-Criticism scale.) Each of the 90 items represents three design facets: *selves* (physical, moral, personal, family, social), *perspectives* (identity, acceptance, behavior), and *direction* (positive, negative). The balanced and crossed design thus includes 30 cells ($5 \times 3 \times 2$) with three replicated items per cell. A critical question is: Where did this framework come from? It was designed by the author of the TSCS to represent the major dimensions and the organization of the domain of self-conception; it is this characteristic that identifies the TSCS as a rationally developed instrument. Fitts (1965, p. 1) reports that seven clinical psychologists were able to classify the 90 items into the three-faceted design with perfect agreement.

The TSCS is scored on a total of 29 different scales. Early critics of the instrument questioned the reasonableness of scoring 29 variables from 100 items and recommended that the correlational structure of the items be examined by factor analytic methods. (See Bolton, 1976c, for a review of the relevant studies.) The use of factor analysis to confirm (or disconfirm) the subscale structure of inventories is one type of application of factor analysis that is used in instrument development and refinement. The other type of application is the direct allocation of items to subscales.

The Factor Analytic Approach

Raymond Cattell has devoted a major segment of his prolific career to the development and the refinement of his conception of the normal personality sphere and the primary instrument for its measurement, the Sixteen Personality Factor Questionnaire (16PF). The 16PF has been used extensively in studies of the psychological characteristics of various disabled populations; see Roessler and Bolton (1978, pp. 29–40) for a review and synthesis of some 20 investigations.

As its title suggests, the 16PF purports to measure 16 primary dimensions of normal personality functioning, as well as 8 secondary (or higher-order) dimensions. How were the scales constructed? In a series of factor analytic studies, Cattell (1946, 1957, 1973), using the interrelationship among items as a basis, progressively refined the item composition of the primary scales. (The technical procedure that is involved is outlined in Chapter 7 and Appendix 7 (page 187).) Because factor analysis of questionnaire items requires considerable judgment on the part of the researcher, it is not surprising that results for the 16PF have been mixed; some results confirmed the hypothesized structure while others questioned its validity. Appendix 2 (page 119) contains brief summaries of the relevant investigations that are organized into favorable and unfavorable results. A summary of pertinent psychometric studies of the 16PF, as well as a general appraisal of the instrument, is available in Bolton (1978a). In good part, the controversy over the factorial validity of the 16PF is due to Cattell, who is a true iconoclast in psychology, having developed his own psychometric personality theory while remaining especially critical of those who have not accepted his orientation. The biographical sketch in Appendix 3 (page 124) illustrates the inseparability of science, politics, and personalities.

Of special interest to rehabilitation researchers is Form E of the 16PF (referred to as 16PF-E). The 16PF-E "...is a special-purpose instrument designed for use with persons of limited educational and cultural background" (IPAT, 1971, p. 1). It consists of 128 binary items that measure 16 primary and 8 secondary personality dimensions. The 16PF-E has been used with a variety of disabled populations, such as mentally retarded adults (Muhlern, 1975), deaf college students (Trybus, 1973), and schizophrenic patients (Serban & Katz, 1975), although the latter application was of questionable validity. Recent factorial studies of 16PF-E that used a large sample of rehabilitation clients support both the primary structure (Burdsal & Bolton, 1979) and the secondary structure (Bolton, 1977a) of normal personality functioning. Furthermore, the 16PF-E is remarkably stable over time (Bolton, 1979c), is reasonably reliable, and makes available a large norm group.comprised of rehabilitation clients (IPAT, 1976).

The Empirical Approach

Available evidence indicates that the Minnesota Multiphasic Personality Inventory (MMPI) is the most popular extant personality inventory for research purposes (and the 16PF ranks second), as measured by the number of references in the psychological literature during the 1969–1971 triennium (Buros, 1975, p. xxvii). An abbreviated version of the MMPI known as the Mini-Mult (Kincannon, 1968) has also proved to be rather popular. (See Faschingbauer and Newmark, 1978, for a review of all MMPI short forms.) The Mini-Mult consists of 71 items, which are phrased as simple questions, and is scored on three validity scales and eight clinical scales (e.g., Hyponchondriasis, Depression, Hysteria, and Paranoia).

Again, the critical question in understanding how the instrument was constructed is: How were the 71 items assigned to the scales and how were they keyed? Is a yes (or no) answer to a particular item indicative of depression, or schizophrenia, or anything? The empirical approach to inventory construction requires that such criterion groups as depressed patients or schizophrenic patients be used to identify scale items. For example, the MMPI Depression scale was constructed by comparing the responses of a sample of 100 psychiatrically diagnosed depressive patients and a group of "normal" persons (hospital visitors) to more than 500 items. Those items that discriminated between the two groups, i.e., the proportions of depressives and normals responding "yes" were significantly different, became the Depression scale and a score can now be calculated for any subject simply by summing the responses that are keyed in the direction (yes or no) suggestive of depression. It should be apparent that scales can be constructed to measure any construct for which a criterion group can be defined. In fact, more than 450 different scales have been developed using the MMPI item pool (Dahlstrom, Welsh & Dahlstrom, 1975, pp. 265–347).

A good example of the use of the Mini-Mult in rehabilitation research is the recent study of 118 spinal cord injured clients reported by Cook (1979). Average scale scores were well within the normal range. Examination of the Mini-Mult profiles provided no evidence of anxiety and depressive reactions; one-third of the sample were classified as deniers, and one-fifth evidenced a tendency to withdraw from people and an inability to express hostility. There were no statistical relationships between psychological adjustment and sex, time since injury, point in the rehabilitation process, or cause of injury. The author contrasted these findings with the results and conclusions of other studies of spinal cord injured persons, most of which had found greater maladjustment in this severely disabled client population.

SUMMARY

Four basic issues that are relevant to the assessment of rehabilitation outcome are 1) economic versus noneconomic measures, 2) self-report versus observer rating measures, 3) unidimensional versus multidimensional measures, and 4) relative versus absolute measures. Because of their special importance in outcome measurement, the second issue, also known as client and counselor perspectives, and the third issue, dimensionality of outcome, were reviewed in considerable depth. It was concluded that the judgment of success is often a function of the observer's perspective and that vocational and psychosocial adjustment are distinguishable dimensions of client change. Also, psychometric problems in the measurement of client change were discussed.

Eber's measures of vocational adequacy at closure and follow-up, the Veterans Administration scale of employment experience, the Rehabilitation Gain Scale, and Hawryluk's gain scale illustrate composite unidimensional measures of rehabilitation outcome. The weakness of these instruments is that they may be averaging several meaningful independent criteria into a combined score that has no specific interpretation. The Human Service Scale and the Client Outcome Measure illustrate the multidimensional approach to the assessment of rehabilitation outcome from the client and agency perspectives, respectively.

The three strategies for constructing multiscale inventories are 1) the rational, or theoretical, approach, 2) the factor analytic, or internal, strategy, and 3) the empirical, or external, procedure. Comparisons among the three approaches suggest that the rational strategy is simpler, is less expensive, and achieves acceptable results with shorter scales. The Tennessee Self-Concept Scale, the Sixteen Personality Factor Questionnaire, and the Mini-Mult illustrate the three approaches to inventory construction.

(Appendix 2, page 119, contains brief summaries of the psychometric studies of the 16PF and Appendix 3, page 124, presents a biographical sketch of Raymond B. Cattell, which is followed by his reactions and comments.)

appendix two
Psychometric Investigations of the 16PF

Few measurement instruments in psychology have been subjected to as much critical research as the 16PF. Interestingly, many of the detractors have used factor analysis — the same psychometric technique that Cattell used to develop and refine his 16PF — to cast doubt on Cattell's conception of the normal personality sphere. Relevant research studies conducted by both critics and supporters are summarized in this appendix.*

THE UNFAVORABLE STUDIES

Levonian (1961) is usually recognized as the first researcher to question the psychometric adequacy of the 16PF. He demonstrated the lack of homogeneity of the 16 scales when he found that "while the average item correlates significantly with fewer than one other item in its factor, it correlates significantly with nearly 8 items outside its factor" (p. 591). Cattell subsequently dismissed this study and similar studies by asserting that high homogeneity was a fetish of misguided itemetric psychometricians and by arguing that moderate heterogeneity was necessary to ensure scale validity (Cattell & Tsujioka, 1964).

Becker (1961) reported a combined factor analysis of the 16PF and three Guilford-Martin inventories. Of the 10 interpretable factors, 7 were defined by 16PF scales: Anxiety, Extraversion, Hostility, Femininity, Independence, Superego Strength, and Intelligence. Becker concluded that "the present evidence suggests that the 16PF is at best dealing with eight factors and only two or three of these with sufficient reliability for individual prediction" (p. 402). It should be noted, however, that at least five of the seven factors listed above are well-replicated second-order factors of the 16PF.

---

*The studies are not reviewed critically nor are the details regarding sample, variables, and method presented. The purpose is simply to illustrate the divergence between the critics and the supporters of the 16PF by noting their results and quoting their conclusions.

In a broader attack on Cattell's normal personality sphere, Peterson (1965) reviewed personality rating evidence as well as questionnaire data. He found little congruence across similarly named factors in several different studies. Even though his analyses were not limited to the 16PF, and his statements often refer innocuously to "most investigators," there is no doubt that Cattell was the target of Peterson's general conclusion: "to date, most narrow primary factors in the personality realm have not convincingly passed the tests of efficiency and invariance" (p. 58).

The steadily increasing capacity of modern electronic computers soon ushered in the age of the large-scale item factor analysis. Eysenck was the first investigator to provide a comprehensive (and generally self-serving) factorial evaluation of the three major personality questionnaire systems. He and his colleagues (Eysenck, White & Soueif, 1969) separately factor analyzed approximately 100 items from the Guilford, the Cattell, and the Eysenck questionnaires. The results of the item factor analysis of 99 16PF items (that were selected by Cattell) led the authors to conclude that "...Cattell's questionnaires...should not be used to measure the Cattell primary factors, whose existence receives no support from this investigation" (p. 228).

A truly large-scale combined factor analysis of 600 items from the Guilford and the Cattell inventories was conducted by Sells, Demaree, and Will (1970, 1971). Since this study was carried out for the purpose of facilitating a theoretical integration of the two personality systems, the results failed to provide definitive ammunition for either the advocates or the opponents of Cattell. Most of the obtained factors were jointly defined by the Cattell and the Guilford items and were identified and named by the authors after a thorough consideration of the item composition.

Without doubt, the most devastating investigation of the 16PF was the item factor analysis reported by Howarth and Browne (1971). A 10-factor rotated solution was judged best and served as the foundation for the authors' conclusion that "...Cattell's questionnaire factor system has been developed on the basis of inadequate investigation of the primary factors..." (p. 138).†

Eysenck (1971) seized upon the results and the strongly stated conclusions of the Howarth and Browne study and used them as the basis for a broad-based denunciation of the 16PF, which included criticisms of the

---

†In a supplementary article Howarth, Browne, and Marceau (1972) summarized an analysis of the 16PF item correlations that was similar to Levonian's (1961) study in method, as well as results. In addition, Howarth et al. concluded that "...some of the items are so badly worded...as to...provide an unnecessary complication to putative content and direction of items" (pp. 86–88). Adcock (1974) also reported an item analysis paralleling the Levonian and Howarth et al. studies.

MMPI and criticisms of other competitors of his own EPI for good measure. Regarding the 16PF, Eysenck concluded that "...the investigator using this scale is in fact getting 16 measures of doubtful meaningfulness, and which are almost certainly non-univocal" (p. 88).

While they are not based on specific empirical studies, the opinions of the reviewers of the 16PF that are published in the *Seventh Mental Measurements Yearbook* merit quotation. Bouchard (1975) concluded that "the dimensions measured do not appear to be special or fundamental in any 'source trait' sense..." (p. 547) and Rorer (1975) stated that "for all practical purposes, the 16PF is composed of 16 scales of indeterminate origin and unknown significance..." (p. 550).

THE FAVORABLE STUDIES

Cattell's (1972) response to Eysenck's (1971) broadside was immediate and predictable. The response included discussions of the item versus parcel factor analysis controversy, the homogeneity "superstition," the seven essential requirements for a sound factor analysis, and Eysenck's alleged short cut to "pseudo" second-order factors.‡ Cattell also presented the results of his own item factor analysis of the 16PF; however, the factor pattern does not contain very convincing loadings for the hypothesized primaries, as Cattell had admitted (p. 176). Nevertheless, after weighing a number of theoretical and practical limitations of this type of analysis, Cattell concluded that "the pursuit of maximum simple structure yields with a high degree of statistical significance the 16 particular factor patterns said to be there..." (p. 184).

The two studies reported prior to the article summarized above require brief mention. Cattell, Eber, and Delhees (1968) factor analyzed the 64 variables resulting from the administration of four forms of the 16PF to a large, heterogeneous sample of adults. They found support for 12 of the 16 personality factors (E, M, N, and O factors were not clearly defined). In fact, the magnitude of the loadings was lower than might have been expected for this type of analysis, i.e., each of the hypothesized primaries was represented by four supposedly parallel measures, and each parallel measure was a composite of 6 to 13 items.

Cattell's unique and unfailing ability to adduce support for the primary dimensions of his normal personality sphere is nowhere more apparent than in his reanalysis of 69 Cattell and Guilford parcels that originated

---

‡ At the same time, Cattell's students jumped to his defense by publishing methodological critiques of the Howarth and Browne (1971) study and other investigations that were critical of the 16PF (see De Young, 1972; Dielman, 1973; Vaughn, 1973).

in a dissertation project by one of Guilford's students (Cattell & Gibbons, 1968). While the original Varimax solution was more consistent with the Guilford system (Gibbons, 1966) the results of Cattell's reanalysis confirmed all 14 of the 16PF factors represented in the data set (Cattell & Gibbons, 1968, p. 118). It should be noted, however, that Gibbons did not concur in this conclusion; he is quoted by Howarth and Browne (1971) as follows: "I have tried to interpret the results from the Cattell-Gibbons oblique rotation and have failed to get a meaningful interpretation" (p. 138, footnote).

One of the more recent studies to appear in the literature was conducted by two of Cattell's students. Burdsal and Vaughn (1974) concluded that the results of their item factor analysis of the 16PF "...was essentially the expected factor pattern. The study did, however, indicate that four of the 16 factors (G, M, N, and Q_1) were probably in need of revision and further research" (p. 223).

Another recently reported item factor analysis of the 16PF by Karson and O'Dell (1974) deserves special attention because it was conducted with Cattell's assistance. Consequently the analysis met his requirements for a sound investigation. The authors were moderate in their interpretation of the results: "But generally, if we stretch our imagination a bit, there does seem to be a fair match between the 16PF items and the constructs the test purports to measure. This match, however, is not strong and by no means fully supports the framework upon which the 16PF is based" (p. 113).

An unpublished item factor analysis by Adcock and Adcock (1975) is noteworthy for the authors' attempt to verify Cattell's 16PF primaries by the interpretation of the *content* of the nonkeyed items that defined the rotated factors. Obviously, their conclusion that the factor pattern "...gives reasonable support for 12 factors being regarded as substantially those described in the 16PF manual" (p. 2) is not comparable to the strictly psychometric conclusions that were reached in the investigations reviewed above.§ In fact, the factor pattern is similar to that of Cattell's (1972) study, with the major exceptions being the emergence of a large second-order factor labeled Emotionality, defined by C, O, and Q_4 items, and the failure to confirm the M, N, O, and Q_3 factors.

---

§In another paper (Adcock, Adcock & Walkey, 1974), the authors clarify this implied distinction: "Certainly all the recent evidence seems to indicate that the items themselves do *not* define the factors to which they are alleged to relate, but one point which appears to have been overlooked is that the factors which *do* emerge are in many cases strikingly similar to the 16PF factors as described" (p. 132). However, Karson and O'Dell (1974) reached the opposite conclusion: "Indeed, the content of the items seemed rather useless in interpreting the factors throughout" (p. 112).

Appropriately, the final study to be summarized was reported by Cattell (1975). A rather complicated parcel factor analysis led him to the global conclusion "...that the 16PF primaries are well confirmed..." (p. 79). Yet, careful examination of the evidence did not warrant such a strong conclusion; at least five factors (E, G, M, N, and Q_1) were far from "confirmed."

These studies are the main studies, both pro and con, that have bearing on the question of the factorial validity of the 16PF.[1] While this necessarily superficial summary would indicate virtually no communality between the critics and proponents of the 16PF, there does seem to be definite convergence at the second-order factor level. Careful examination of the factor patterns generated by Becker (1961), Howarth and Browne (1971), Karson and O'Dell (1974), and Sells et al. (1971) reveals several of the Cattellian secondaries, and not only the two universally recognized trait dimensions of extraversion and anxiety. It is true that the results of the various studies usually include fragmented secondaries mixed with some of the primaries; this is most certainly the effect of choosing to rotate an intermediate number of factors, i.e., more than 8 and less than 20. It is also true that several of the Cattellian primaries barely emerged as recognizable, even in the proponents' investigations. Among the favorable studies, support for E, G, M, N, O, Q_1, and Q_3 has been weak in one or more investigations.

Careful and reasonable evaluations of the investigations summarized above in conjunction with the results of two factor analytic studies of 16PF-E (Bolton, 1977a; Burdsal & Bolton, 1979) led the author to the following conclusion:

> While the available evidence for the factorial validity of the 16PF is far from unanimous, it certainly does not justify the negative conclusions reached by some psychologists. When evaluated by reasonable standards, the 16PF compares favorably with any other inventory that purports to measure variations in normal personality functioning. (Bolton, 1978a, p. 1080)

---

[1]Two additional investigations that I did not have access to are recorded in the interest of thoroughness: articles by Grief (1970) and Timm (1968) are cited by Eysenck (1972, p. 269) as failing to support the psychometric validity of the 16PF.

appendix three
Professor Raymond B. Cattell: An Appraisal

At this fifth anniversary meeting I believe that it is especially appropriate to review the monumental career of the founder of the Society of Multivariate Experimental Psychology, Professor Raymond B. Cattell. My presentation has three objectives:

1. To overview Professor Cattell's long career in order to give an idea of his enormous productivity and extensive contributions to quantitative psychology.
2. To speculate on some reasons for his controversial status and relative lack of recognition, a situation that is nicely stated by Pervin (1975): "...it is strange that a man who has produced so much and who is so convinced of his being on the right path should be ignored by so many psychologists" (p. 359).
3. To suggest some possible directions and projects for reducing the large disparity between Professor Cattell's extensive contributions and the minimal recognition that he has received.

CAREER OVERVIEW

Many psychologists believe that Professor Cattell's career began with the publication of *The description and measurement of personality* (1946), which served as the foundation for his conception of the normal personality sphere. Some may know that he wrote a manual entitled *A guide to mental testing* (1936) 10 years earlier. In fact, as Professor Cattell has pointed out in one of his autobiographical statements, he has lived two psychological careers. *The description and measurement of personality*

This appendix is based on the author's presidential address to the Society of Multivariate Experimental Psychology, Southwestern Division meeting, Fort Worth, Texas, April 21, 1977.

(1946) was the first major product of the second career, which began when he moved to the University of Illinois in 1944.

His pre-Illinois career, which covered the 15 years from 1929 (when he received his Ph.D.) to 1944, was more productive than the entire careers of 99% of all psychologists. In addition to heading a child guidance clinic, teaching at several British and American universities, conducting empirical research on personality and temperament, and developing several psychological tests, he published at least seven books: *Psychology and social progress* (1933), *Your mind and mine: An introduction to psychology* (1934), *A guide to mental testing* (1936), *The fight for our national intelligence* (1937), *Crooked personalities in childhood and after: An introduction to psychotherapy* (1938), *Psychology and the religious quest* (1938), and *General psychology* (1941).

His University of Illinois career can be divided into three periods, which I have designated as foundation (1944–1959), consolidation (1960–1969), and synthesis (1970–   ). Although it is impossible to do justice to the breadth and scope of Professor Cattell's voluminous productivity by simply listing his major books, the following titles are impressive:

1. Foundation: *The description and measurement of personality* (1946), *Personality: A systematic, theoretical, and factual study* (1950), *Factor analysis* (1952), *Personality and motivation structure and measurement* (1957).
2. Consolidation: *The meaning and measurement of neuroticism and anxiety* (1961), *The scientific analysis of personality* (1965), *Handbook of multivariate experimental psychology* (1966), *The prediction of achievement and creativity* (1968).
3. Synthesis: *Abilities: Their structure, growth, and action* (1971), *A new morality from science: Beyondism* (1972), *Personality and mood by questionnaire* (1973), *Motivation and dynamic structure* (1975), *Handbook of modern personality theory* (1977), *The scientific use of factor analysis* (1978).

For the record, his publications are estimated to be of the following magnitude: 30+ books, 300+ research articles, 25+ book chapters, and 12+ psychological tests and manuals. In order to give a more concrete perspective on Professor Cattell's contributions, I mention just a few specific achievements: the distinction between crystallized and fluid intelligence, the normal personality sphere and the questionnaires for its measurement at all age levels, the scree test for number of factors, maxplane and rotoplot rotational procedures, P technique factor analysis for the study of individuals, culture-fair intelligence tests, objective measurement of the components of motivation, dimensional analysis of small group functioning and national morale, multiple abstract analysis of variance technique, and plasmodes to evaluate factor analysis procedures.

In summary, it is apparent that Professor Cattell's contributions, which span almost half a century, reflect a tremendous expenditure of energy and a true dedication to the advancement of scientific psychology. Why, then, has recognition not been commensurate with his achievements?

THE PARADOX

This question introduces my second objective, which is to speculate on possible explanations for Professor Cattell's paradoxical status within the American psychological establishment. I believe that it is fair to say that the methodological cornerstone of Professor Cattell's approach to psychology is factor analysis. As noted above, he has been a major contributor to the development and the refinement of the procedure, as well as an ardent defender and voracious user. Factor analysis has enabled him to "map out" numerous psychological domains, e.g., normal personality, intellectual abilities, motivation, and psychopathology.

Thus, it seems reasonable to initiate the list of potential explanations or causes underlying the paradox with three "unresolved issues" or differences of opinion regarding factor analytic methodology.

1. Professor Cattell has long argued that properly conducted factorial studies have the power to discover *causal* traits in human functioning. While some psychologists relegate factorial results to the descriptive level (see Mischel, 1976) and a few hold that factors are meaningless, empty abstractions, most psychologists would probably take a moderate position: factors are potentially useful constructs that require further validation in subsequent investigations.

2. Professor Cattell favors a large number of fairly specific factors, in contrast to many psychologists who prefer fewer constructs of broader generality (see Allport, 1937; Eysenck, 1972; Comrey, 1973). The particular point that disturbs a number of critics is Professor Cattell's penchant for intricate interpretations of factors defined by a few relatively small loadings. It would seem that some type of hierarchical arrangement could resolve the differences in preference for complexity or specificity, but this is apparently not the case. Disputes among factor theorists concern the basic nature and existence of factors.

3. Professor Cattell uses a highly refined rotational procedure that involves an element of human judgment. Many psychologists look askance at techniques that entail subjective decisions, preferring various types of computer rotations to simple structures that meet a strict criterion of "scientific objectivity." Yet, a number of prominent psychometricians maintain that psychological meaningfulness of the obtained solution is more important than a blind simple structure criterion (see Guilford, 1977).

There are in addition several possible reasons for Professor Cattell's lack of wide acceptance:

1. Professor Cattell's writings are highly mathematical, and thus especially difficult for the nonquantitatively oriented reader.
2. Objective observers of Professor Cattell's work discern an element of faith in his research. For example, Hall and Lindzey (1970) conclude that Cattell's confirmatory interpretations of his empirical studies are often unwarranted. And Pervin (1975) notes that Cattell goes far beyond the data to formulate his theoretical principles.
3. Professor Cattell has not conformed politically. By directing his own research laboratory and test publishing company he has probably incurred the jealousy of many colleagues. He has not been active in the American Psychological Association ("the overgrown amoeba we call the APA"), the Psychometric Society, or other psychological establishment organizations. In fact, to the annoyance of many contemporaries, he founded his own professional society, The Society of Multivariate Experimental Psychology. He has literally developed his own "school of psychology" and operated independently of everyone else.
4. As Professor Cattell admits in his autobiographical statements, his personal style has not been especially conducive to winning friends and influencing people. While he aims to convince others with rational arguments, in fact, he often intimidates and overwhelms his critics. In his writings he appears to be overly critical of the work of other psychologists, particularly those whose findings are not supportive of his own theories.
5. While his writing style is engaging and colorful, his phraseology, labels, and analogies often seem unfair to others. For example, he has characterized clinicians as "soft-headed" psychologists and as refugees from the physical sciences. And he has suggested that the relationship between humanistic/clinical psychologists and scientific psychologists parallels that of nurses to doctors! In one of my favorite

examples, Professor Cattell analogizes a hypothetical situation involving 10 cases of whiskey to illustrate difficulties with Guilford's orthogonal rotations.

In summary, Professor Cattell's idiosyncrasies encompass personal style and professional orientation, as well as technical psychometric issues. Disregarding the ethical issue of judging the man on irrelevant grounds, what can be done to ensure a fair evaluation of his contributions?

SOME SUGGESTIONS

This question brings me to my third objective, which is to suggest some ways of addressing the paradox that was outlined above. My recommendations are as follows:

1. Preparation of a thorough nonmathematical summary of Professor Cattell's work. Both a historically oriented chronology documenting his introduction of thematic test methods, response sets, culture-fair testing, etc., and a logical summary of his theories and developments would be useful.
2. Integration of his ideas and theories into the mainstream of personality theory, psychometrics, genetics, etc. When seen in the broader context of contemporary psychology, Professor Cattell's contributions would become more visible than when they are viewed independently.
3. Design and conduct of a series of objective evaluations of Professor Cattell's many methodological and substantive contributions. Whenever possible, replication of his critical studies by nonpartisan investigators would be especially helpful.

While several of these suggestions could be carried out in conjunction with masters or doctoral research, or as faculty research projects, my guess is that the necessary "translations" of Professor Cattell's writings into a form that can be appreciated by the majority of psychologists will never be completed. Furthermore, I would also venture the opinion that proper recognition from the academic establishment will not be forthcoming. The unfortunate irony is that if Professor Cattell had been more diplomatic and politically oriented, his views would probably have been much more widely accepted. Ideally, of course, personal and political factors should not enter into the appraisal of scientific and professional merit, but in reality they do. Hence, I must conclude that very few psychologists of present and future generations will be able to appreciate one of the true creative geniuses of our time.

POSTSCRIPT: PROFESSOR CATTELL RESPONDS

Dear Professor Bolton,

Your letter invites a candid response to the position you so powerfully stated in your Presidential Address to the Southwestern Society for Multivariate Experimental Psychology. You referred particularly to an unnecessary lag in the advance of psychology as a science and to the fact that the new theoretical concepts developed by me and my colleagues through multivariate experimental methods had not been seen by the popular mass of psychologists as occupying the central structural position in theory which their intrinsic scientific soundness would indicate.

The hundred or more basic researchers with whom I have published over 50 years will appreciate your perception that it is time to call attention to a log-jam in the general stream of psychology. But while anyone interested in seeing clinical and personality psychology grow out of its prescientific, prequantitative confusion and uncertainty will deplore the situation as much as you do, yet the diagnoses of the causes and therefore of the way out may be varied.

One straw that might show the direction of the current is that my work, like that of, for example, Piaget, caught on earlier in Europe and Canada than in the U.S. If I may mention tangible evidence I would point to my election (along with Piaget and Skinner) to the half dozen distinguished foreign associates of the British Psychological Society (and my nomination this year to the German Psychological Society) and to the fact that requests for reprints from countries like Germany, France, and Czechoslovakia just about add up to those from the U.S. To cut a long analysis short I believe one reason for the low theoretical and mathematical interest of the average American psychologist goes back to the lesser mathematical and logical-analytical education in the American high school, compared to the German gymnasium, the French lycée, and the British selective secondary school.

Another cause could well be the flood of commercially oriented undergraduate texts, often written with the help of a journalist, which seek popularity with the students, and therefore with their teachers, by avoiding any difficulties and precision thinking or equations. A recent book, *Current Personality Theories,* drops the names of over 80 "originators of personality theories" but has not a single formula or statistical figure from cover to cover. Undergraduates in chemistry, physics, biology, and engineering are expected to manage formulae and calculations, but many psychology teachers seem bent on retaining psychology as a refuge for those students who cannot.

Finally, as Kuhn has well illustrated, we must expect radically different ideas, however well supported, to break through the crust of accepted scholarship only with deplorable delays. It took 20 years from, for example, the basic discoveries of Hertz to the relatively obvious applications by Marconi. Fifty years elapsed from Faraday's discovery of the principle of the dynamo to the first commercial use of the dynamo. Traditional medical men took a generation to accept and incorporate the theories of Harvey and Pasteur, while nearly 150 years elapsed from Copernicus until astronomers began calculating on a sun-centered planetary system.

Without placing ourselves in that eminent category I and my colleagues in multivariate experimental psychology can take heart from their eminent illustrations. The demonstration that trait structure can rest firmly on factor analytic research is 70 years old in the domain of abilities, 40 years in general personality structure, and 20 years in the domain of dynamics. In the last mentioned, use of P-technique — the only known objective technique for unravelling dynamic roots of clinical symptoms — is still strange to clinicians. A string of concepts could be reeled off from multivariate research that are operationally precise and practically useful, but stand in the arc of ignorance of many allegedly qualified students today. They include the relation of lower to higher order traits in depth psychometry (as in the split of exvia into surgency, affectia, etc primaries); the behavior specification equation and the use of situation vectors; the distinction in test use of homogeneity, reliability, and transferability coefficients; the relations of Q, L, and T data personality traits; the examination of heritability by the MAVA method; the distinction of epogenic and ecogenic age curve components; the separation of integrated and unintegrated motivational components in attitudes; the analysis of personality observations by perturbation and trait view theories (which include "social desirability" in a wider context); the distinction and measurement of anxiety, stress, depression, and other states and emotions by differential R-technique; and the principles of structured learning theory.

I understand that you are writing a book on research methods. I am sure from your other writings that it will have a balanced combination of statistical clarity and first hand acquaintance with the "nitty-gritty" realities of actual research problems. It will be a tangible contribution to loosening the logjam and moving to more scientifically based theory in psychology, issues that you and I and many others are painfully aware. I am convinced that if students were introduced more sympathetically, gradually, and in relation to their real psychological interests to the issues of design, statistics, and conceptual inference, it would be a very great service to psychology.

Sincerely,
Raymond Cattell

AN INDEPENDENT APPRAISAL

In his recent review of the 16PF for *The eighth mental measurements yearbook,* Walsh (1978, pp. 1081–1083) made a number of very favorable comments about Professor Cattell that greatly strengthen the picture outlined above:

No one has ever undertaken a more ambitious and vigorous search for the fundamental dimensions of human behavior than Raymond Cattell. In seeking behavioral scientists with whom to compare him, one is tempted to place him in the company of James McKeen Cattell, Charles Spearman, and L. L. Thurstone. Yet these men — like him, original thinkers, prodigious workers, and monumentally productive scientists — sought answers to questions of a much more limited nature than the one to which Cattell has addressed himself: the number and nature of a minimally sufficient set of factors from which essentially all of human behavior may be predicted. For, while Cattell and colleagues have sought to measure "personality" factors, their definition derives from the whole "person" rather than from some more limited frame of reference. The factors which the 16PF purports to scale range from intellectual ability to affective states, ego functioning, coping style, and group orientation, as well as some of the more usually accepted "personality variables." Cattell and a galaxy of co-workers have pursued this venture for more than 35 years now, and many of their most central results, important conclusions, and methodological advances are embodied in the current and earlier versions of the 16PF.

The primary tool with which Cattell has pursued his researches is factor analysis. Having begun his career at a time when the work of Spearman was still current and that of Thurstone was a bright new achievement, he incorporated many of their factor analytic orientations, techniques, and procedures into his own technical armamentarium. At the same time, he made advances of his own and was always open to the insights of others. . . .

The 16PF is in many ways a monument to the tremendous energies which Cattell has expended in his search for the basic dimensions of behavior. . . . The excellent normative data constitute one of the two real strengths of the instrument. The other is Cattell's unparalleled example of the kind of commitment, energy, and dedication which must be brought to any ambitious scientific endeavor. [Walsh, James A. "Review of the Sixteen Personality Factor Questionnaire," pp. 1081–1083. In the Eighth Mental Measurements Yearbook. Edited by Oscar Krisen Buros. Highland Park, N.J.: Gryphon Press, 1978. pp. xliv, 2182. Reprinted with permission of the publisher.]

chapter six
Prediction of Outcomes

In any rehabilitation setting some clients are more likely to be successful than other clients. Furthermore, some clients are more responsive to certain combinations of services, while other clients respond better to different treatment programs. In other words, clients respond differentially to rehabilitation services. In this chapter, several topics relevant to the prediction of differential client response to rehabilitation services are considered. Also, the important issue of the long-term adjustment of ex-clients is reviewed.

A PERSPECTIVE ON PREDICTION

One of the major goals of the behavioral sciences is the prediction and the control of individual behavior. Hence, a great deal of research effort has been expended on attempts to predict successful adjustment in various areas of human functioning, e.g., marriage, school, or work. It is realized, however, that the ability to predict success (or failure) does not guarantee control over the outcome. But prediction is a necessary precondition for control by intervention. In the context of human service programming for individual clients, the term *control* refers specifically to the ability to *prevent failure* by intervening to disrupt unfavorable predictions.

Horst, Wallin, and Guttman (1941) state the rationale for prediction research very well: "The goal of research in prediction is to reduce as much as possible the individual, social, and economic waste resulting from trial and error methods of selection of persons for various types of activities" (p. 101). When failure is believed to be highly probable for an individual, it is then possible for service planners to design a program to avoid an unsuccessful outcome. That is, the ability to predict failure is the first step toward intervention to prevent that failure. Obviously, then, the variables upon which the prediction is based must be assessable *before* the individual engages in the activity in which failure is being predicted. It follows that the research problem in prediction is to discover those critical variables that are associated with success/failure so that they can be employed to estimate the probability of success or failure *before* services are rendered. The first half of this chapter is concerned with various issues in the prediction of rehabilitation client outcomes.

Before proceeding, it is necessary to acknowledge a dissenting point of view that is not uncommon among practitioners from the "humanistic" school. The assumption that appears to underlie this orientation is the belief that human behavior is too complex to be analyzed into quantitative prediction equations. This attitude is illustrated by the critical remarks of the eminent sociologist Pitirim Sorokin:

> They attempt to put the business of prediction on a solid scientific basis. . . . This part is utterly disappointing and objectionable. Its main defects (include). . .an overenthusiastic faith in the infallibility of the ritualistic operations of a mechanical and quasi-quantitative nature in producing truth. . . . Who, except Almighty God, can combine and especially comeasure these incommensurable and uncombinable variables in one set of the multiple factors of happiness in marriage? (Sorokin, 1942, 78–79)

PREDICTION AND SERVICE DECISIONS

It can be reasonably argued that the central professional activity in the provision of rehabilitation services is prediction. All decisions, whether they are administrative judgments or counseling decisions made with the client's participation, involve an element of uncertainty and thus constitute predictions. The first critical decision-making situation that is faced by an applicant for rehabilitation services is eligibility determination, which requires a judgment of feasibility. Feasibility refers to the rehabilitation counselor's prediction of successful outcome after appropriate services are provided for the client. The feasibility prediction is an example of the *institutional* (or selection) decision. Although seemingly contrary to humanitarian rehabilitation philosophy, situations do exist in which limited resources and limited personnel necessitate the selection of those applicants who are most likely to benefit from the services and become rehabilitated (or possibly, the selection of those who are most in need of service). The other type of prediction is the *individual* (or classification) decision. The goal of classification procedures is the assignment of each rehabilitation client to the optimal treatment for him/her, i.e., the treatment that will maximize the probability of a successful outcome. Ideally, prediction in rehabilitation would be entirely of the individual decision type. Realistically, both selection decisions and classification decisions will be required for several years to come. Either way, it should be clear that the scientific study of prediction in rehabilitation is important for the improvement of services to all clients.

TWO SUMMARIES OF PREDICTION STUDIES

Two summaries of prediction studies are presented in this section. The first summary (Rubin, Bolton & Salley, 1973) is based on a comprehensive review of studies of correlates of client outcome and is concerned with *results,* i.e., the summary attempts to specify the variables that are predictors of rehabilitation success. The second summary (Bolton, 1972b) is based on a restricted review of prediction studies and focuses on the *methodology* of prediction.

Correlates of Client Outcome

The summary of correlates of client outcome is presented in five parts: 1) client demographic variables, 2) client ability variables, 3) client personality variables, 4) patterns of service, and 5) the rehabilitation counselor.

Client Demographic Variables   The studies suggested that the most potent demographic predictors of employment are age, marital status, amount of education, and age at onset of disability. Overall, it would appear that clients who are older and unmarried, have little formal education, and are older when they suffer disability are more difficult to rehabilitate. The review also suggested that clients with a psychiatric disability are more difficult to rehabilitate than clients with a physical disability. As would be expected, within the psychiatrically disabled group, the more severe the disability the lower the probability of rehabilitation. Some client variables, although mentioned less often, appear to be indicative of increased client difficulty: fewer dependents, less healthy relationship with family, poorer health, less formal vocational training, public or private relief as the primary source of income, no home ownership, and socially disadvantaged.

Client Ability Variables   The studies using client ability variables to predict client outcome are difficult to summarize meaningfully because of the lack of consistent criteria from study to study. Of the seven studies that reported significant results, only three utilized an employed/unemployed criterion. The WAIS appears to be the most significant predictor with higher scores associated with employment. The WAIS was also found to be predictive of completion of training and work performance in a sheltered workshop. Finally, the Ravens Progressive Matrices Test was found to be predictive of employment for a mentally retarded sample, and psychomotor performance was predictive of hospital discharge for a psychiatrically disabled sample.

Although it does not fall into the category of predictive investigations as they are typically defined, the now-classic study of adjustment to blindness by Bauman and Yoder (1966) does provide information that is relevant to the goals of predictive research. It would be impossible to improve on their concluding statement:

> Indeed, if it were necessary to summarize all the findings of this study in a single thought, that thought would be that no quality of vision, health, education, or family and social interaction has so much to do with adjustment as have the qualities measured by the Intelligence Quotient and personality inventory scores. Each of the preceding may at times influence IQ and, especially, personality scores. But regardless of what shaped it, that aspect of the client which is measured by these tests, in the end, most consistently shows relationship to adjustment, even when the most fundamental measure of adjustment is economic. (p. 75)

Client Personality Variables   The review suggested that clients' level of personal adjustment is a significant predictor of employment. Interestingly, this was found to be the case in mixed disability samples as well as in samples of the psychiatrically disabled. Also worth noting is the fact that, although three studies did not find a relationship between client outcome and adjustment at initiation of services, they reported a significant relationship between adjustment at termination and client outcome (better adjusted, more likely to be employed). This finding suggests that personality measures could be meaningfully utilized as intermediate outcome criteria.

Patterns of Service   Very little systematic research has been conducted in this area. More research is needed, especially on patterns of service for the various client disability groups. From the available studies, it appears that cost variables (both total and specific), counselor time variables (both total and specific), and specific services that can be provided or arranged by the rehabilitation agency are related to various aspects of client outcome (e.g., rehabilitation gain, client satisfaction, and job placement). The interested reader is referred to two recent studies by Growick (1976) and Growick and Strueland (1979).

The Rehabilitation Counselor   Research indicates that the rehabilitation counselor has a multi-role job. Counselors appear to allocate the greatest amount of time to face-to-face contacts with clients in which much emphasis is placed on the exchange of information, while relatively little focus is placed on the use of affective subroles. The research also suggests that levels of a counselor's interpersonal skills are related to the client's depth of self-exploration, the client's motivation to achieve the goals of the rehabilitation plan, and the client outcome.

Multivariate Prediction Studies

The second summary is based on the review of prediction studies of client outcome, which is included in Appendix 4 (page 151). The studies had to meet two criteria in order to be included in this review: 1) the criterion predicted was a rehabilitation outcome, e.g., employment, hospital discharge, and community placement, and 2) a composite prediction formula was developed, which reported predictive efficiency as a correlation, or percentage, of correct classification. Based on the studies that met the two criteria the following conclusions were reached:

1. Predictive studies have been fairly popular in rehabilitation; more than 30 studies were reviewed that met the two somewhat restrictive criteria.
2. The majority of studies have employed biographical data as predictive variables, with standardized tests a distant second place. (This is not unexpected given the universal availability of biographical data.)
3. Prediction of rehabilitation outcomes based on biographical data consistently exceeds chance levels. The average correlation of predictor composites of biographical data is estimated to be in the low 0.40s.
4. In no study that was reviewed did the predictor composite ever account for as much as one-half of the criterion variance in a cross-validation sample. (A correlation of 0.71 accounts for one-half of the variance.) This limited predictability is *not* unique to rehabilitation, but rather is the rule in applied psychological research.
5. Predictive studies in rehabilitation are generally not comparable due to mixed disability samples and differences in referral criteria, criterion definitions and measurements, predictor variables (even biographical data is not comparable because every agency collects slightly different information or records it differently), and methods of data analysis.
6. Only a few studies included treatment data in addition to client characteristics in the prediction equations. Therefore, most results reflect the (unknown) *interaction* of client characteristics and differential treatments. It is generally not possible to say what caused success or failure for the various client groups. The Counselor-Client Interaction Project, reviewed in Chapter 4, was one attempt to consider several sources of information in their interactive combinations. Also,

the numerical example that is used to illustrate multiple regression procedures in Appendix 5 (page 157) includes some treatment variables.

THREE REHABILITATION EXAMPLES

Three examples of traditional prediction studies are overviewed in this section. The first study involved multiple predictors and criteria, but the analysis was limited to simple pair-wise correlations, and the results were interpreted from the pattern of significant correlations. The last two investigations utilized multivariate statistical procedures.

Community Adjustment of Retardates

Rosen, Kivitz, Clark, and Floor (1970) reported the results of a study that correlated a set of 29 demographic measures, psychometric scores, and behavioral ratings with 22 criteria of community functioning for a sample of 65 institutionalized persons who received vocational and social rehabilitation training and were discharged to independent community living. The average age of the subjects at discharge was 29 years and their mean length of institutionalization was 15 years. Immediately prior to discharge, all subjects spent 6 months to 1 year in a traditional halfway house program, living at the institution, but working in the community.

Prior to their discharge, subjects completed a battery of psychological tests, which included measures of general intelligence, perceptual-motor abilities, academic achievement, and mechanical abilities. During their participation in the halfway house program, the subjects were also rated by their employers on four separate scales of work potential and social adjustment.

Criterion measures were derived from personal interviews conducted with the subject in his/her home 6 months to 1 year after discharge. The interview procedure used a structured questionnaire and rating scale techniques to assess functioning in three major categories: economic, vocational, and personal-social adjustment.

Each of the 29 predictor variables was correlated with the 22 criteria of community adjustment. Because of the large number of correlations (638), most of which were relatively low (only 30 were significant at the 0.01 level), the results were discussed in general terms:

1. Tests of perceptual-motor abilities were better predictors of postinstitutional adjustment than verbal intelligence and achievement tests.

2. Only the behavioral ratings of institutional adjustment concerned with employability were significantly related to the criterion variables.
3. Ratings by community employers in the halfway house program showed no significant relationship with the criteria.
4. Ratings of social adjustment within the institution did not relate to any of the social or vocational criteria of adjustment in the community.
5. Job-related criteria showed the majority of predictive relationships; criteria of social adjustment were not readily predicted.

Employment of Epileptics

Schwartz, Dennerll, and Lin (1968) investigated the relationship between combinations of neuropsychological and psychosocial variables and the employment status of a sample of epileptic clients. The study was part of a larger project that was designed to provide an empirical base for the development of an evaluation and classification system for the identification of employment problems of epileptics. The 181 subjects were volunteers in an outpatient diagnostic and research center for epilepsy. The subjects were approximately evenly divided between employed (88) and unemployed (93). The predictor variables were of two types. The neuropsychological variables included subtests of the Wechsler Adult Intelligence Scale (WAIS) and the Halstead-Reitan Battery (HB). The psychological variables were the subtests of the California Personality Inventory (CPI) and the Edwards Personal Preference Schedule (EPPS).

Three different combinations of the predictor variables were assembled using multiple discriminant analysis and multiple regression analysis. (Both techniques are described in Appendix 5, page 156.) The first analysis included five WAIS subtests, five CPI scales, and nine HB tests: 77% of the employed group and 80% of the unemployed group were correctly identified. The third analysis used the 15 EPPS scales: 63% of the employed group and 64% of the unemployed group were correctly classified. A stepwise multiple regression analysis selected five variables (three WAIS subtests, one CPI scale, and one HB test) that had a correlation of 0.58 with the employed/unemployed criterion.

Schwartz, Dennerll, and Lin noted that predictability would be expected to improve when variables such as frequency of current seizures and neurological status were included in the evaluative battery. They suggested a reexamination of the belief that changing employer attitudes and adequate seizure control represent a sufficient approach to the employment problems of epileptics.

Personal Adjustment of Stroke Patients

The study by Ben-Yishay, Gerstman, Diller, and Haas (1970) produced a battery of psychometric measures that successfully predicted three rehabilitation criteria for left hemiplegic patients. The subjects were 69 rehabilitation patients who suffered a cerebrovascular accident and were rendered left hemiparetic or hemiplegic. All subjects came from middle or uppermiddle socioeconomic backgrounds and had attained successful vocational or business careers prior to their disability. The mean age for the subjects was 60 years.

About one week after admission for rehabilitation, each subject completed an intensive battery of psychological tests. A total of 42 predictor variables were derived from the testing procedures. The 42 variables represented five types of psychological data: 1) clinical-demographic, 2) sensory motor, 3) standard WAIS scores, 4) special WAIS-cues scores, and 5) Bender-Gestalt scores. Stepwise multiple regression analyses were conducted for various combinations of the five predictor data sets and the three criteria — length of time in program, status of ambulation, and self-care skills — that were assessed at the time of discharge from the rehabilitation program.

Fifty-four of the patients were used as the construction sample and 15 patients constituted the *cross-validation* sample. A compact prediction battery, requiring just 45 minutes of testing time and using 27 variables, produced correlations of 0.83, 0.84, and 0.84 with the three rehabilitation criteria for the construction sample. When the regression equation was applied to the cross-validation sample, the resulting correlations with the three criteria were 0.62, 0.67, and 0.84. The authors concluded that this study established the feasibility of using psychological tests to predict the length of the rehabilitation program, as well as functional competence for ambulation and self-care after departure for left hemiplegic patients.

The statistical methodology of prediction research, including multiple regression analysis, pattern analysis, rational procedures, and cross-validation, is outlined in Appendix 5 (page 156).

CLINICAL VERSUS STATISTICAL PREDICTION

The long-standing controversy between clinical and statistical prediction was formalized by Meehl (1954) who reviewed 20 studies that compared clinical and statistical techniques of predicting various behavior outcomes. He concluded that in one-half of the studies the two methods were equal and that in the other half the clinical method was definitely inferior.

The controversy has continued during the past two decades, with proponents of both methods producing arguments and evidence to support their views.

Holt (1958) considered Meehl's analysis invalid because his clinical/statistical dichotomy was not meaningful. Holt argued that there are so many ways for clinical judgment to enter the prediction process that there are many types of clinical and actuarial combinations, and that Meehl had oversimplified the issue by classifying everything that is not 100% actuarial as being clinical prediction. Holt proposed a synthesis of clinical and statistical methods, which he called the "sophisticated clinical" method.

Sawyer (1966) refined Holt's argument and classified prediction methods in a two-dimensional table that provides a necessary framework for comparisons. The two dimensions are mode of data collection (type of measurement) and mode of data combination; eight prediction methods result. Sawyer applied the framework to the analysis of 45 studies, which produced 75 comparisons, and concluded that there is definite superiority for mechanical (statistical) modes of both data collection and data combination. His results supported Meehl in that the mechanical mode of combination is always equal to or superior to the clinical mode, regardless of whether data are collected by clinical or mechanical means.

Watley (1966) pointed out that most clinical versus statistical studies have focused on the predictive accuracy of the average clinician in comparison to the statistical method and that the results should not be interpreted to suggest that all counselors are less accurate than statistical methods of prediction. The one conclusion that seems warranted is that statistical procedures are vastly superior to global clinical predictions of complex behavioral outcomes in situations where large numbers of persons receive services according to a fairly standard routine; such is often the situation in the state/federal rehabilitation program. The investigation summarized next illustrates the typical methodology and result of clinical versus statistical prediction studies.

Prediction of Successful Psychiatric Rehabilitation

Roehlke (1965) compared counselors' predictions and statistical predictions of the outcome of rehabilitation of former psychiatric patients who were accepted for vocational rehabilitation services in Missouri. She used the biographical inventory technique to develop the statistical predictor from data in the clients' case folders on a normative sample of 44 clients. Actual outcome (dichotomous) was known for all clients. The biographical variables included psychological and vocational evaluation information, as well as personal history and demographic data. The single most important variable in differentiating between the two criterion groups was the diagnostic category. Two sets of scoring keys (one based on 25 variables and the other based on 13 variables) were used to classify two cross-validation samples into successful or unsuccessful closure status. The percentage of correct classification in the cross-validation samples ranged from 67% to 90%. Roehlke concluded that a reasonable overall estimate of the predictive efficiency of the statistical method was 80%.

The case folders of the 20 clients in the primary cross-validation sample were presented to 12 clinical judges. Each judge's predictions of outcome were compared with the actual outcomes, and the accuracy of prediction was calculated. The best of the 12 judges predicted the correct outcome for 55% of the cases; many did much worse. (On this sample the best statistical predictor resulted in 90% correct classifications.)

It is apparent that when the same case materials are used as the basis for separate predictions (of rehabilitation outcome of psychiatric patients) by statistical and clinical methods, the statistical method is vastly superior. This general conclusion has been reached in dozens of other studies; it is just not reasonable to expect the human brain to be able to analyze and correlate a set of data as efficiently as a statistical method, which is designed for maximal predictive efficiency.

LONGITUDINAL FOLLOW-UP STUDIES

The ultimate goal of rehabilitation treatment is the successful life adjustment of disabled persons. Regular contact with ex-clients and their families and employers is the only way to evaluate the long-range impact of rehabilitation services. Systematic follow-up studies are relatively rare in the rehabilitation counseling literature, although more studies are being conducted since the Vocational Rehabilitation Act of 1973 mandated the assessment of service effectiveness. Bauman and Yoder (1966) characterized the situation well: "Although some other research fields recognize the importance of studying data over long periods of time, this has not been usual in rehabilitation research" (p. 76).

Long-term follow-up studies are often expensive to conduct because people move to new residences, change jobs, etc. Furthermore, many ex-clients do not wish to be reminded of past difficulties and may even fear revelation to their current friends or employers, especially when the disability is a stigmatizing one, such as mental illness. Naturally, those clients who have been unsuccessful do not wish to be confronted with their failures. It should be obvious that follow-up studies in rehabilitation are subject to a variety of potentially biasing factors. Nevertheless, they are essential to determining the effectiveness and value of treatment programs.

The Longitudinal Investigation

Because longitudinal research projects can provide the only direct evidence regarding human development and adaption, these projects occupy a special place in theoretical and applied psychology. The major objectives in longitudinal investigations are: 1) the assessment of the permanence (stability), or conversely, the modifiability, of psychological characteristics over time, and 2) the evaluation of the long-term effects of interventions (planned or fortuitious) on psychological adjustment. These purposes distinguish the two basic longitudinal designs. Both designs require an initial assessment and at least one follow-up assessment of the same subjects, on the same variables, several years later. The difference is that the first design simply measures stability (or variability) over time as a result of naturally occurring conditions, but the second design is concerned with changes that may have been produced by the intervention. Clearly, the provision of rehabilitation services constitutes the planned intervention of concern in this section.

Classical Longitudinal Studies

The best known example of the non-intervention longitudinal investigation is Lewis Terman's life span study, which began in 1922, of 1,500 intellectually gifted children. Two recent reports on the surviving subjects, who are now 68 years old, are available in articles by Sears and Barbee (1977) and Sears (1977). Another well-known series of longitudinal studies are E. K. Strong's investigations of the stability of vocational interests over periods of 20 years and longer (see Strong, 1951). McClelland, Constantian, Regalado, and Stone (1978) interviewed a sample of young adults whose mothers had been respondents in a study of child-rearing practices in the early 1950s. And Vaillant (1977) describes the current life adjustment of 95 men who were students at Harvard in the early 1940s. The interested reader is referred to Bloom (1964) for a review and a synthesis of longitudinal studies in psychology and human development.

A model for the conduct of the experimental longitudinal investigation is available in the series of reports by Shore and Massimo (1966, 1969, 1973). They interviewed 20 participants in a vocationally oriented psychotherapeutic treatment program at intervals of 2, 5, and 10 years after the termination of the program (Massimo & Shore, 1963). A truly long-term follow-up study (30 years) of 400 youngsters who were subjects in the experimental Cambridge-Sommerville Youth Study (a preventive treatment program) reached the disconcerting conclusion that intensive personal counseling had negative effects (McCord, 1978; *Science News,* 1977). These two longitudinal intervention studies are somewhat atypical in that they employed random assignment to treatment and control groups; the typical investigation does not include an untreated control group because of the ethical problems of withholding services. In rehabilitation research, there would also be legal complications if appropriate services were not provided as expeditiously as possible to all eligible applicants.

LONGITUDINAL STUDIES IN REHABILITATION

Several longitudinal follow-up investigations of former vocational rehabilitation clients have been carried out. In one of the earliest studies, Scheltzer, Dawis, England, and Lofquist (1958) contacted 91 ex-clients of the Minnesota DVR and found that two-thirds of the former clients were employed full time. Fox, Miller, and Lawrence (1967) found that 16 of 20 successfully closed former clients of the Michigan DVR were employed 2 to 5 years after closure. A 4-year follow-up survey by McWilliams and Eldridge (1973) revealed that 78% of a sample of successful rehabilitants of the Tennessee DVR had retained employment.

Sankovsky and Newman (1972) sent questionnaires to 276 vocational training graduates of a comprehensive rehabilitation center 1 to 2 years after program completion. Based on a 70% response rate, one-third of the sample were found to be unemployed at follow-up, and one-third of the sample had worked less than one-half of the time since leaving the center. The most frequently cited problems in finding work were: employer resistance (18%), lack of skill or experience (16%), transportation problems (15%), and severity of disability (11%).

Neff (1959) reported a 1-year follow-up study of 197 ex-clients of the Chicago Jewish Vocational Service's Vocational Adjustment Center: two-thirds of the clients had been placed on jobs after satisfactory completion of their workshop programs and one-third had worked virtually continuously during the following year. Furthermore, while age, disability, and previous employment were unrelated to rehabilitation outcome, a supportive family attitude was associated with the client's successful vocational adjustment.

Gay, Reagles, and Wright (1971) developed a 20-item instrument that was completed by 193 clients at acceptance, at closure, and from 2 to 4 years after closure. The 20 items, which included work status, earnings, and several items tapping social and community participation, were combined into a global status score. Although three-quarters of the sample either maintained or increased their overall adjustment from closure to follow-up, the major contributing items were the vocational items.

THREE REHABILITATION EXAMPLES

The follow-up investigations of former rehabilitation clients that were briefly summarized above strongly support the positive benefits of vocational rehabilitation services on the employability of disabled persons. Few studies, however, have addressed the question of clients' long-term psychosocial adjustment or have examined clients' occupational adjustment in depth. The three investigations that are described in detail in this section merit special attention because of their scope and methodology.

The Minnesota Survey

Tinsley, Warnken, Weiss, Dawis, and Lofquist (1969) reported the results of a follow-up survey of the employment experiences of 4,000 ex-clients of the Minnesota DVR who completed the Minnesota Survey of Employment Experiences. At the time of the follow-up contact, which was between 2 and 5 years after closure, 81% of the rehabilitated clients were employed, in contrast to a 28% employment rate at acceptance. For comparative purposes, 54% of the nonrehabilitated clients who responded to the questionnaire were employed at follow-up, versus 25% who were employed at acceptance. At follow-up, 45% of the rehabilitated group were employed in professional, technical, managerial, clerical, and sales occupations, versus 26% employed in such occupations at acceptance. Over 91% of the employed former rehabilitants worked full time (35 hours or more) at their jobs. A sample of the employed rehabilitants were found to be just as satisfied with their jobs as their coworkers and were rated by their supervisors as only slightly less satisfactory on the average than their coworkers. And while the average annual incomes for this large sample were only $450 lower than their coworkers, both the ex-clients and their coworkers had incomes that were substantially lower (more than $2,000) than the average U.S. annual income. This last finding confirms the well-known fact that public rehabilitation programs serve a larger proportion of disabled individuals from lower socioeconomic backgrounds. A subsequent analysis of this same data by Tinsley and Gaughen (1975) provided further support for the conclusion that rehabilitation services have a substantial and lasting impact on the vocational adjustment of clients.

Adjustment of Blind Clients

Bauman and Yoder (1966) summarized the results of a 14-year follow-up of 406 clients of six state agencies for the blind. The sample contained three subgroups of clients that had been evaluated by their counselors in 1950 as well-adjusted, undetermined, and poorly adjusted, respectively. It is important to note that the essential characteristic of "good adjustment" was *self-supporting*, although other factors were also considered. At follow-up in 1964, 85% of the well-adjusted ex-clients were still in that category. The finding that 63% of the poorly adjusted group retained that evaluation at follow-up indicates that, while there was some improvement, the majority of these clients were unable to overcome their limitations. Thus, these data suggest that the long-term adjustment of blind ex-clients is relatively stable. However, some clients did evidence improvement in their situations, while others deteriorated.

Two factors were related to positive changes in the adjustment of these blind persons. First, of the ex-clients who had originally not been self-supporting, but had subsequently demonstrated movement in that direction, 72% had received either vocational training or placement services (or both). Second, positive family attitudes toward blindness were associated with improved adjustment on the part of the ex-clients, while overprotective and rejecting family attitudes were related to worsened adjustment over time. This second finding corroborates the similar conclusion reached by Neff (1959). Finally, a remarkable statistic supports the validity of this 14-year follow-up study: 92% of the original subjects interviewed in 1950 ($N = 443$) were located and reinterviewed in 1964 ($N = 406$).

The Arkansas Longitudinal Study

In the only follow-up study in which standardized personality inventories were administered on a test/retest basis (Bolton, 1979b), 32 clients of the Arkansas Rehabilitation Services completed the Sixteen Personality Factor Questionnaire, the Tennessee Self-Concept Scale, and the Mini-Mult at the time of acceptance for services and again at follow-up more than 6 years later. Information regarding vocational adjustment and social participation was also collected at follow-up. The statistical analyses were conducted at two levels: 1) an analysis of overall sample data using traditional significance tests on group data, and 2) an analysis of individual clients' changes on the criterion variables. Extensive comparisons of the research sample indicated that it was representative of the state/federal rehabilitation program client population and, therefore, that the results of the investigation are generalizable to the service impact of state rehabilitation agencies. The following conclusions were reached:

1. Rehabilitation services appeared to have a significant overall effect on the vocational adjustment of the research sample: the proportion of clients who were employed increased from 22% to 62%, while those in "not working" and "other" categories decreased.

2. However, not all clients benefited from vocational rehabilitation services: eight former clients (25%) in the research sample were not working and were also inactive at follow-up, and five of the group were receiving some form of public assistance. The other three change patterns were: improvement in work status ($N = 14$), retention of employment ($N = 6$), and not working but active ($N = 4$).

3. The beneficial effects of rehabilitation services on the psychological adjustment of the research sample were suggested by significant overall improvement on two scales: Psychosis and Number of Deviant Signs. Since both of these scales are empirically derived, and thus more resistant to social desirability responding, these positive changes were especially impressive. Although there was a significant decrease on Super-Ego Strength (SES), the mean score at follow-up was still higher than the norm group mean.

4. Analyses of the individual client's changes on the 20 psychological scales indicated that rehabilitation services probably had a substantial influence on long-term psychological adjustment, but not in a consistent manner. Some clients made significant improvements in various aspects of personality functioning, while other clients deteriorated significantly. Four times as many clients made significant changes as would be expected due to the unreliability of the measurements.

5. Two of the 20 psychological variables were exceptionally stable over the 6-year interval, Alertness (0.75) and Extraversion (0.67); and four other variables were moderately stable, Independence (0.58), Psychosis (0.58), Hysteria (0.52), and Super-Ego Strength (0.49). In contrast, the self-concept variables were the least stable, indicating that self-esteem may be more amenable to modification as a result of rehabilitation services.

6. On three global self-ratings completed at follow-up, clients typically viewed their physical health as less satisfactory overall than their emotional adjustment, and most characterized their family relationships as good. This sample of former clients reported a wide range of participation in social activities, from zero activities to a total of 16. The correlation of 0.67 between emotional adjustment and social par-

ticipation indicates that socially active former clients perceived themselves as better adjusted.

7. Consistent relationships among work status, Physical Self, Number of Deviant Signs, Hypochondriasis, social participation, and rated physical health suggest the existence of a core dimension of vocational-psychosocial adjustment underlying rehabilitation success. However, the modest magnitude of the relationships between improved vocational adjustment and improved psychosocial adjustment indicates that although these two types of criteria may be mutually facilitative, they represent distinguishable aspects of client outcome.

8. In summary, the results of this investigation suggest that the provision of rehabilitation services may have a significant impact on the long-term vocational and psychosocial adjustment of clients. However, not all clients benefit in all areas of functioning, but the vast majority do evidence improvement in some types of psychological or vocational adjustment.

FOLLOW-UP METHODOLOGY

Bitter, Kunce, Lawver, Miller, and Ray (1972) conducted a study to systematically examine three follow-up data collection procedures: telephone, mail, and personal visits. They were concerned with the relative effectiveness of each of these procedures, as well as their combined effect in providing a representative sample from the follow-up population. The following conclusions were drawn from the results of the investigation:

1. Telephone follow-up is the most effective and efficient approach to contact with former clients.

2. Only two telephone attempts are usually necessary for most subjects who have a telephone.

3. Where there is no telephone, a personal visit to the subject's home or place of employment is highly effective for successful contact.

4. Most former clients can be reached during daytime working hours; however, it is worthwhile to attempt contact in the evenings and on weekends. Also, the frequency and recency of service delivery contacts with former clients contribute significantly to successful follow-up.

5. Letters, both regular mail and certified, are unsuccessful follow-up techniques.

6. Systematic follow-up procedures can provide a representative sample. Age, education, marital status, disadvantaged status, and occupational classification for previous employment make little difference in contributing to follow-up success. (Bitter et al., 1972, p. 69).

Individuals who are planning rehabilitation follow-up studies are advised to review the recent handbook by Reagles (1978) for specific suggestions and guidelines for carrying out all aspects of this important type of investigation. A shorter presentation is available in the monograph by Engelkes, Livingston, and Vandergoot (1975).

SUMMARY

The results of prediction studies can be used as a basis for making selection or classification decisions. Classification decisions are concerned with the optimal assignment of clients to treatments and, thus, with the improvement of the efficiency of rehabilitation service programs. Two summaries of prediction studies focusing on results and methodology concluded that 1) biographical composites correlated consistently, but modestly, with client outcomes, and 2) application of the results of most studies would be of limited value due to the omission of treatment variables. Traditional studies were illustrated by the prediction of 1) community adjustment of retardates, 2) employment of epileptics, and 3) personal adjustment of stroke patients. A review of the long-standing statistical versus clinical prediction controversy concluded that statistical procedures are vastly superior to global clinical predictions of complex behavioral outcomes.

The ultimate goal of rehabilitation treatment is the successful life adjustment of disabled persons. Thus, longitudinal follow-up studies are essential to determining the effectiveness and the value of treatment programs. The major objectives of longitudinal investigations are 1) the assessment of the permanence, or conversely, the modifiability of psychological characteristics over time, and 2) the evaluation of the long-term effects of interventions on psychosocial adjustment. Following reviews of classical longitudinal studies and longitudinal follow-up studies of former vocational rehabilitation clients, three rehabilitation follow-up investigations are described in some detail. The Minnesota study of employment experiences of former clients, Bauman and Yoder's 14-year follow-up of blind clients, and the Arkansas longitudinal study illustrate the methodology and results of follow-up studies in rehabilitation. The chapter concludes with some suggestions for the conduct of follow-up research.

(Appendix 4, page 151, includes brief summaries of the multivariate prediction studies in rehabilitation and Appendix 5, page 156, outlines the statistical methodology of prediction research, including multiple regression analysis, pattern analysis, rational prediction procedures, and cross-validation.)

appendix four
Summary of
Multivariate Prediction Studies

Prediction studies in rehabilitation that meet the two criteria explained in Chapter 6 — the prediction of a rehabilitation outcome and the development of a composite prediction formula — are classified as samples of 1) mixed disability clients, 2) emotionally disturbed clients, 3) physically disabled clients, and 4) mentally retarded clients. Within these categories the studies are ordered with respect to the type of predictor data employed: biographical data, psychological tests, counselor ratings, and global counselor judgments.

MIXED DISABILITY CLIENTS

DeMann (1963) used routinely collected biographical data to predict rehabilitation success for a sample of state agency clients. Eight selected biographical variables were combined in a linear discriminant function that correctly classified 65% of rehabilitants and nonrehabilitants in a cross-validation sample. Ehrle (1964) developed a composite predictor formula from 20 selected biographical items that correctly classified 68% of a cross-validation sample of suitably employed and unemployed clients. Eber (1966) used 10 selected biographical variables to predict two criteria derived from a factor analysis of 61 client variables. Multiple regression equations for a sample of 500 clients closed in Alabama in 1962 produced correlations of 0.49 with vocational adequacy at closure and 0.43 with vocational adequacy at follow-up. Bolton, Butler, and Wright (1968) combined 10 biographical variables in a multiple regression equation that correlated 0.48 with earnings during the first week after placement for 2,500 clients closed in Wisconsin in 1966. Stein, Bradley, and Buegel (1970) used biographical data and ratings of severity of disability of 1,200 VA rehabilitation clients to predict a composite index of employment success at a 2-year follow-up. The multiple correlation coefficient was 0.46. Kunce and Miller (1972) used 12 biographical variables to predict rehabilitation outcome, work status, and earnings for 6,099 state agency clients. Multiple correlations for the three criteria were 0.31, 0.37, and 0.45, respectively, and the unit-weighted biological composites correlated 0.24, 0.26, and 0.35 with the criteria.

Ayer, Thoreson, and Butler (1966) used 14 MMPI scales with biographical data and IQ to predict rehabilitation outcome for 79 clients. The multiple correlation of 0.65 was not significant at the 0.05 level. (None of the MMPI scales correlated higher than 0.10 with closure status.) Arnholter (1962) administered the Rorschach to 35 clients referred to a vocational adjustment workshop program at entrance and again at completion of the 12-week program. The protocols were objectively scored on maladjustment and rigidity scales. Of the several statistical comparisons calculated, one was significant: a greater proportion of those clients employed at the 6-month follow-up had decreased pretest/posttest rigidity scores (a total of 70% correct classifications). Flynn and Salomone (1977), using the MMPI, reported an attempt to predict employment for 256 clients of a large rehabilitation center. Their double cross-validation discriminant analyses provided little evidence of predictability: between 57% and 60% of the employed clients were correctly identified.

Bolton et al. (1968) used counselor ratings of severity of employment handicap to predict earnings during the first week after placement. Multiple regression equations were developed for each of 28 counselors who closed at least 35 clients. The unbiased (shrunken) multiple correlations ranged from 0.71 to 0.00, with an average of about 0.40. Arnholter (1962) found that the global judgments of employability made after a 12-week workshop program predicted employment status at 6-month follow-up for 35 referrals with 80% accuracy. Neff (1959) also found that staff judgments of employability were moderately predictive of employment at 1-year follow-up for 200 referrals to a workshop program. From Neff's data, the author calculated a contingency coefficient of 0.33.

EMOTIONALLY DISTURBED CLIENTS

Mortenson (1960) developed two scoring keys composed of 116 and 34 biographical items for predicting rehabilitation outcomes for ex-psychiatric patients. On a cross-validation sample, the long and short keys correctly classified 86% and 70% of the clients into successful (employed) and unsuccessful closure groups. Roehlke (1965) used a composite of biographical items to classify correctly 80% of a cross-validation sample of ex-psychiatric patients into successful and unsuccessful closure groups.

Lindemann, Fairweather, Stone, and Smith (1959) developed a composite index of five biographical variables to predict hospital discharge for a sample of neuropsychiatric patients. The index correctly classified 77% of the original sample. Lorei (1967) used a combination of biographical data and attitudinal ratings to predict two outcome criteria for 215 male VA hospital patients. The criteria were: 1) proportion of follow-up year spent out of the hospital and 2) full-time employment for 6 months. Multiple correlations for various subsamples ranged from 0.24 to 0.37 for the hospitalization criterion and from 0.42 to 0.53 for the employment criterion. Neff and Kultov (1967) also predicted hospitalization and employment criteria for ex-psychiatric patients. They combined biographical data and ratings in several multiple regression equations for a sample of 120 ex-psychiatric patients, half of whom had participated in a rehabilitation program. The highest shrunken multiple correlations were 0.46 for hospitalization and 0.47 for employment. It was noted that the treatment program had slight influence in comparison to the other predictive data. Soloff and Bolton (1968) calculated multiple regression analyses for the Work Therapy Center data (Soloff, 1967). Biographical data predicted hospital discharge and employment criteria for chronic schizophrenic patients in a state hospital: the highest shrunken multiple correlations were 0.41 and 0.36 for the two criteria. Again, the treatment program had modest predictive influence in comparison to the biographical data. Buell and Anthony (1973) combined 10 demographic variables using multiple regression analysis to predict posthospital employment for 78 ex-psychiatric patients. The obtained multiple correlation of 0.72 was based to a great extent on one predictor, previous employment history. A replication study using another sample of 79 ex-psychiatric patients produced almost identical results (Anthony & Buell, 1974).

Burstein and associates (1967; 1968) used a battery of psychomotor tests to predict hospital discharge and employment for samples of chronically ill mental patients in a state hospital. A composite performance score correctly classified 75% and 62% of the samples for the two dichotomous criteria. Lowe (1967) attempted to predict employment for 70 ex-psychiatric patients using the WAIS, the Rorschach, and the MMPI. None of the 39 test scale comparisons were significant on cross-validation. Drasgow and Dreher (1965) used the Rorschach, the MMPI, and the Kuder neuropsychiatric keys to predict job placement for a sample of VA neuropsychiatric referrals for rehabilitation services. A composite index correctly classified 83% of the failures; the Kuder neuropsychiatric keys alone were 80% accurate in predicting failure. Goss (1968) used the Kuder Preference Record (Form CH) to predict employment for a sample of 67

VA psychiatric patients. When the sample was divided into four diagnostic groups, an average of 75% correct classifications was made. Barry, Dunteman, and Webb (1968) used psychological test scores and interview ratings in a multiple regression analysis of 125 VA patients to predict a criterion rating of motivation for recovery and return to work (which was based on data obtained at 1-year follow-up): the multiple correlation was 0.67.

PHYSICALLY DISABLED CLIENTS

Kunce, Iacono, and Miller (1974) used nine biographical variables to predict placement salary for blind clients in five state agencies. (All cases were closed in one year.) The five cross-validated correlations ranged from 0.47 to 0.64. Miller, Kunce, and Getsinger (1972) combined biographical data and ability data to predict six employment criteria for 106 hearing-impaired clients. The highest correlation of 0.28 was with employment persistence. Gressett (1969) used biographical data, the WAIS, and the Hypochondriasis scale of the MMPI to predict employment for 40 male cardiac patients. Multiple correlations for various predictor sets were in the 0.50s. The Hypochondriasis scale was the best single predictor with a correlation of 0.43. Ben-Yishay et al. (1970) predicted discharge from a rehabilitation program for stroke victims rendered left hemiplegics. Several WAIS and Bender-Gestalt scores were combined with biographical data in a regression equation that produced a cross-validated multiple correlation of 0.62. (Discharge was independent of ambulation and self-care abilities.) Schwartz et al. (1968) used the WAIS, the Halstead-Reitan Battery of Neuropsychiatric tests, the California Personality Inventory, and the EPPS to predict employment for 181 epileptics. A discriminant function correctly classified 80% of the sample. Bolton (1975b) analyzed the relationships between biographic, psychometric, and service variables and employment at follow-up for three samples of deaf clients. Optimal multiple regression equations accounted for between 20% and 35% of the variance in employment.

Miller and Allen (1966) combined counselor ratings on four factors (medical severity, age, previous occupational level, and previous educational level) in a multiple regression equation that correlated 0.50 on cross-validation with closure status for a sample of Old Age and Survivors Insurance (OASI) referrals. Soloff and Bolton (1969) used a short form of the CJVS Scale of Employability to predict job placement for older disabled workshop clients. The point biserial validity coefficients for two samples were 0.29 and 0.50. Miller et al. (1972) found significant correlations between counselors' judgments of employability and six employment criteria for 106 hearing-impaired clients; the highest correlation of 0.65 was with employment persistence.

MENTALLY RETARDED CLIENTS

Jackson and Butler (1963) predicted successful community placement for 191 young institutionalized female retardates. A multiple regression equation, including three biographical variables and verbal IQ, correlated 0.43 with the criterion. Kilburn and Sanderson (1966) found that the Raven Coloured Progressive Matrices test correlated 0.60 with successful job placement for a sample of 21 retardates. Bitter and Bolanovich (1970) used a 40-item rating scale to predict employment for mentally retarded workshop trainees. The average biserial correlation for several counselors was 0.70. Pooled judgments of employability made by the counselor at the end of a 36-week training program correlated 0.76 with the criterion. (A biserial correlation of 0.75 is equivalent to a Pearson correlation of 0.60).

appendix five
Multivariate Prediction Techniques

Multiple predictor/single criterion data sets predominate in applied psychology. The criterion may be a single variable or a composite constructed from several variables. Regardless, the primary goal is to combine the independent variables in some fashion so that a maximum proportion of criterion variance is explained. Linear multiple regression (LMR) is the standard procedure that is employed for the analysis of multiple predictor/single criterion data sets in educational, industrial, and clinical applications. Although a variety of statistical prediction techniques have been developed and tested, none have proved superior to multiple regression in the overall robustness of application. However, under certain conditions less sophisticated methods may be preferable.

Statistical prediction techniques can be classified in a fourfold table using the two dichotomous dimensions of linear/nonlinear and additive/ interactive. The linear/nonlinear dichotomy refers to the form of relationship between each predictor and the criterion: a *linear* relationship exists between two variables when the points in the scatterplot tend to fall along a straight line (as opposed to *curvilinear* relationships). The additive/interactive dichotomy concerns the nature of the relationship between the predictor variables and the criterion: an *additive* relationship exists when the relationship between two variables is not influenced by other variables. An example of an interaction would be where the correlational relationship between clients' age and placement salary was different for orthopedically disabled and mentally retarded clients. Type of disability would be said to *moderate* the relationship between age and placement salary.

Each of the four combinations that result from these two dichotomous factors can be illustrated by a currently available statistical prediction procedure:

1. *Linear/additive* Linear multiple regression (LMR)
2. *Nonlinear/additive* Reciprocal averages prediction technique (RAPT)

3. *Linear/interactive*   Moderated multiple regression (MMR)
4. *Nonlinear/interactive*   Automatic interaction detection (AID)

Several studies comparing multiple regression analysis with the more complex procedures have been conducted, e.g., Weiss (1963), Weiss and Dawis (1968), and Stein, Bradley, and Buegel (1970) reported comparisons of RAPT and LMR; Saunders (1956) and Neff and Kultov (1967) compared MMR and LMR; and Tucker (1959) and Pickerel (1954) compared pattern analysis and LMR. In general, the results of these studies indicate that while the elaborate statistical procedures account for more criterion variance in the construction sample, they tend to "shrink" considerably on cross-validation. They apparently are too sensitive to sample uniqueness. In this section three prediction techniques with the greatest potential applicability in rehabilitation counseling — multiple regression, automatic interaction detection, and rational procedures — are outlined and illustrated.

MULTIPLE REGRESSION ANALYSIS

Linear multiple regression is by far the most common statistical prediction technique. It is used to maximize the correlation between a weighted combination of predictor variables and a criterion variable. In symbols:

$$Y = b_1 \cdot X_1 + b_2 \cdot X_2 + \cdots + b_n \cdot X_n$$

where Y is the criterion, the bs are the *regression weights* and the Xs are the predictor variables. The regression weights are determined by the *least squares criterion,* which minimizes the errors in the prediction of the criterion. Multiple discriminant analysis is very similar to multiple regression, the only difference being that the former uses a nominal or categorical criterion (e.g., disability type and occupational classification), while the latter requires a continuous criterion (e.g., earnings and days in training).

Because multiple regression is the standard technique used in prediction studies, a numerical example is outlined and discussed at this point. Seventy-six deaf clients who were enrolled in vocational training programs at the Hot Springs Rehabilitation Center constitute the data sample for the example (Bolton, 1975b). Each client had scores on 13 predictor variables (five biographical, five psychometric, and three treatment) and the criterion, which was employment status at follow-up. (Two-thirds of the clients were successful.) The predictor variables are listed in Table 5.1, which presents the intercorrelations among all 14 variables. The far right-

Table 5.1 Intercorrelations among predictor and criterion variables for 76 deaf clients

Step	1	2	3	4	5	6	7	8	9	10	11	12	13	14
1. Sex	—	0.08	0.07	0.13	0.31	0.25	0.27	0.12	-0.26	0.09	0.03	-0.11	0.00	0.29[a]
2. Age		—	-0.24	0.27	-0.07	0.05	0.08	-0.18	-0.12	0.07	0.16	-0.05	-0.16	0.16
3. Race			—	-0.24	-0.25	-0.21	-0.17	0.14	-0.05	-0.12	-0.16	0.25	0.06	-0.06
4. School				—	-0.15	0.19	0.08	-0.14	-0.14	-0.16	0.13	-0.13	-0.04	0.00
5. Previous work					—	-0.38	-0.29	0.01	-0.38	-0.19	-0.16	0.34	0.17	0.38[b]
6. Basic educational skills						—	0.85	0.34	0.45	0.46	0.14	-0.13	-0.22	-0.14
7. Reading comprehension							—	0.24	0.32	0.49	0.04	-0.12	-0.04	-0.16
8. Psychomotor skills								—	0.55	0.10	0.10	0.04	-0.31	0.09
9. Nonverbal reasoning									—	0.26	-0.10	0.10	-0.16	-0.02
10. Communication skills										—	-0.04	0.03	-0.08	-0.06
11. Total days											—	-0.55	-0.39	-0.10
12. Completed training												—	0.39	0.31[b]
13. Overall adjustment													—	0.06
14. Employment														—

[a] $p < 0.02$.
[b] $p < 0.01$.

158

hand column contains the zero-order correlations between the 13 predictors and employment. Briefly, the three significant correlations indicate that males, clients with previous work experience, and clients who completed training were more likely to become employed.

The *stepwise* multiple regression procedure was utilized to assess the predictive relationship between subsets of the 13 independent variables and the criterion. The stepwise procedure selects predictor variables, one at a time, adding at each step the variable that makes the greatest contribution to the composite equation. Thus, it becomes possible to make statements regarding the *jointly occurring* combination of client characteristics that are predictors of employment. However, the resulting optimal set of predictor variables often does not include all of the variables that, singly, correlated highest with the criterion, therefore, the interpretation may be complicated.

When the stepwise procedure was applied to the data in Table 5.1, a cumulative series of regression equations was produced. The regression weights and multiple correlations for each of the first six steps are presented in Table 5.2. The third row (step) indicates that when the three predictor variables, sex, previous work, and completed training are weighted approximately equally, almost one-fourth (23.6%) of the variance in employment status can be predicted. The appropriate conclusion is that the male client, with previous work experience, who completed his training program was more likely to become employed.

The fourth, fifth, and sixth steps become increasingly difficult to interpret (examine the pattern of regression weights and zero-order correlations together); however, the 6-variable equation, which accounted for one-third of the criterion variance, could be used in a strictly empirical fashion to identify those clients who will need special attention. Before any prediction equation is used in a service program it should be cross-validated on an independent sample of subjects, as illustrated by the Ben-Yishay et al. (1970) study.

AUTOMATIC INTERACTION DETECTION

In contrast to multiple regression analysis, pattern analytic techniques sort subjects into homogeneous groups on the basis of similarity of their predictor variable profiles. One pattern analytic technique that has recently been applied to rehabilitation data is Automatic Interaction Detection. Automatic Interaction Detection (AID) is not restricted to the linear/additive model and is thus a more flexible statistical procedure. It can account for nonlinear relationships, as well as interactions among variables.

Table 5.2 Stepwise multiple regression analysis for 76 deaf clients[a]

Step	1	2	3	4	5	6	7	8	9	10	11	12	13	R	R^2	P-tot.	P-ent.
1	0.254				0.384									0.381	0.145	<0.005	<0.005
2	0.262		−0.176		0.314							0.204		0.428	0.183	<0.005	< 0.05
3					0.217							0.262		0.486	0.236	<0.005	<0.005
4	0.349		−0.196		0.253		−0.012					0.303		0.526	0.277	<0.005	< 0.05
5	0.399		−0.204		0.166		−0.017					0.323		0.556	0.309	<0.005	< 0.05
6					0.228				0.010			0.281		0.583	0.340	<0.005	< 0.05

[a]The predictor variables are listed in Table 5.1; R is the multiple correlation coefficient; R^2 indicates the proportion of variance predicted; P-tot. is the significance of the total set of variables for each step; P-ent. is the significance of the last variable entered for each set.

160

The results of an AID analysis are presented in the form of a tree diagram. The tree structure is generated by repeatedly dichotomizing the original data sample. Each predictor variable is treated as a set of categories. At each step, all predictor variables are examined to determine the optimal split into two subsets of predictor categories. The process continues by successively splitting groups until the variance that can be explained falls below a minimum value. Nonlinear relationships between predictors and the criterion can be assessed because the predictors are categorized and the interactions among predictors are accounted for by nonsymmetrical selection of predictor variables. The interested reader is referred to the books by Sonquist (1970; Sonquist, Baker, & Morgan, 1971) for additional information.

An example of the results of an AID analysis of rehabilitation client data is presented in Figure 5.1. The sample consisted of 8,566 clients served and closed by the Arkansas Rehabilitation Service in fiscal year 1971. The potential predictors that were used were 10 demographic variables that are routinely collected at the time of intake (age, sex, race, marital status, education, referral source, disability, number in family, family income, and source of support). The criterion was employed versus unemployed. The cumulative sequence of variable splits defines the final client groups, with group size and proportion successful at the endpoint. (Thirty-two percent of the variance in outcomes was accounted for by the final groups.)

The results of the AID procedure are in a form that is easily interpreted by practitioners. After the counselor ascertains the basic demographic information for a given client, he/she can trace the client's profile on the tree to determine what group the client is a member of, and therefore determine the client's a priori probability of successful outcome. This predictive information should be useful in planning a rehabilitation program for the client. In general, the lower the estimated probability of success, the greater the need for intensive services. The next question that may occur to the reader is: Which combination of services is appropriate for the various client groups?

Unfortunately, the example presented above does not make an answer to this question possible because treatment data were not included in the AID analysis. In fact, the results as presented reflect the combined interactive effect of client characteristics and differential treatments (unless all clients received the same services, which is highly improbable). However, the AID procedure does provide a mechanism for introducing treatment data as a second stage, or possibly integrated with the client data, in order to isolate the client-treatment interactions.

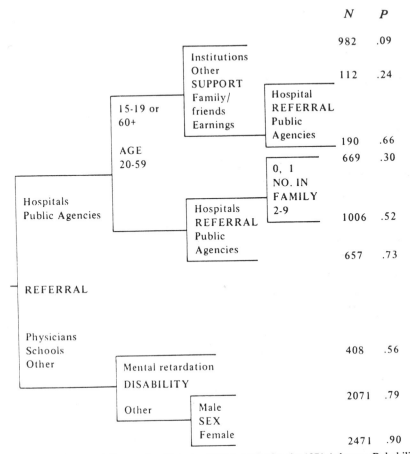

Figure 5.1.   Automatic Interaction Detector (AID) results for the 1971 Arkansas Rehabilitation Service Sample.

Several steps would be necessary if a client-treatment interaction model were to be developed and implemented in a clinical service program:

1. The formulation of primary rehabilitation treatments, where a treatment is defined as a particular combination of services.
2. The random assignment of a sample of clients to the primary treatments in order to provide a basis for the evaluation of client-treatment interactions.
3. The development of an assignment model for allocating clients to optimal treatments at the time of acceptance for rehabilitation services.

4. The adoption of a flexible attitude on the part of counselors regarding the use of statistical aids. Practitioners are generally reluctant to substitute mechanical procedures for their clinical judgment. But for reasons discussed in the section on clinical versus statistical prediction, they should be willing to incorporate statistical probability estimates in their decision-making processes.

Interestingly, Eber (1967; 1968) initiated a project to study rehabilitation counselors' uses of computer generated predictions of client outcome in a state agency field office. However, the project was apparently terminated before the evaluation was completed. A recent article by Byrd (1978) concluded that AID is a potentially useful program evaluation tool for analyzing client and service delivery data routinely collected by state rehabilitation agencies.

RATIONAL PREDICTION PROCEDURES

Kunce and his associates (Kunce & Miller, 1972; Kunce & Worley, 1970; Miller, Kunce, & Getsinger, 1972) have demonstrated the potential usefulness of a prediction procedure that begins with the *rational* selection of predictor variables, as opposed to the empirical selection that was illustrated in the multiple regression example. In addition, the Kunce et al. rational procedures are noteworthy for the use of a simple additive point scheme, instead of complex predictor weighting techniques, and for the recommended applications of the prediction results.

The investigation by Kunce and Miller (1972) provides the strongest evidence for the generalizability of rational prediction methods. Two exceptionally large client samples were used: all clients closed by two midwestern states' rehabilitation agencies during fiscal year 1968 (samples of 6,000 and 4,000 clients). The twelve variables that were *hypothesized* to be predictive of employment were selected from the standard R-300 form. The point that deserves emphasis concerns the identification of the 12 predictor variables; guided by "common-sense decision rules" the authors "searched for personal information that could be anticipated to relate to prevalent employment-hiring practices" (p. 505). They did *not* select the 12 variables because the variables were correlated with the outcome measures.

The variables chosen were: age, selective service, race, number of dependents, education, earnings at acceptance, employment at acceptance, welfare status, SSDI status, physical disabilities, marital status, and previous client. Each variable was reduced to two or three categories and scores of 0, 1, and 2 points were assigned to the intervals. Index scores were calculated by adding the total number of points for the 12 variables for each client.

The criteria were also obtained from the R-300 records: rehabilitation outcome, work status at closure, and earnings at closure. The index scores correlated 0.24, 0.26, and 0.35, respectively, with the three outcome measures for the 6,000 client sample. Using multiple regression analysis to optimally weigh the 12 predictor variables yielded correlations of 0.31, 0.37, and 0.45 with the criteria. Unfortunately, the multiple regression equations were not cross-validated on the 4,000 client sample, nor were the criterion correlations for the index scores reported.

In two other articles Kunce presented evidence that the simple addition procedure for aggregating multiple predictor variables into an index score has greater generalizability across the samples than does the more sensitive multiple regression weighting technique. In other words, if the index score criterion correlations and the multiple regression equations had been calculated for the 4,000 client sample, the index score correlations would have remained about the same, while the criterion correlations for the multiple regression equations would have diminished or "shrunk."

Because about 90% of all clients in these very large and most certainly representative research samples were placed in either competitive or sheltered employment, Kunce and Miller (1972) argued that the index scores should *not* be used to make feasibility predictions, i.e., to "select" clients for rehabilitation services who have a greater probability of successful outcome. Even those clients who had the lowest index scores achieved an 81% success rate on the placement criterion. Kunce and Miller did recommend several possible uses of index scores:

1. Index scores provide a means for describing agency or counselor "caseload difficulty."
2. Index scores may be useful diagnostically in determining client strengths and limitations.
3. Index scores may be useful in developing rehabilitation plans, for example, competitive or sheltered employment.
4. Index scores might assist in the identification of superior programs (i.e., achieving outcomes greater than expected).
5. Delineation of personal variables that related to occupational adjustment provides a counseling tool to identify barriers to successful employment. Some of these variables suggest remedial deficits in the client (e.g., educational) and deficits that must be worked with in the community (e.g., racial attitudes). (p. 508)

In another study, Kunce, Iacono, and Miller (1974) demonstrated the applicability of index scores to the evaluation of rehabilitation programs by comparing success rates after adjusting for overall differences in caseload difficulty. Their procedures are, of course, equally applicable to the long-standing problem of comparing counselors with caseloads of varying composition. Because it is a rather specialized topic, albeit one of intense interest and concern, an indepth discussion is provided in the chapter on weighted case closures.

ISSUES IN PREDICTION RESEARCH

As described previously, the weights that are calculated for the predictor variables in a multiple regression equation are determined in such a way that the resulting multiple correlation is as large as possible. However, when the prediction equation is applied to another (cross-validation) sample, the multiple correlation will almost always be reduced, a phenomenon that has been referred to as "shrinkage." Three aspects of multiple regression procedures may contribute to the degree of shrinkage, or loss of predictive efficiency, in cross-validation samples: 1) the use of small, atypical subject samples, 2) the selection of a few predictors from a much larger set of variables, and 3) the differential weighting of the predictor variables in the final equation. The effects of these possible weaknesses in prediction studies have been systematically investigated and, although opinions are not unanimous, suggestions and guidelines for dealing with some problems have emerged.

Kunce (1971; Miller & Kunce, 1973) compared multiple regression analysis and rational prediction procedures using rehabilitation client samples of varying sizes. The major purpose was to examine the effects of the subject/variable ratio on the predictability of an outcome measure in cross-validation and validity generalization samples. Two conclusions that were reached in the Miller and Kunce (1973) study are especially relevant: 1) a rule of thumb of at least a 10 to 1 subject/variable ratio should be followed in multiple regression analysis, and 2) if the number of subjects per variable are too few to meet the 10 to 1 ratio, then a rational weighting procedure may provide results that are as generalizable as those from complex weighting procedures (p. 162). Concerning the second conclusion, Wainer (1976) presented a general proof that using equal weights instead of the optimal regression weights for the predictor variables would result in higher cross-validated multiple correlations. However, subsequent responses to Wainer by Laughlin (1978) and by Pruzek and Frederick (1978) and Wainer's (1978) rejoinder leave the practical usefulness of his proof in some doubt. Finally, Darlington (1978) has outlined a new class of prediction techniques, called reduced-variance regression techniques, that appear to offer a compromise between rational weighting procedures and traditional regression analysis.

A study by Parker (1974) also addressed the potential problems with multiple regression procedures that were noted above. Four prediction techniques, multiple regression of raw scores, multiple regression of factor scores, the single best predictor, and Kunce's rational procedure, were compared on a cross-validation sample of 145 rehabilitation clients. The single best predictor and the rational procedure were the most effective predictors of employment status, with the multiple regression procedures much more susceptible to shrinkage, particularly the multiple regression of raw scores.

A reasonable conclusion that emerges from these studies of prediction methodology is that multiple correlations are often inflated estimates of the true predictive relationships that exist. One procedure for "adjusting" multiple correlations is to use one of the several "correction for shrinkage" formulas that have been developed (see Guilford, 1965, pp. 400–401 and McNemar, 1969, pp. 207–208). Comprehensive studies by Herzberg (1969) and Schmitt, Coyle, and Rauschenberger (1977) indicated that these formulas generally provide accurate estimates of the population values. The exception occurs when the best subset of predictors is selected from a larger set of variables using statistical (as opposed to rational) criteria, e.g., as in the Ben-Yishay et al. (1970) study and the stepwise multiple regression example that used deaf clients. In this situation there is no substitute for empirical cross-validation, where the subject sample is randomly divided into two subsamples and the optimal prediction equation is developed on one and applied to the other to estimate the true predictive efficiency of the equation. (See Wiggins, 1973, pp. 46–49 for an extended discussion of this issue.)

Because most of the multiple correlations that are reported in rehabilitation research investigations are not cross-validated, the reader can assume that they are overestimates of the population values. The degree of the shrinkage that would occur depends upon sample size, the subject/variable ratio, and the extent of variable selection. When rational prediction techniques are used, shrinkage is not a serious problem.

chapter seven
Factor Analysis

The purpose of this chapter is to prepare the reader to critically analyze factor analytic studies by: 1) introducing methodological procedures and discussing issues in the interpretation of results, and 2) illustrating the application of factor analysis in rehabilitation research by summarizing several studies from the literature. A comprehensive review of factor analytic studies in rehabilitation is included in Appendix 6 (page 181). It should be emphasized that this presentation is not concerned with mathematical or psychometric problems in factor analysis, e.g., commonality estimates, number of factors, and type of extraction or rotation, but with fundamental principles of design and interpretation. However, an overview of technical procedures and issues is included in Appendix 7 (page 187).

PURPOSES OF FACTOR ANALYSIS

Factor analysis is a psychometric procedure that is used to reduce a large set of variables to a smaller number of basic dimensions. If the variability among a sample of individuals on 20 measurements can be reduced to five underlying factors, a substantial gain in economy of description and presentation would be achieved. Thus, the first purpose of factor analysis is *parsimony*. Furthermore, if the five factors possess more generalized meaning, that is, if they are amenable to sound psychological interpretation, then a second purpose is realized, that of *conceptual clarity*. These two purposes correspond to the two sequential steps that comprise factor analytic methodology: 1) *condensation,* or the reduction to major components of variability, and 2) *rotation,* or the rearrangement of the major components so that the psychological meaning of the factors is optimized.

Literally hundreds of factor analytic studies are reported in the social science literature each year (see Hinman & Bolton, 1979). The potential usefulness of the results of these studies to rehabilitation practitioners can be illustrated by addressing a familiar question: "How can theories of personality be used by counselors in their work with clients?" Personality theories offer the rehabilitation professional *conceptual frameworks* for integrating information about clients and designing treatment programs that will, hopefully, alleviate diagnosed deficiencies in clients' psychosocial and vocational functioning. Most personality theories have their genesis in *clinical* experience. In contrast, the results of factor analytic studies provide systematic conceptual structures that are *empirically* based. However, their potential utility to rehabilitation counselors is similar to that of traditional personality theories, i.e., they provide ways of viewing clients' functioning in the rehabilitation setting.

HISTORICAL BACKGROUND

Factor analysis was invented by a psychologist, Charles Spearman, more than 70 years ago. He advocated a particular approach that produced a large general factor, "g," for general intelligence. Factor analysis achieved prominence as a psychometric technique in the 1920s and 1930s in the fields of differential and educational psychology, primarily through the efforts of Truman Kelly, Godfrey Thompson, and L. L. Thurstone. In the 1940s and 1950s factorial methods were extended to the realm of personality, chiefly by Raymond B. Cattell, H. J. Eysenck, and J. P. Guilford. During the 1950s and 1960s factorial methods were increasingly employed in fields other than psychology, e.g., anthropology, economics, physiology, political science, and sociology.

Maximum research benefit probably has not been realized from this flexible statistical technique. The primary reason for the less than optimal use of factorial methods is that factor analysis has never been accepted by the mainstream community of behavioral researchers. The history of factor analysis has been laced with pseudo-controversies and exaggerated claims. Extreme proponents of the technique have offered it as a universal truth-finding procedure, while no lesser psychologists than Gordon Allport and Ann Anastasia have denied factors any psychological reality. In an amusing, mildly satirical article entitled "The Principal Compulsions of Factor-analysts," Cureton (1939) described the situation as follows:

> Factor theory may be defined as mathematical rationalization. A factor-analyst is an individual with a peculiar obsession regarding the nature of mental ability or personality. By the application of higher mathematics to wishful thinking, he always proves that his original fixed idea or compulsion was right or necessary....
>
>   The fixed ideas, after a sufficient number of rotations, become theories regarding the nature of mind and personality. The compulsions lead to the development of mathematical systems of analysis. (pp. 287 & 289)

THE SCIENTIFIC ROLE OF FACTOR ANALYSIS

Factor analysis is, in simplest terms, a data reduction technique. Its primary objectives are the achievement of descriptive parsimony by the elimination of redundancy, and the enhancement of reliability and generalizability of psychometrically defined constructs by the isolation and definition of major dimensions of variation. Three potential applications of factor analytic methodology are: 1) the specification of the major dimensions that span behavioral domains, 2) the discovery and definition of clusters or types of persons, and 3) the delineation or grouping of items into reliable (homogeneous) subscales. Each of these applications may serve the fundamental purpose of data reduction, or they may be used to test hypotheses and to confirm or disconfirm theory.

An initial step in the systematization of knowledge in any discipline or area of investigation, such as rehabilitation counseling, is the discovery and the operational definition (measurement) of basic theoretical constructs. Skinner (1961) has made this point in no uncertain terms: "First it must be made clear that the formal properties of a system of variables can be profitably treated only after the dimensional problems have been solved" (p. 252). Any doubts that factor analysis should play a central role in the solution of dimensional problems have been dispelled by another well-known experimental psychologist, Underwood (1957): "But it is only recently that systematic attempts have been made to break down complex psychological dimensions into their component dimensions. In general, some form of factor analysis or derivative therefrom is being used most successfully in this very important work" (p. 44).

FACTOR ANALYSIS IN REHABILITATION RESEARCH

In commenting on research methods in the study of the psychological effects of disability, Shontz (1970) observed that "one notes the lack of factor analytic research in the literature. Properly replicated, basic, intensive and extensive multivariate research. . . could go a long way toward clarifying the descriptive problem and identifying the most important variables for future study" (p. 60). Kutner (1971) extended Shontz's evaluation of the role of factor analysis. Although he made a disparaging reference to "factorial cryptolanguage" while discussing the results of factor analytic studies of attitudes toward the disabled, Kutner's (1971) overall appraisal was positive: ". . . we are emerging into a period of research in disability in which attitudes toward the disabled are seen as involving complex component parts each of which may conceivably have differing origins, have various modes of expression, and be subject to modification in varying degrees" (p. 153).

The potential contribution of factor analytic research in the psychology of disability was also independently recognized by two groups of investigators in mental retardation. The inconsistency of the results of research on the self-concept of the mentally retarded led Schurr, Joiner, and Towne (1970) to conclude that "...if different sets of observations are used to represent self-concept, an attempt should be made to dimensionalize them so that an overall factor structure might become clear" (p. 42). Collins, Burger, and Doherty (1970) recommended that "...future research in this area should investigate specific dimensions of the self-concept rather than employ a single global measure" (p. 289).

Briefly summarizing, it is clear that factor analytic investigations are viewed as potentially useful in rehabilitation research. Furthermore, the statements quoted above suggest a realistic appraisal of the role of factor analysis in isolating and defining psychological constructs of value in rehabilitation.

A NUMERICAL EXAMPLE

Factor analytic procedures are performed on intercorrelation matrices. An intercorrelation matrix is the systematic arrangement of all possible correlations among a set of variables. For example, three variables produce three correlations, four variables result in six correlations, and five variables result in ten correlations. As the number of variables increases, the number of correlations multiplies rapidly, e.g., ten variables generate a matrix of 45 correlations, 20 variables result in 190 correlations, and 40 variables result in 780 correlations. Obviously a statistical procedure is required to search for patterns of relationships in intercorrelation matrices. Although the computational procedures are complex, the logic of factor analysis is relatively straightforward.

Variables that are correlated among themselves or clustered together suggest the existence of a common, underlying factor or mutual influence process. Thus, when several clusters of variables appear in an intercorrelation matrix, corresponding factors or dimensions may be hypothesized. Factor analysis is simply a procedure for translating the intercorrelation matrix into a form in which the clusters of variables are easily identified. The intercorrelation matrix in Table 12 was selected from a larger matrix and the variables were ordered so that the clusters stand out. The 17 variables were chosen from 26 measures that sampled the *domain* of communication skills and nonverbal intellectual and psychomotor abilities of

Table 12. Intercorrelations among 17 communication-ability variables

Communication-ability variable	1	2	3	4	5	6	7	8	9	19	11	12	13	14	15	16	17
1. Speechreading	—	0.65	0.71	0.62	0.36	0.42	0.31	0.41	0.33	0.27	0.41	0.34	0.33	0.30	0.24	0.32	0.32
2. Reading		—	0.57	0.90	0.56	0.59	0.52	0.60	0.54	0.54	0.65	0.60	0.58	0.34	0.27	0.37	0.46
3. Speech			—	0.55	0.26	0.30	0.17	0.25	0.28	0.29	0.40	0.35	0.37	0.29	0.11	0.22	0.26
4. Writing				—	0.49	0.54	0.47	0.58	0.43	0.47	0.58	0.52	0.53	0.35	0.31	0.42	0.45
5. Manual Signs (Receptive)					—	0.89	0.92	0.81	0.39	0.39	0.34	0.38	0.35	0.21	0.20	0.22	0.25
6. Fingerspelling (Receptive)						—	0.87	0.90	0.37	0.39	0.37	0.41	0.36	0.28	0.26	0.32	0.36
7. Manual Signs (Expressive)							—	0.86	0.35	0.42	0.34	0.38	0.34	0.31	0.34	0.35	0.37
8. Fingerspelling (Expressive)								—	0.33	0.40	0.38	0.42	0.42	0.38	0.36	0.45	0.52
9. Ravens PMT (1–12)									—	0.62	0.58	0.56	0.47	0.05	0.09	0.10	0.29
10. Ravens PMT (13–24)										—	0.71	0.67	0.54	0.30	0.18	0.28	0.40
11. Ravens PMT (25–36)											—	0.74	0.68	0.22	0.26	0.32	0.49
12. Ravens PMT (37–48)												—	0.61	0.29	0.19	0.36	0.46
13. Ravens PMT (49–60)													—	0.17	0.09	0.26	0.38
14. Purdue Pegboard (Right)														—	0.70	0.66	0.64
15. Purdue Pegboard (Left)															—	0.77	0.69
16. Purdue Pegboard (Both)																—	0.71
17. Purdue Pegboard (Assembly)																	—

Table 13.   Rotated factor matrix for 17 communication-ability variables[a]

Communication-ability variable	I	II	III	IV
1. Speechreading	_0.85_	0.20	0.16	0.17
2. Reading	_0.62_	0.38	0.53	0.19
3. Speech	_0.86_	0.04	0.21	0.09
4. Writing	_0.64_	0.34	0.43	0.24
5. Manual Signs (Receptive)	0.16	_0.92_	0.22	0.04
6. Fingerspelling (Receptive)	0.22	_0.90_	0.21	0.14
7. Manual Signs (Expressive)	0.06	_0.92_	0.22	0.21
8. Fingerspelling (Expressive)	0.18	_0.85_	0.23	0.30
9. Ravens PMT (1–12)	0.15	0.22	_0.74_	0.06
10. Ravens PMT (13–24)	0.06	0.21	_0.81_	0.17
11. Ravens PMT (25–36)	0.25	0.11	_0.84_	0.19
12. Ravens PMT (37–48)	0.17	0.17	_0.80_	0.21
13. Ravens PMT (49–60)	0.24	0.17	_0.73_	0.08
14. Purdue Pegboard (Right)	0.19	0.12	0.05	_0.83_
15. Purdue Pegboard (Left)	0.04	0.15	0.02	_0.90_
16. Purdue Pegboard (Both)	0.14	0.15	0.15	_0.87_
17. Purdue Pegboard (Assembly)	0.11	0.16	0.36	_0.79_

[a]The highest loading in each row is underlined.

deaf rehabilitation clients. The interested reader is referred to the original articles for details regarding the studies (Bolton, 1971; 1973). The 17-variable intercorrelation matrix has been partitioned into sections that separate the four clusters. Inspection of the matrix indicates that the correlations within the clusters (triangles) are higher on the average than the correlations between or across clusters (squares).

If the variables in the intercorrelation matrix were not arranged so that the clusters were readily apparent, the process of searching for the underlying dimensions would be rather difficult. Factor analytic procedures examine the matrix of correlations, locate the clusters of variables and generate a summary table called a rotated factor matrix, which tells the investigator two things: 1) the variables that comprise the clusters, and 2) the extent to which each variable contributes to the cluster. The rotated factor matrix presented in Table 13 summarized the intercorrelations of the 17 communication and nonverbal ability variables. Each number in the body of the table is a correlation coefficient (if the rotation is orthogonal; see below) and is referred to as a factor pattern coefficient or loading. The pattern of coefficients defines the vertical columns, which are the factors. A cursory examination of Table 13 reveals that it contains essentially the same information as Table 12, i.e., four clusters are easily identified. However, the rotated factor matrix provides more detail regarding the exact composition of the factors.

The four factors spanning the communication / nonverbal ability domain of deaf rehabilitation clients were labeled as: I. Oral-Verbal Communication, II. Manual Communication, III. Nonverbal Intelligence, and IV. Psychomotor Skill. These results were consistent with the findings of comparative and developmental studies in deafness (see Furth, 1966, 1971). The following general conclusions were supported: 1) oral communication skills develop independently of manual communication skills, 2) residual hearing is slightly related to intelligence and substantially related to the development of oral-verbal skills, and 3) linguistic development and intellectual development are independent processes. The results were also consistent with eight previous factor analytic investigations of deaf persons in Scandinavia, Great Britain, and the United States in that nonverbal intelligence and language-communication variables always defined separate factors (Bolton, 1972c).

FACTOR ANALYTIC DESIGN

Most factor analytic studies are *exploratory* investigations in which little or no hypothesizing is done regarding the possible factors that might be expected to emerge. In contrast, *confirmatory* studies are conducted to test hypotheses or theories about the structure of behavioral domains. In practice a continuum exists, with most research uses of factorial methods being close to the exploratory pole. However, in any research some tentative hypothesizing must be done in order to define the domain of concern and to sample the measurable variables comprising the domain. One can generally have more confidence in the results of studies that tend toward the confirmatory pole of the continuum. However, all factor analytic studies must be interpreted cautiously, as the two studies summarized below demonstrate.

Horn (1967) factor analyzed 74 *random* variables that were arbitrarily given names of different ability and personality variables. The sample consisted of 300 hypothetical subjects. Several of the resulting factors made good sense and were appropriately labeled. In a similar study, Armstrong and Soelberg (1968) analyzed 20 personality traits (actually *random* variables) for a sample of 50 hypothetical subjects. The nine factors that resulted were not only easy to name, but the authors were able to recall various studies in the literature that lent support to the solution! The obvious point that these studies demonstrate is that the results of factor analysis are *always* interpretable to the researcher.

There are two general classes of techniques that may be utilized in the second stage of factor analysis: 1) *orthogonal* rotation, which maintains independent (uncorrelated) factors, and 2) *oblique* rotation, which allows the factors to be correlated. A difference of opinion regarding the general applicability and value of orthogonal versus oblique factors has long existed among psychologists. However, the oblique solutions are probably favored now by the majority because they more closely approach solutions to problems in which the structure is *known* to be oblique.

THREE REHABILITATION EXAMPLES

The three broad categories of applications of factor analysis that were mentioned above, dimensioning variables, clustering persons, and allocating inventory items to subscales, are illustrated in this section.

Dimensions of the Rehabilitation Process

Eber (1966) conducted a large-scale multivariate investigation of the rehabilitation counseling process in Alabama. The primary purposes of the study were 1) to demonstrate the applicability of multivariate statistical procedures to a complex interactive service system, and 2) to achieve a clearer identification of a vocational rehabilitation system. Eber began by delineating three major areas of functioning and by selecting variables to represent them: the client, the counselor, and the community. After each domain was reduced to its major dimensions, the predictability of two criterion factors was assessed from the information available at various stages in the rehabilitation process, e.g., preferral, referral, and acceptance for service. The presentation here is limited to the factor analysis of client data. Sixty-one variables representing intake, service, closure, and follow-up data were factor analyzed for a sample of 502 clients. The 10 factors that resulted are summarized in three sets:

Client Characteristics

    I.   Adequacy of vocational adjustment at acceptance (earnings and work status at acceptance, etc.)

    II. Sex (maleness, weight, height, etc.)

    III. Maturity (married, work history prior to disability, etc.)

    IV. Acceptance by the client of welfare or public assistance services (amount of public assistance received at acceptance, during rehabilitation, at closure, and at follow-up)

V.   Psychiatric disability (history of psychiatric hospitalization, history of psychiatric contact, etc.)

Patterns of Service

VI.   Vocational training service (rapid service, service to severely disabled clients, etc.)

VII.   Long-term vocational training (expenditure of training and maintenance funds)

VIII.   Physical restoration services (expenditure of surgical or medical funds and hospital funds)

Criterion Factors

IX.   Vocational adequacy at closure (work status and earnings at closure)

X.   Vocational adequacy at follow-up (employment at follow-up, promotion record, weekly wages, etc.)

Using various sets of independent variables, Eber developed multiple regression equations that correlated 0.58 and 0.67 with criterion factors IX and X. Thus, considerable predictability within the system was achieved. This study provides a conceptual basis for a better understanding of the rehabilitation process.

Three Rehabilitation Counselor Styles

In conjunction with the Counselor Client Interaction Project outlined in Chapter 4, Bolton (1974c) factor analyzed the verbal interview profiles of 54 rehabilitation counselors. The verbal interaction profiles, which were derived from audio recordings of actual counseling interviews, consisted of 12 categories, e.g., information giving, listening, supporting, and advising. Factor analysis of the intercorrelation matrix of counselors isolated three verbal interaction styles:

1.   Information providers (who give general administrative information, specific details about services, and information tailored to the client's needs)
2.   Therapeutic counselors (who listen, explore, reflect, and provide support to their clients)
3.   Information exchangers (who solicit information from clients, provide educational and occupational information, discuss various topics, and offer advice)

Comparisons of the three groups of counselors on biographical variables supported the conclusion that academic training, counseling orientation, and job function are related to the verbal interaction style that rehabilitation counselors use. Two subsequent validation studies (Bolton, 1976d; 1977e) demonstrated that case performance characteristics, such as client disability, case services used, and client closure rate, and client self-reported psychological adjustment were associated with the three counseling styles.

Dimensions of Employability

Gellman, Stern, and Soloff (1963) developed the Workshop Scale of Employability for the primary purpose of predicting employment outcomes for rehabilitation clients in vocational adjustment workshops. A secondary objective was the identification of the major dimensions of client functioning in the workshop setting. In conjunction with the validation studies, the Workshop Scale was completed for samples of clients in workshops in three midwestern cities. The 52-item intercorrelation matrices from each workshop were factor analyzed independently. Similar factor structures emerged in each of the analyses. Six common factors were identified using a repeatability criterion requiring that an item have loadings of 0.30 or greater in two of the three analyses in order to define a factor. The six factors are:

1. Attitudinal conformity to work role
2. Speed of production
3. Maintenance of quality
4. Acceptance of work demands
5. Interpersonal security
6. Clerical ability

Since the factor structures that resulted from the three independent analyses were very similar, and given the broad, representative item sample, it can be concluded that these six factors represent the major behavioral dimensions of client functioning in vocational adjustment workshops. Considering that the Workshop Scale is an observer rating instrument, it might be more appropriate to refer to the factors as dimensions of *staff perceptions* of client behavior. (See the discussion of perspectives in Chapter 5.)

Because inventory items contain more *specific* variance, which typically includes substantial *error* variance, factor analyses of item correlation matrices are more difficult to replicate than are the analyses of composite variables. In other words, since items share less common variance than do composite variables, rotated factor patterns tend to be less stable across samples. An outstanding illustration of this problem is the continuing controversy surrounding the factorial validity of the Sixteen Personality Factor Questionnaire (16PF). A summary of the dozen or so relevant studies is included in Appendix 2 (page 119). Viewed in this context, the repeatability criterion used in the factor analytic study of the Workshop Scale is seen to be an important safeguard against nonreplicable results.

TWO FUNDAMENTAL ISSUES

Much of the controversy and disagreement about the value of factor analysis in psychological research centers on two basic issues. Both of these issues are concerned with the meaning and the interpretation of factors.

Descriptive Dimensions versus Causal Influences

One popular position maintains that factor analysis provides a parsimonious description of a set of variables and argues that no psychological meaning can be assigned to the factors. Anastasi (1938) summarized the majority opinion 40 years ago: "It should be apparent that no method of factor analysis (can)...reveal causal relationships....It is doubtful whether anyone who has worked with factor analysis would regard factors as causal" (p. 392). Representing the minority school of thought, Cattell believes that factors are more than psychometric constructs limited to descriptive purposes: "But — although not all factorists agree — many psychologists, including me, assume also the correctness of an underlying scientific model that recognizes the factors to be more than dimensions — in fact determiners, influences, or causes." (1973, p. 9)

It is possible to cite research that supports the potential of factor analysis to discover basic psychological traits. An excellent example is Osgood's research on the measurement of meaning, which has covered a period of 25 years and has resulted in more than 1,000 publications. In a wide variety of studies it has been demonstrated that judgments on a set of bipolar adjective scales reliably resolve into three major factors or dimensions of meaning: evaluation (good-bad), potency (strong-weak), and activity (fast-slow) — E-P-A. These factors have occurred in a diversity of judgmental situations, both within and across language-culture communities around the world. Thus, it can be said with some confidence that these three factors are universal dimensions of human semantic systems. Osgood (1969) has argued that the E-P-A factor structure reflects an underlying affective meaning system that is innately determined:

> In my opinion, it is the innateness of the emotional reaction system of the human animal that underlies the universality of the affective E-P-A compo-

nents of meaning. In other words, the "innateness" of E-P-A...is really the panhumanness of emotional reactions, and these obviously have evolutionary significance for the survival of any species. (p. 195)

In order to address the issue of the proper interpretation of factors scientifically, Cattell and his associates conducted two tests of factor analytic procedures on data with known physical dimensions. The "subjects" of the first investigation were 80 balls of varying size and weight (Cattell & Dickman, 1962). Four ball "traits" — size, weight, elasticity, and string length — representing four expected physical influences were factor analyzed together with 28 measures from the behavioral domain of "balls-suspended-on strings." An oblique rotation produced the factor pattern that was hypothesized from a mathematical and kinematic analysis of the variables. The second test (Cattell & Sullivan, 1962), using 80 cups of coffee as the "subjects," extended the physical model from the mechanical and spatial dimensions of balls to concepts of temperature, sweetness, and chemical concentration. The research strategy, the data analysis, and the results paralleled those for the ball study. The authors concluded that "the main hypothesis that the factor analytic model yields patterns corresponding to the known patterns of causal influence...is strongly supported" (Cattell & Sullivan, 1962, p. 192).

This conclusion did not go unchallenged. Overall (1964) argued that the variables analyzed in the ball and coffee cup examples had been "contrived" in such a way as to guarantee that the results would correspond to the "preconceived" primary dimensions. He then presented his own counter example and concluded that "...there is no need to assume that simple structure factors will correspond to any particular set of fundamental dimensions of the objects nor, for that matter, to assume that such fundamental dimensions exist in nature" (p. 276). It should be noted that Overall extended the issue of the meaning of factors into the realm of philosophy of science by raising the question of the existence of a fundamental structure of nature.

However, for the purposes of applied psychological research, it suffices to recognize the agreement that exists: factors may, in fact, represent causal constructs or primary dimensions of behavior; on the other hand, they may have only descriptive significance. Because this cannot be known in advance (except with artificial examples), it is necessary, then, to conduct validation studies that incorporate the factors as either independent variables, to examine their causal effects, or as dependent variables, to study how they are influenced by experimentally manipulated variables. Mischel (1976) summarized this position well: "...while the factor analytic search...may yield mathematically pure factors, their psychological meaningfulness...cannot be assumed...they must be demonstrated" (p. 147). In summary, factors should be validated in subsequent research in the same way that any other new variables are.

Group Structure versus Individual Characteristics

On this issue there is little disagreement between the critics and the proponents of factor analysis. The issue, which is simply that of the nomothetic versus the idiographic approach to the study of human personality, centers on whether the assumption of a common trait model renders factor analytic research useless in understanding individual behavior. As with the first issue, some historical perspective might be enlightening.

One of the arch enemies of factor analysis, Gordon Allport, phrased the issue in unflattering, yet, colorful terms: "An entire population is put into the grinder, and the mixing is so expert that what comes through is a link of factors in which every individual has lost his identity" (1937, p. 244). In other words, the factors only represent a hypothetical average subject who, Allport would probably have argued, does not exist. One of the most prominent advocates of factor analytic methodology, J. P. Guilford, said the same thing in somewhat more neutral language: "...the degree of generality that we find for a trait by factor analysis is a feature of the average person in the group, not necessarily a description of how any one person's traits are organized" (1975, p. 813). Finally, Wiggins (1973) stated the issue as a postulate of trait psychology: the trait structure yielded by factor analysis, "although defined with reference to groups of subjects, is thought to characterize the internal organizations of individuals...the majority of trait theorists seem to accept this assumption with equanimity" (p. 369).

While some clinicians and personologists may question the value of the nomothetic approach to the study of behavior, most researchers do not. This is because any scientific approach to human behavior requires that a standard set of independent and dependent measures be taken on all subjects in the research sample. Fiske (1971b) stated this simple fact as an axiom: "the nomothetic approach is necessary for basic research" (p. 24). The same variables, traits, or characteristics must be measured in all subjects in a scientific research study, because science is concerned with generalizable laws, not individual uniqueness and idiosyncratic behavior.

As with so many issues, there is no final answer to the question of the proper psychological interpretation of factors. For any particular area of investigation, several points must be considered: 1) the extent of previous theorizing, 2) the consistency of previous research results, 3) the nature of the variables measured, and 4) the adequacy of the variable sampling procedures. Considering all of the available evidence and expert opinions, it is reasonable to conclude that factor analytic research can contribute to the isolation and operational definition of relevant psychological constructs that are essential to progress in understanding and improving the rehabilitation counseling process.

SUMMARY

Factor analysis is a procedure that is used to achieve two purposes: 1) parsimony, which results from condensing a set of variables to a smaller number of basic dimensions of variation, and 2) conceptual clarity, which results from rotating the major dimensions so that their psychological meaning is optimized. Factor analytic studies provide practitioners with systematic conceptual frameworks for viewing clients' behavior in the rehabilitation setting. Although the history of factor analysis has been fraught with controversy, the technique has generally been regarded as potentially useful in rehabilitation research.

A numerical example based on 17 variables selected from the domain of communication skills and nonverbal abilities of deaf clients is used to illustrate factor analytic procedures. The distinctions between exploratory and confirmatory studies and orthogonal and oblique rotational techniques are clarified. Three examples of factor analytic investigations in rehabilitation illustrate three major types of applications: 1) dimensions of the rehabilitation process (analysis of variables), 2) rehabilitation counselor styles (clustering of persons), and 3) dimensions of employability (analysis of items). Two fundamental issues in the interpretation of factors, descriptive dimensions versus causal influences and group structure versus individual characteristics, are discussed and suggested guidelines are outlined.

(Appendix 6, page 181, contains brief summaries of the factor analytic studies in rehabilitation and Appendix 7, page 187, overviews technical procedures and issues including design, number of factors, type of rotation, multimethod analysis, and analysis of change.)

appendix six
Summary of
Factor Analytic Studies

The published factor analytic studies in the area of rehabilitation counseling research are summarized in this appendix. The studies are classified into five groups: 1) rehabilitation counselor role and performance, 2) rehabilitation clients, 3) instrument development, 4) attitudes toward disability, and 5) rehabilitation environments. Inclusion in this appendix does not constitute endorsement of the methodological procedures or results of the investigations; readers are encouraged to critically examine any study before accepting the results as valid or useful for any particular purpose.

REHABILITATION COUNSELOR ROLE AND PERFORMANCE

Bronson, Butler, Thoreson, and Wright (1967) factor analyzed scores on 17 variables that measured the professional concerns of 280 rehabilitation counselors. Three dimensions of professional concern resulted: technical concerns, professional resources, and client-community relationships. In a study of perceived counselor proficiency, Rubin, Richardson, and Bolton (1973) analyzed 82 counselors' ratings of 29 job behaviors and identified three dimensions of proficiency in performing the rehabilitation counselor's job role: affective orientation, dealing with information, and being direct and initiating action.

Muthard and Salomone (1969) analyzed a 119-item task inventory that had been completed by 378 counselors. Eight duty factors resulted: placement, affective counseling, group procedures, vocational counseling, medical referral, eligibility case finding, test administration, and test interpretation. Using a hierarchial clustering technique, Berven and Hubert (1977) reanalyzed the Muthard and Salomone (1969) task inventory data and generally confirmed the original findings. Berven and Hubert combined two factors, (medical referral and eligibility case finding) and divided one factor (group procedures) into two clusters (group counseling and professional development).

181

Keil and Berry (1969) studied the role expectations for the rehabilitation counselor in a mental health setting. An 83-item role inventory was completed by 128 professionals. A cluster analysis produced nine roles: communication channel, humanistic, therapist, community, team subordinate, patient-employer intermediary, vocational counseling, integrated team member, and provider of basic services. In their investigation of leader behavior and job satisfaction in state agencies, Aiken, Smits, and Lollar (1972) factor analyzed 16 variables from three inventories measuring leadership behavior, interpersonal relationships, and job satisfaction for a sample of 280 counselors. Six aspects of the job were identified: interpersonal, involvement, leader directed, financial reward, exertive, and autonomous functioning.

Bolton (1974c) analyzed the verbal interview behavior of 54 rehabilitation counselors and isolated three counseling styles: information providers, therapeutic counselors, and information exchangers. Two validation studies, using case performance data and measures of clients' psychological change, were supportive of the original distinctions among the three styles of counseling (Bolton, 1976d; 1977e). Zadny and James (1977b, pp. 13–14) reported the results of a factor analysis of R-300 closure data for 287 counselors. They identified two of the four factors: indexing net productivity (quantity) and reflecting the nature of closures (quality).

REHABILITATION CLIENTS

Baumeister and Bartlett (1962a; 1962b) factor analyzed subtest scores of the WISC for several samples of retardates. In addition to three standard Wechsler factors (general, verbal, and performance), they found a *stimulus trace factor, which loaded on arithmetic, picture arrangement, coding, and digit span.* They validated the interpretation of this factor as short-term memory in a later study (Baumeister, Bartlett & Hawkins, 1963). For a more recent analysis and discussion of the stimulus trace factor see Van Hagen and Kaufman (1975). Shulman (1967) analyzed the WISC for a sample of retardates who were participating in an experimental vocational development program. The resulting factors were: perceptual part-whole performance, verbal elaboration, verbal-numerical, and sequential performance.

Miller (1977) analyzed 17 measures of intellectual ability and cognitive style for a sample of 60 congenitally blind male rehabilitation clients and found two large factors, verbal and nonverbal intelligence, and three test-specific factors, category width, flexibility, and repression-sensitization. Bolton (1971) factor analyzed 14 nonverbal ability measures and 10 communication ratings for a sample of 87 deaf rehabilitation clients. Four factors resulted: nonverbal reasoning, manual communication, oral-verbal communication, and psychomotor skill. A subsequent analysis (Bolton, 1973) split oral-verbal communication into two highly correlated factors: oral-verbal communication and residual hearing. The results of these studies were consistent with eight previous factorial investigations in that nonverbal intelligence and language communication variables always defined separate factors (Bolton, 1972c).

Kassebaum and Baumann (1965) analyzed the concept of the sick role for a sample of 201 chronically ill patients with heart disease, diabetes, or psychoneurosis as their primary diagnoses. Four dimensions of the sick role emerged: dependence, reciprocity, role-performance, and denial. Mathews (1966) conducted a Q factor analysis of the responses of 70 clients to the Handicap Problems Inventory, producing six dimensions of psychological impact of physical disability: feelings of personal rejection, need to be treated as normal, denial of disability, guilt, despair, and self-acceptance.

Bolton (1972a) analyzed the Q-sort personality descriptions of 42 deaf clients and isolated four behavioral styles, creative, rigid-inhibited, undisciplined, and acceptance-anxious. Bolton's behavioral styles corresponded to the four styles comprising a classification system that was synthesized from a survey (Rosenberg & Colarelli, 1969) of clinical and psychometric research on a variety of client populations. Using the 16PF-E protocols of a sample of 135 clients in a comprehensive rehabilitation center, Rice and Glenn (1973) conducted a Q factor analysis that resulted in three personality types: normal-adjusted, assertive-aggressive, and passive-aggressive.

Bolton (1974b) factor analyzed pretest/posttest change scores that reflected self-reported psychological adjustment and R-300 vocational improvement. Improved vocational functioning was independent of two psychological adjustment factors. A subsequent replication (Bolton, 1978d) supported the distinction between economic-vocational and psychosocial dimensions of client change during the rehabilitation process. Eber (1975) summarized his earlier research on vocational aspects of client outcome (Eber, 1966) in which 24 variables were reduced to two oblique factors: short-range success (closure) and long-range success (follow-up).

INSTRUMENT DEVELOPMENT

Gellman, Stern, and Soloff (1963) constructed a rating scale instrument, the Scale of Employability, for the purpose of assessing the potential employability of rehabilitation workshop clients. Replicated factor analyses (three different workshops) were conducted for the 52-item Workshop Scale and the 44-item Counseling Scale. The five workshop factors were: attitudinal conformity to work role, maintenance of quality, acceptance of work demands, interpersonal security, and speed of production. The six Counseling Scale factors were: adequacy of work history, appropriateness of job demands, interpersonal competence, language facility, prominence of handicap, and ethnic identification.

Factor analysis has been used extensively in the instrument development phase of the Minnesota Work Adjustment Project (Dawis, 1976). Using more than 5,000 subjects, Gay, Weiss, Hendel, Dawis, and Lofquist (1971) factor analyzed the 20 vocational need scales of the Minnesota Importance Questionnaire (MIQ) and found six factors, or general need reinforcer patterns: management, autonomy, conditions of work, altruism, achievement, and recognition. The Minnesota Satisfactoriness Scales (MSS) are composed of 28 items that are completed by a worker's supervisor (Gibson, Weiss, Dawis & Lofquist, 1970). Factor analysis grouped the 28 items into four scales: performance (productivity), conformance (interpersonal relations), dependability (disciplinary problems), and personal adjustment (emotional health). The Minnesota Satisfaction Questionnaire (MSQ) is a 100-item, 20-scale instrument for measuring employee satisfaction with the job (Weiss, Dawis, England & Lofquist, 1967). Factor analyses for several occupational groups (both disabled and nondisabled) generally revealed two factors: intrinsic satisfaction and extrinsic satisfaction.

Bolton (1975c; 1976e) factor analyzed the 71 items of the Mini-Mult for a sample of 312 rehabilitation clients and produced three subscales: low morale, somatization, and psychotic distortion. In developing the Human Service Scale (HSS), Kravetz (1973) analyzed a large pool of items that was eventually reduced to 80 items that are scored on seven subscales — physiological, emotional security, economic security, family, social, economic self-esteem, and vocational self-actualization — that paralleled five of Maslow's need categories. The Sixteen Personality Factor Questionnaire-Form E (16PF-E) was designed for use with persons of limited educational background and has been normed on rehabilitation clients. A series of analyses by Bolton (1977a; Burdsal & Bolton, 1979), using a sample of 449 rehabilitation clients, supported the factorial validity of the primary and secondary factors of 16PF-E. Westerheide, Lenhart, and Miller (1974) factor analyzed the 24 items that comprise the Service Outcome Measurement Form (SOMF) and found five factors: economic/vocational, physical functioning, psychosocial, family relationships, and education. Vandergoot (1976) replicated the SOMF factor structure with some slight alterations.

Harrison and Budoff (1972) analyzed 137 items from the Laurelton Self-Concept Scale together with 23 locus of control items for a sample of 172 adolescent educable mentally retarded persons (EMRs). They identified 11 major factors: physical self, maladjustment, combativeness, scholastic inadequacy, narcissism, obedience, depression, motivation, identification with authority, social adjustment at school, and social inferiority. Bolton (1976c) factor analyzed the responses of 312 rehabilitation clients to the Tennessee Self-Concept Scale (TSCS) and found modest support for the five aspects of self that the TSCS purports to measure: physical, moral, personal, family, and social.

ATTITUDES TOWARD DISABILITY

The most extensive dimensional investigations of attitudes toward disability have been conducted by Siller and his associates (Siller, 1970; Siller, Chipman, Ferguson & Vann, 1967; Siller, Ferguson, Vann & Holland, 1967). The results of their studies suggest that there are eight distinct aspects of attitudes toward a wide variety of disabilities: interaction strain, rejection of intimacy, generalized rejection, authoritarian virtuousness, inferred emotional consequences, distressed identification, imputed functional limitations, and denial of severity. Kohler and Graves (1973) subsequently replicated the four second-order factors that were originally identified by Siller, Ferguson, Vann, and Holland (1967): net affect, authoritarian virtuousness, distressed identification, and cosmetic aversion.

In an earlier study, Siller and Chipman (1964) factor analyzed the Attitudes Towards Disabled Persons Scale (ATDP) and two related measures for several samples. The ATDP factors were identified as: hypersensitive-depressed, benevolent inferiority, depression-strained interaction, and negative atypicality. Whiteman and Lukoff (1964) analyzed the Attitudes Toward Blindness Questionnaire for two subject samples and identified five factors: personal attributes, social attributes, evaluation of blindness, nonprotectiveness, and interpersonal acceptance.

Jenkins and Zyzanski (1968) factor analyzed the 16 Semantic Differential for Health scales that were completed by 436 adults for each of three diseases, polio, cancer, and mental illness, and found three consistent factors across the diseases: personal involvement, human mastery, and social acceptability. Hansen and Parker (1972) identified five factors in their analysis of a 30-item questionnaire measuring attitudes toward income maintenance: federally administered subsidization, work ethic, subsidization of the needy, elimination of poverty, and economic equality.

REHABILITATION ENVIRONMENTS

Rosen, Weiss, Hendel, Dawis, and Lofquist (1972) revised and expanded the taxonomy of occupational reinforcer patterns associated with the Minnesota Theory of Work Adjustment. Their cluster analysis of the need reinforcer profiles for 148 occupations produced 12 groups. The correspondence between a client's vocational needs, as measured by the Minnesota Importance Questionnaire, and the reinforcer patterns of the 148 occupations can be quantified via an index of similarity.

Eber (1966) factor analyzed 69 sociological, or community, variables for 67 Alabama counties. Six influence factors resulted: large educational institution, older population, business and industry, family farm economy, plantation economy, and poverty. It was demonstrated later in the study that community characteristics contributed to the predictability of rehabilitation outcome.

appendix seven
Factor Analysis:
Technical Procedures and Issues

Factor analysis is a highly complex topic that cannot be treated adequately in one chapter of a book. Two recent textbooks by Comrey (1973) and by Gorsuch (1974) are recommended for the nonmathematically oriented reader who may wish to pursue the subject. The mathematically sophisticated reader is referred to texts by Cattell (1978), by Harman (1976), and by Mulaik (1972) and to Cattell's (1966) comprehensive review of multivariate research methodology. The following articles contain briefer introductions to factor analysis: Cattell (1965a; 1965b), Eysenck (1952, 1953), Guilford (1952), McNemar (1951), and Weiss (1970; 1971).

This Appendix contains overviews of factor analytic procedures and selected technical considerations that are relevant to the understanding and the interpretation of factorial investigations.

FACTOR ANALYTIC PROCEDURES

There are two basic factor analytic designs: the clustering of persons (Q) and the reduction of items or variables (R). The total variance of a variable or person is partitioned into *common* variance (which is shared with other variables) and *unique* variance (which includes unreliable or error variance). The common variance is the basis for separating variables or persons into homogeneous clusters, which are assumed to reflect underlying patterns or constructs. Factor analytic procedure follows a two-stage sequence: the variable or person set is *condensed* into a minimum number of mathematical composite dimensions, and then the composite dimensions are *rotated* to achieve a psychologically interpretable final solution.

The process of designing and conducting a factorial investigation can be separated into four major phases:

1. *Definition of the behavioral domain*   The behavioral domain should meet three criteria: 1) the behaviors comprising the domain should be

precisely specifiable, 2) a process for sampling and measuring the relevant behaviors should be available and feasible, and 3) the results should have reasonable probability of generalization beyond the behavioral sample that is used.

2. *Measurement of the behavioral domain*   The optimal approach to measurement of the behavioral domain begins with a systematic sampling plan and uses multiple measurement methods where necessary. If a Q analysis is planned, an ipsative (forced-choice) measurement procedure is recommended. However, experimentally dependent variables should not be used in R designs.

3. *Reduction of the correlation matrix*   After the domain has been measured, the variables (or persons) are intercorrelated. The square matrix, which summarizes the relationships among the variables, is reduced to a minimum number of independent composite variables, or underlying dimensions of variation. These new composite dimensions are then rotated to a meaningful final position, according to the "simple structure" criterion.

4. *Validation and interpretation*   There are three general approaches to the validation and interpretation of the results of factor analytic investigations: 1) the interpretation of each factor or cluster by rational analysis of the salient items or variables, 2) the correlation of the factors with (or comparison of the person-clusters on) variables external to the original factor analysis, and 3) the evaluation of the factorial structure in terms of hypotheses, theory, or previous research. Most factor analytic studies conclude with an interpretation by rational analysis. However, investigations that do not use external validation or evaluation of hypotheses cannot provide confirming evidence of the structure of behavioral domains because the final solution often depends on the judgment of the investigator.

SELECTED METHODOLOGICAL ISSUES

This section 1) discusses the two major decisions that occur in the reduction and transformation of the intercorrelation matrix, the selection of the number of factors to retain and the choice of type of rotation, and 2) outlines two problems that arise in certain factorial designs, method variance and the quantification of change.

Number of Factors

Cattell and Vogelmann (1977) carried out a comprehensive comparison of the two most widely used criteria for deciding on the number of factors, the Kaiser-Guttman (KG) rule and the scree test. As a first step, both criteria require that unities be placed in the diagonal of the correlation matrix and that the successive latent roots, or eigenvalues, be extracted. The KG rule states simply that those factors with associated eigenvalues greater than 1.0 be retained, while the scree test involves an examination of the eigenvalue plot to ascertain the "break" in the curve that signifies the last real factor. To evaluate the relative accuracy of the KG and the scree, Cattell and Vogelmann constructed 15 numerical examples that varied in 1) the number of variables, 2) the number of factors, 3) the degree of obliquity, 4) the presence of simple structure, 5) the presence of error, and 6) the size of communality. Both expert and novice judges were employed to apply the scree test to the 15 examples. In most cases, the scree test produced a more accurate estimate of the true number of factors than did the KG rule.

In general, the KG rule tends to underestimate the number of factors when relatively few variables, i.e., less than 20, are being analyzed and to overestimate the number of factors when a large set of variables is involved and/or the variables are less reliable, as is almost always the case with items. The best advice regarding the number of factors decision is to rotate two or more sets if necessary and to evaluate the final solutions in terms of their interpretability and simple structure. However, it is probable that solutions using substantially different number of factors (on the order of twice as many) represent different levels of generality in the domain being investigated, e.g., see the studies by Bolton (1977a) and Burdsal and Bolton (1979) that confirmed the eight secondary factors and the 16 primary factors of the 16 PF-E, respectively, by locating the scree at different points in the eigenvalue distribution.

Type of Rotation

Three related issues are subsumed under this heading: orthogonal versus oblique rotation, choice of oblique procedure, and targeted, or procrustean, rotations. Guilford (1975) has been the most consistent proponent of orthogonal (uncorrelated) factors because "this situation means less redundancy of meaning and a greater amount of information per factor" (p. 805). On the other hand, the main argument in favor of oblique (correlated) factors is that important variables in biometry, physiology, and psychology are often correlated, e.g., height and weight, systolic and diastolic blood pressure, or verbal and performance IQ. Cattell and others have argued that orthogonality imposes an unrealistic restriction on factorial solutions. For example, a varimax transformation was unable to reproduce the known solution to the ball problem summarized in Chapter 7 because two of the "traits" correlated 0.70.

If an oblique rotation is preferred, the researcher can choose from at least a half dozen analytic programs available in the standard packages, e.g., BMD, SPSS, SAS. The question that arises is obviously how to select the most appropriate program for a given problem. Hakstian (1971; Hakstian & Abell, 1974) reported the results of two studies comparing several oblique rotational procedures, e.g., oblimax, promax, maxplane, biquartimin, Harris-Kaiser, and direct oblimin, and concluded that "no *single* computing procedure...can be expected to yield uniformly optimal oblique solutions *for all kinds of data*" (1974, p. 444). In other words, there is no infallible oblique program available. It logically follows that several solutions should be generated and compared — but according to which criteria?

In addition to using the standard simple structure criteria, i.e., Thurstone's (1947) five rules that emphasize low factorial complexity of the variables and good overall interpretability of the factors, in deciding among several rotational solutions, Hakstian and Abell (1974) suggest that low overall factor obliquity is preferable, "all other things being equal." So it seems that Hakstian and Abell agree with Guilford that orthogonal factors are desirable. Ironically, Guilford (1975) believes "that many factors *are* oblique" (p. 804), but does not trust oblique rotations to give correct estimates of interfactor correlations!

The special class of rotations known as procrustean procedures deserve brief mention. In these methods, the investigator prepares a "target matrix" that incorporates hypotheses about the factorial solution; the rotation is then forced as closely as possible to the hypothesized solution. Horn and Knapp (1973) analyzed data from Guilford's structure-of-intellect (SI) research to demonstrate that procrustean methods can be used to provide support for randomly determined theories. However, the results of subsequent studies (Guilford, 1977, p. 18) based on a large number of computer-generated random target matrices indicated that the SI-targeted rotations were better than the chance-generated rotations. At least one study in the rehabilitation literature has used procrustean methods. Siller (1970) rotated 120 attitude items to two targets, eight hypothesized attitude dimensions, and nine disability types, and found a better fit for the eight attitude factors.

Cronbach (1971) summarizes the rotational situation well: "Factor analysis is a treacherous technique, largely because it can rearrange the same data in many ways" (p. 470). Recognizing the numerous pitfalls that occur in the application of factor analytic methods, the following suggestions seem warranted. First, use the scree test and the KG rule, in conjunction with knowledge about the complexity of the domain from previous research, to select one or more sets of principal components for rotation. Second, begin with an orthogonal rotation, probably varimax, and the promax oblique rotation, which simply "adjusts" the varimax rotation toward obliquity, and examine and compare the various solutions for the different number of factors. Third, following the standard simple structure criteria referred to above, select the best solution in terms of overall interpretability. Sometimes, however, the results of two or more solutions are irreconcilable, and this must be reported (see Bolton, 1978d).

Multimethod Factor Analysis

A fairly common occurrence in factor analytic research designs is the inclusion of variables from two or more data sources, or perspectives (methods). The different sources may only be tests or questionnaires with different formats, purporting to measure the same or different variables, or they may be represented by self-report and observer rating instruments.

Jackson (1969) proposed a procedure for factor analyzing multimethod matrices that was employed in a number of published studies, and which he later characterized as "admittedly arbitrary and ... an unfortunate departure from the basic framework of factor analysis" (Jackson, 1975, p. 260). Several other procedures for analyzing multimethod data have been proposed; these are critically reviewed by Schmitt, Coyle, and Saari (1977). The combined factor analysis of variables from two or more distinct sources, i.e., multimethod factor analysis, is generally not the most appropriate method of data analysis because the within-methods variance tends to be large relative to the across-methods covariation and, therefore, the resulting factors are usually source-specific (see Barry et al., 1968).

Several approaches to the analysis of multimethod data sets are recommended: 1) examine the cross-correlation matrices for evidence of convergence and divergence of measures, 2) conduct separate factor analyses of the variables from each data source or instrument and intercorrelate the rotated factors (see Nesselroade & Baltes, 1975, for an effective application of this approach), 3) calculate the largest canonical correlation for each pair of data sets to determine the maximum predictive relationship across sets or methods, and 4) assess the total variance overlap between the various sets of measures by carrying out a redundancy analysis (Weiss, 1972). In summary, there is no direct solution to the vexing problem of method variance, especially when different viewpoints or perspectives are represented; hence, a number of analyses should be carried out and reported.

Factor Analysis of Change

Factor analyses of change scores are conducted for the purpose of isolating and defining the primary dimensions of improvement/deterioration that treatment programs influence. As discussed in Chapter 5, in rehabilitation counseling there appear to be two broad classes of client change dimensions: vocational-economic and personal-social (Bolton, 1974b, 1978d). Researchers in psychotherapy have devoted considerable effort to the quantification and dimensionality of change, as documented in the review of Green, Gleser, Stone, and Seifert (1975). But, the critical question that remains concerns the type of change scores that should be factor analyzed.

Cattell (1963) has been a consistent advocate of the use of raw scores in factorial studies of change. The results of a recent investigation of state and trait anxiety by Nesselroade and Cable (1974) support the use of raw difference scores: "for some types of change, difference score factor analysis is not misleading but actually rather precise in not only revealing change dimensions but in suppressing dimensions of stable inter-individual differences" (p. 281). However, other investigators find compelling justification for the use of residual change scores in dimensional studies (Berzins, Bednar & Severy, 1975). In the most recent investigation of dimensions of client outcome, the author concluded that residual change scores were more appropriate measures of improvement/deterioration than raw difference scores (Bolton, 1978d).

Like most of the technical issues outlined in this Appendix, there is no final answer concerning the best index of change for use in factor analytic studies. The optimal strategy would appear to be to conduct parallel analyses using raw and residual change scores and to select the most interpretable and internally consistent results for reporting purposes. However, it should be emphasized that the scientific model mandates that *all* analyses and results be explained and summarized in the research report.

The obvious conclusion that emerges from these discussions is that the appropriate use of factor analytic methodology in rehabilitation research, of necessity, requires an element of human judgment and subjectivity. Fortunately, there exists a substantial amount of relevant literature to assist the researcher in understanding the statistical and empirical bases for these unavoidable decisions.

chapter eight
Rehabilitation Program Evaluation

Daniel W. Cook and Paul G. Cooper

By common definition, the word evaluation denotes a judgment, a determination of the relative value of some object, person, or idea. Evaluation is a universal and pervasive activity that can be subjective, "beauty is in the eye of the beholder," or objective, "the ad sold 100 automobiles." Program evaluation is a relatively recent area of specialization, which has evolved out of public awareness that, in an era of scarce resources, social programs must be held accountable.

In the simplest sense, program evaluation implies that some information is applied to some standard so that a decision can be reached. More specifically, Trantow (1970) has defined program evaluation as:

> ...essentially an effort to determine what changes occur as the result of a planned program by comparing actual changes (results) with desired changes (stated goals) and by identifying the degree to which the activity (planned program) is responsible for the changes. (p. 3)

While program evaluation can be defined in a relatively straightforward manner, it is actually a very complex task. For example, Bennett and Weisinger (1974) have pointed out that program evaluation might focus on program *effectiveness,* the achievement of specified outcomes; *effort,* the program resources expended; and/or *efficiency,* the relative amount of effort expended in reaching specified outcomes. Program evaluation may be conducted for reasons other than accountability, such as policy planning and program development, program improvement, or program expansion.

PROGRAM EVALUATION MODELS

Basically, program evaluation provides information so that decisions can be made. Strictly speaking, information does not imply knowledge, i.e., an understanding of what is known. Rather, information, in order to be valid and useable, needs to be organized in some way. The most prevalent method of organizing information in program evaluation is through model building. Models may be specified for formative evaluations or for summative evaluations. Summative evaluations may make use of an evaluation research model or a goal attainment model.

Formative Program Evaluation

Formative evaluation includes policy planning, needs assessment, resource allocation, and procedures for program monitoring. Formative evaluations are used, in effect, to plan the best program possible, and the problem is to choose the best course of action possible. Ackoff, Gupta, and Minas (1962) have suggested a formative evaluation model designed to limit unknown program outcomes by transforming "uncertainty conditions" into "risk conditions," or probability statements, of certain types of outcomes. Based on known or estimated probabilities, evaluators can formulate the best program possible. Edwards, Guttentag, and Snopper (1975) have suggested a "decision-theoretic" approach to formative evaluations. Basically, Edwards et al. (1975) have tried to link inferences about reality and the values of decision makers to decision making. By attending to value utility, in conjunction with the probability of goal achievement, evaluators are said to be able to identify different probabilities for achieving different objectives under different decision values.

Summative Program Evaluation

Summative program evaluation emphasizes program effectiveness, or outcome, and the adequacy of program performance, or quality. Summative evaluations are time specific and serve as a check on the decisions made during the formative evaluation. Summative evaluations may use different assessment procedures and methodologies. For example, in evaluating a new service delivery system to see if it should be incorporated in the overall program, an experimental methodology might be used in which group differences, relative group change, and achievement of goals are analyzed with respect to the generalizability of program outcomes. In evaluating established programs, program effectiveness might be determined through program monitoring.

Evaluation Research

Suchman (1967) was one of the first to point out that a program intervention implies a causal relationship between the program and some expected outcome. Cook and Cooper (1978) have presented a research model for program evaluation in vocational rehabilitation. A research approach using traditional methodologies focuses on the program as an independent variable, which, in the case of rehabilitation, should impact on the dependent variable — the consequences of disability. Rather than focusing exclusively on *how* a program functioned, the research orientation can also suggest *why* it did, or did not, work. An added advantage of evaluation research is that it forces the evaluator to focus on measurable program outcomes.

A variation of the research approach to program evaluation is the emphasis on defining program outcomes in terms of the relative achievement of each individual served by the program. This approach has its basis in psychotherapy, particularly in the field of behavioral analysis. The idea is that program worth can be established when client changes are the result of program intervention relative to preprogram client needs. Using this highly individualized approach, intermediate, as well as final, outcomes are important. In that individual client needs and outcomes are measurable, and in that the evaluation is based on ameliorating specific client problems, a highly individualized approach is a promising approach. However, Franklin and Thrasher (1976) have noted "that often the success of a program is *not* the same as the sum of successes of individual clients" (p. 13). That is to say that in programs such as vocational rehabilitation, there are other legitimate program evaluation concerns, not the least of which is the cost-benefit ratio of bringing different individuals to their highest level of functional ability.

Evaluation of Program Goal Attainment

Within vocational rehabilitation much program evaluation utilizes the goal attainment model in which program worth is established if a program meets its stated goals. In other words, the question is did the program accomplish what it said it would do? The logic behind this approach is readily apparent: the program is evaluated in terms of its effectiveness in meeting predetermined objectives. Unfortunately, in practice the process is never so clear cut. Goals are often value judgments, and people can honestly disagree as to the value of a goal. Then too, goals may be explicit (number of case closures in a specified time) or implicit (maintaining an organizational power structure). Goals may be established at different organizational levels, may be quite different at each level, and may even be incompatible. For example, goals established outside the rehabilitation agency may focus on administrative concerns and emphasize program justification and cost accountability. Such program goals have obvious implications for program survival. On the other hand, goals established at the agency level might stress program improvement and focus on client outcomes. Using the goal attainment approach, the evaluator often must refine general statements of purpose (goals) in order to measure actual program impact. Program goals can, of course, focus the evaluation on *program structure,* the allocation of resources within the program; *program process,* such as the adequacy of service delivery; or *program impact,* the program-induced changes compared to the desired changes.

Program evaluation goals may be classified as either internal or external. Internal goals emphasize management information, allocation of resources, and program improvement as well as outcome. External goals, on the other hand, focus on accountability and compliance with federal regulations. Assessing the extent to which both types of goals are met is a legitimate function of program evaluation. Bennett and Weisinger (1974) have described two goal attainment models. First, the Input-Process-Outcome model divides analysis and evaluation into three self-explanatory categories. The second model, called the Responsibility model, classifies evaluation activities into three levels of responsibility — institutional (program level), technical (service delivery level), and managerial (program management level). Bennett and Weisinger (1974) suggested that each level of a rehabilitation program be evaluated with respect to each criterion of program worth, i.e., effectiveness, efficiency, and effort.

DATA SOURCES IN VOCATIONAL REHABILITATION

In reality, there are only two distinct methodological approaches to evaluating a program. The first approach is purely subjective whereby an authority makes a judgment or issues an opinion as to the worth of a program. The second approach is objective, based on scientific measurement, and is preferred because it generates quantifiable data open to public inspection and to subsequent confirmation or refutation.

Selection of evaluation measurement devices should follow the principles discussed in this volume. Program evaluation generally should not use measurement instruments merely because they are available. An exception may occur when an evaluator is asked to assess the merits of a program after the program is in existence. In this case, the evaluator would, of course, be limited to those data that are routinely collected. In the selection of measurement instruments, the evaluator is concerned with the purpose of the evaluation (e.g., assessing agency effectiveness via accrued client benefits), the type of change that is expected (absolute or relative), and the unit of analysis (agencies or individuals). Ideally, program objectives can be specified in behavioral terms. If so, program outcomes can be defined operationally. For example, a person is considered trained upon completion of a certain number of tasks, or an individual is considered employed when certain preset criteria are met. Unfortunately, some of the most relevant objectives are the most complex and, behaviorally speaking, the least precise. It is here that the evaluator becomes concerned with the selection of the evaluation instruments to meet the purpose of the evaluation. In selecting an evaluation instrument, the evaluator needs to be concerned with reliability and validity, cost, time needed to complete the instrument, and special modifications that are required if handicapped persons are to complete the instrument. Four kinds of measures — questionnaires, rating scales, psychological inventories, and existing records — are considered as they relate to program evaluation in vocational rehabilitation.

Questionnaires

Questionnaires used via the survey technique are one of the most popular ways to collect client information. Questionnaires have great appeal because they represent a low cost method for collecting data on a relatively large sample. The major drawback of questionnaires is their vulnerability to response bias. Persons responding may answer any one question in terms of its social desirability; that is, answering a question as one thinks the majority of people would answer it.

Questionnaires have an intuitive appeal in supplementing other forms of evaluation data and they are valuable for obtaining the client's point of view. As an after service follow-up device, questionnaires can be used to assess program effectiveness, e.g., client satisfaction with services. Indeed, questionnaires have been very popular in vocational rehabilitation and have been used extensively in client follow-up studies, as discussed in Chapter 6.

Because of their intuitive appeal and apparent ease of construction, questionnaires continue to be popular. There are, however, some problems in using questionnaires in evaluation research. Reliability and validity are often not estimated for questionnaires, mainly because they tend to be used in one-time-only studies. Such one-time-only application also limits inter- and even intra-agency comparability. When used as a measure of the client's point of view and as a correlate of other evaluation measures, questionnaires provide a worthwhile addition to the evaluation effort.

Rating Scales

Ratings and rating scales are important program evaluation measurement devices in rehabilitation. There are two fundamental procedures used in ratings — one is a ranking relative to other persons on the same behavior; the other is scaling a person's behavior with respect to predetermined levels of the behavior. The scaling procedure usually locates a person's behavior somewhere along a continuum of successive intervals, e.g., from poor to average to good. The degree to which rating scales are behaviorally anchored (i.e., use discrete descriptions of observable behaviors to define the intervals), and the degree to which raters have the opportunity to observe the behaviors, influence both scale reliability and validity. As rating scales depart from observable behaviors and require the raters to infer abstract traits or characteristics in those behaviors being rated, the scales tend to become less reliable. Reliability, in this case, means the degree to which two or more observers agree in their ratings. Of course, the more abstract the rated behavior, the less likely are two persons to agree on its occurrence.

Rating scales are particularly vulnerable to errors stemming from human characteristics that people often exhibit when asked to judge others. Most people, in rating other persons, tend to be overly generous in their judgements. This "error of leniency" acts to reduce the discrimination power of the scale. "Halo effects," or rating someone based on an overall impression, tend to displace all ratings toward that overall impression. These and other rater errors, such as the error of central tendency, or avoidance of scale extremes, subject ratings to a systematic bias that limits the usefulness of the approach.

In vocational rehabilitation, rating scales are popular measurement devices. Because they can be constructed to fit practically any situation, rating scales are most prevalent in facilities and training centers where they serve as measures of program effectiveness. The Client Outcome Measure, detailed in Chapter 5, is an example of a rating scale used in vocational rehabilitation.

Psychological Inventories

Psychological inventories are often used to evaluate vocational rehabilitation programs when the program is expected to impact on client psychological well-being. And psychological inventories, in that they relate to inferred abstract constructs, such as one's self-concept, are the only measurement devices available when such constructs are important in the evaluation scheme. Unfortunately, relatively few of the thousands of psychological inventories available were developed specifically with rehabilitation concerns in mind.

An example of a psychological inventory developed for use in rehabilitation is the Human Service Scale (HSS), which is also described in Chapter 5. If program goals include improved client psychological adjustment, the HSS could be a valuable criterion measure for assessing program efficiency (services expended in meeting scale-defined client needs), effectiveness (documenting sustention of benefits through postservice attainment of needs), and quality (number of needs met).

Psychological inventories can add to the evaluation scheme in that they provide estimates of the client's inner states, i.e., personality and attitudes. Other advantages of psychological inventories are that inventories may be administered before and after services to assess degree of improvement, that test scoring is objective leaving little room for subjective judgements, and that inventories often have standardized norms, which facilitate interpretation. Disadvantages include limitations in meeting particular program needs, prohibitive administration time, and excessive costs.

Existing Records

Existing records are forms that are used to categorize bits of data routinely collected by agencies and facilities. Generally, existing records are required for governmental reporting and are used in policy planning and programming. In rehabilitation the best known of these forms is the Statistical Reporting Form R-300.

Traditionally, program evaluation in vocational rehabilitation has consisted of monitoring the flow and outcomes of clients served by the program. Within the program, clients are tracked via the R-300, which consists, in part, of a series of two-digit codes that correspond to a client's status at any point in the rehabilitation process. The R-300 has over 60 client related variables, has various program related variables, and is readily available and comparable across and within state agencies.

It is possible, using R-300 data, to describe various program *input* characteristics (types of persons referred, referral sources, etc.), *process* characteristics (time in different statuses, type and cost of various services), as well as client *outcome*. There are four types of outcomes or client closure statuses. A 08 closure status refers to a client deemed ineligible for services at referral. Clients who are eligible for services, and complete a rehabilitation plan, but progress no further in the program are closed status 30 — unsuccessful closure, some services received. Clients who receive necessary services, and are ready for employment, but do not get a job are closed status 28. Finally, persons who progress through the system and remain employed for 60 days after service, are closed status 26 — successfully rehabilitated.

The vocational rehabilitation program broadly defines employment not only to include competitive employment but also to include employment in a sheltered workshop and employment as a "homemaker." However, employment remains the sole index of program related client success. Because other legitimate client outcomes, such as physical and emotional well-being, accrue from program intervention but are not accounted for, the sole use of the 26 closure status has been severely criticized (Conley, 1973; Viaille, 1968). The Rehabilitation Services Administration has begun to attend to the importance of quality, as well as quantity, in measuring program outcomes as exemplified by the current attempts to design program evaluation standards (defined in the next section) and to develop systems for weighting case closures (see Chapter 9).

The most common use of the R-300 is in summary statistical reporting. The annual report titled *State Vocational Rehabilitation Agency Program Data* is a federal document utilizing R-300 data. Using the R-300 data, the West Virginia Rehabilitation Research and Training Center (Moriarty, 1977) has developed the Profile Analysis Technique (PAT), which can be used to compare different rehabilitation agencies or even different counselors. The PAT makes use of data transformations to plot such things as time in status, case closure, and the number of rehabilitants per counselor. In and of themselves, the R-300 data elements lack meaning. In the PAT procedure, the raw data are transformed to normed scores that have a common reference point, facilitating inter- and intra-agency comparisons. This procedure is described in the next chapter. Other existing records can aid the program evaluator. Most vocational training facilities routinely collect information on their clients. Federal, state, and community organizations often collect program related materials that provide another rich source of data.

PROGRAM EVALUATION STANDARDS

As a result of the emphasis placed on standards for program evaluation by the Rehabilitation Act of 1973, a great deal of time, effort, and money have been devoted to the development of measurable standards for the vocational rehabilitation program. This developmental effort has been marked by a series of research or training grants (Berkeley Planning Associates, 1978a; Rubin, 1975; The Urban Institute, 1975) resulting in the formation of a set of eight performance standards and four procedural standards (Berkeley Planning Associates, 1978b). Since the vocational rehabilitation program is constantly changing, it cannot be expected that the evaluation standards will remain static. It is not only probable, but desirable, that the standards for evaluation continuously evolve to reflect the changing emphasis and priorities of the program. The current standards suggested by Berkeley Planning Associates (1978b, p. 7) represent one stage in a continuously changing system of evaluation criteria:

Performance Standards

1. Vocational Rehabilitation (VR) shall serve the maximum proportion of the potentially eligible target populations, subject to the level of federal program funding and priorities among clients.
2. The VR program shall use resources in a cost-effective manner and show a positive return to society of investment in vocational rehabilitation of disabled clients.
3. VR shall maximize the number and proportion of clients accepted for services who are successfully rehabilitated, subject to the meeting of other standards.
4. Rehabilitated clients shall evidence increased economic independence.
5. There shall be maximum placement of rehabilitated clients into competitive employment. Noncompetitive closures shall be in accordance with the Individualized Written Rehabilitation Program (IWRP) goals and shall represent an improvement in gainful activity for the client.
6. Vocational gains shall be attributable to VR services.
7. Rehabilitated clients shall retain the benefits of VR services.
8. Clients shall be satisfied with the VR program, and rehabilitated clients shall appraise VR services as useful in achieving and maintaining their vocational objectives.

Procedural Standards

9. Information collected on clients using the R-300 and all other data reporting systems used by the Rehabilitation Services Administration (RSA) shall be valid, reliable, accurate, and complete.
10. Eligibility decisions shall be based on accurate and sufficient diagnostic information, and VR shall continually review and evaluate eligibility decisions to ensure that decisions are being made in accordance with laws and regulations.
11. VR shall ensure that eligibility decisions and client movement through the VR process occur in a timely manner appropriate to the needs and capabilities of the clients.
12. VR shall provide an Individualized Written Rehabilitation Program for each applicable client, and VR and the client shall be accountable to each other for complying with this agreement.

Although there can be little disagreement as to whether the 12 standards represent desirable characteristics for a vocational rehabilitation program, a great deal of controversy has centered around the methods used to measure the standards. For example, standard 6 states that "Vocational gains shall be attributable to VR services." Unfortunately, it is certainly not a straightforward task to measure the extent to which this standard is met. Berkeley Planning Associates (1978b) have suggested a comparison of the average wage change for successfully rehabilitated clients with the average wage change for clients accepted for services but not closed successfully. Although this approach is clearly a compromise, procedures more technically precise might require randomly allocated services, a requirement totally unacceptable to most program administrators. A cursory examination of the other program standards quickly reveals that the measurement difficulties are not limited to standard 6.

An additional difficulty impeding the development of program evaluation standards centers around the cost of measurement. Even when the technology for measurement is available and no programmatic conflicts are encountered, the cost of evaluation relative to some standards can be prohibitive. For example, the first standard requires an estimate of the "target population," or number of disabled individuals, in each state. The technology for conducting the surveys necessary for this estimation is well established. Unfortunately, in the opinion of many program administrators, the potential benefits of such survey techniques do not justify the cost. Hence, a compromise technology has been suggested (Rubin, 1975) that meets the cost criterion but that may not possess all the technical qualities desirable in an estimation procedure.

In summary, the task of developing program evaluation standards is twofold. First, the standards must be adequately defined; second, the technology for assessing compliance with the standards must be developed. Unfortunately, the current state of the art precludes simultaneous resolution to problems due to cost constraints, programmatic conflict, or lack of knowledge. Thus, the evaluator is restricted to operationally defining the standards in terms of specific quantities for which feasible measurement technology exists. That is, the current state of the art requires a compromise between the conceptual clarity of a standard and the precision with which compliance with that standard may be assessed. In the next two sections some of the inherent conceptual and methodological problems in implementing the mandated evaluation standards are reviewed.

MEASURING CLIENT SATISFACTION

Vocational rehabilitation continues to place more emphasis on evaluation from the consumer's point of view. Indeed, one of the program evaluation standards mandated by the 1973 Rehabilitation Act accentuated the importance of measuring client satisfaction with the vocational rehabilitation program. Cook (1977) has reviewed the literature on client satisfaction with rehabilitation services, has pointed out methodological issues inherent in assessing consumer satisfaction, and has given recommendations for measuring client satisfaction.

Client Satisfaction Research

In their review of the literature, Reagles, Wright, and Butler (1970b) found few citations dealing specifically with client satisfaction and rehabilitation. Bassett (1974) reported that 1 year after the Rehabilitation Act of 1973, over one-half of the state rehabilitation agencies were employing measures of client satisfaction. Currently, practically all the state agencies measure some form of client satisfaction.

Rubin (1975) reported on two studies designed to research the ramifications of measuring client satisfaction with vocational rehabilitation. The first study (Rubin, 1975, pp. 297–307) sought to measure client satisfaction with seven areas of concern, including satisfaction with outcome, service delivery, and services received. This study found that of the clients surveyed, those in active statuses, about 90% were "satisfied." A subsequent factor analysis revealed "that the questionnaire tapped a single dimension [general satisfaction] rather than the seven dimensions it was originally designed to measure" (Rubin, 1975, p. 303).

A number of other studies have also suggested that most clients who go through the rehabilitation process and are either in active status or have been closed "rehabilitated" are satisfied with the overall rehabilitation program. The second study reported by Rubin (1975, pp. 326–338) addressed the question: "To what degree do persons exposed to the rehabilitation process, but closed not rehabilitated, express satisfaction with services received?" It was found that persons who received rehabilitation services, but were closed not rehabilitated, were in fact satisfied with the rehabilitation process and services received, especially with regard to the psychological benefits of services received.

Several additional studies have addressed more specific attributes of client satisfaction. Reagles et al. (1970b) found that "client satisfaction depends upon the intensity of intervention by the counselor in using the resources of the total rehabilitation process" (p. i). That is, amount of purchased services, counselor contacts, and counselor advocacy were related to positive client satisfaction. Roessler and Mack (1975b) compared different social and rehabilitation service delivery systems and found that clients were generally satisfied with services received. They did find that more than 50% of the clients expressed dissatisfaction with orientation to the services that they might have received. Thus, unless clients know what services are available, it is hard for them to estimate if they received the necessary services.

Recommendations for Assessing Client Satisfaction

Studies on client satisfaction with rehabilitation services have found that most clients are generally satisfied with the program. Studies have also suggested that client satisfaction is a function of amount and type of counselor intervention, joint counselor/client planning, and agreement on goals. In conducting client satisfaction studies, the following recommendations are offered:

1. Decide on the goals of the assessment and the type of client satisfaction to be measured.
2. Choose an existing client satisfaction instrument or develop a device specific to program needs. In either case, the instrument should be reliable and valid, i.e., measure "real" concerns rather than asking "did you like us?"
3. Determine if the clients were aware of the full range of rehabilitation services available.
4. Use good sampling and survey techniques to assure that the findings are accurate. Include clients closed not rehabilitated in the assessment.
5. Utilize client satisfaction as one measure of outcome. The relationship between satisfaction and other aspects of outcome is not well understood. (Cook, 1977, p. 113)

EXAMPLES OF PROGRAM EVALUATION STUDIES

Program evaluation in vocational rehabilitation may have as its central purpose program accountability, program monitoring, or evaluation of innovative program components and new service delivery projects. In the remainder of this chapter, five studies reflecting different types of program evaluation activities are discussed. Each study is described using a standard format, including a short overview, a review of the methodology used, and a summary of results and conclusions. Specifically, the first and second studies addressed two of the aforementioned evaluation standards, assessing undue delays or the timely movement of clients through rehabilitation services, and an evaluation of the efficiency of conducting the required review of client eligibility decisions. The third study examined, through case flow modeling, the projected programmatic impact of serving the most severely disabled. The fourth study evaluated the efficiency and effectiveness of innovative diagnostic services, and the fifth study evaluated the effectiveness of a rehabilitation service project designed to provide services to the spinal cord injured.

Assessing the Extent of Undue Service Delays

The Rehabilitation Services Administration requires that state vocational rehabilitation agencies ensure that undue delays are avoided in providing clients with services. Additionally, the agencies are required to comply with special performance standards, which specify limits on the time that clients may spend in certain service statuses. In an attempt to establish feasible methods for determining the extent of undue delays, Cooper and Greenwood (1976) conducted a study of undue delays in seven agencies in HEW-RSA Region VI.

Method   A two-phase study design was adopted. The first phase consisted of the collection and the analysis of detailed time-in-status information from the participating agencies. The second phase consisted of a case review procedure designed to collect more detailed information relevant to undue delays. Instruments were developed for collecting both the time-in-status information and the case review data from the participating agencies. The time-in-status instrument consisted of a tape/card format for the state agencies to use in reporting the number of months that each client spent in the various statuses. The case review instrument contained blanks for a reviewer to enter the date a client entered a particular status, the length of any undue delay that may have occurred in that status, and the reason for the delay. On the basis of their knowledge of each case reviewed, the reviewers specified whether or not the case was unduly delayed in any given status.

Important Results and Conclusions   Analysis of the time-in-status data indicated that there was considerable variability among agencies with respect to the average time in any given status. Additionally, it was found that severely disabled clients tended to remain in referral status and in service statuses longer, and were on the caseloads for longer periods of time. This suggests that agencies serving a higher proportion of severely disabled clients can expect those cases to move more slowly. In the case review sample, the reviewers found undue delay in 48% to 71% of the cases reviewed. The reviewers, for the most part, attributed the cause for the delays to the counselor. For the region as a whole, the counselor was judged to be responsible for about five times as many delays as the client, and was responsible for nearly ten times as many delays as the agency.

Review of Ineligibles and Nonrehabilitants

An annual review of ineligibles and nonrehabilitants is mandatory for vocational rehabilitation agencies. The purpose of the review, as set forth in federal regulations, is to ensure that vocational rehabilitation agencies guarantee each individual ready access to the benefits of the program, redress for grievances, and employment commensurate with ability. However, the cost of conducting the reviews in terms of counselor time and other resources was an issue of widespread concern, which led Cooper, Greenwood, and Davis (1979) to examine the effectiveness of the review process as a means for guaranteeing access to program benefits.

Method   Three major questions were addressed by the evaluation. First, what was done to complete the review, what did it cost, and what were the results? Second, what were the characteristics of the individuals receiving reviews? Finally, what was the previous history of the "review" clients in the rehabilitation system? To provide the data necessary to answer these questions, an annual review report form was designed. For each case reviewed, the form included the counselor action taken to review the case (mail, telephone, or personal contact), an estimate of time required for the action, and the outcome of the action. The annual report forms for all clients reviewed during the 1977 fiscal year were collected at the end of the year, and therefore represented a retrospective report by the counselors.

Important Results and Conclusions   The annual review in the three participating agencies did not prove to be an efficient mechanism for ensuring benefits to clients closed due to lack of vocational potential. Of the 2,332 cases reviewed, only 17 cases reentered a caseload following counselor action as part of the annual review of ineligibles and nonrehabilitants. If the resources required to conduct reviews requiring no counselor action are ignored, then it required a total of approximately 166 working days to result in 17 cases reentering the caseload, assuming that all 17 returned as a result of counselor intervention. Of the 17 cases, most were expected to be closed ineligible or nonrehabilitated. The small probability of success and the high cost of the annual review procedure strongly suggest that this process is not an efficient technique for ensuring vocational rehabilitation benefits to those closed due to lack of potential for achieving a vocational goal.

Case Flow Modeling

The vocational rehabilitation of disabled persons has traditionally been conceptualized as a process that proceeds by stages — a client moves from the acceptance and plan development stages, through the rehabilitation service stage, to a closure status. Because the resources required for successful rehabilitation of severely disabled clients differ from those required for the rehabilitation of nonseverely disabled clients, Cooper and Davis (1979) developed a model of case movement from which predictions of case flow parameters can be made for projected changes in the proportion of the state caseload that is severely disabled. Since these changes may directly result from alterations in policy, services provided, or client population characteristics, case flow modeling may be used to evaluate the probable effects of policy decisions.

Method   The research sample consisted of 2,428 cases served by two district offices of a state vocational rehabilitation agency from July 1, 1976 to July 1, 1977. Approximately 48% of the clients were severely disabled. A general statistical model, a Markov process, was fitted to a collection of data and used to predict case flow characteristics under three alternative conditions. In the first condition it was assumed that emphasis on the severely disabled would decrease, resulting in a caseload with only 10% severely disabled clients. In the second condition it was assumed that the proportion would remain the same, so that 48% of the caseload would be severely disabled. The third condition reflected a substantial increase in the number of severely disabled served, with a caseload consisting of 90% severely disabled clients. A comparison of case flow characteristics under these three alternative conditions served to illustrate the utility of statistical modeling in planning programs for the severely disabled.

Important Results and Conclusions   The model-fitting effort resulted in the general conclusion that case flow modeling is indeed a feasible tool for program planning and evaluation in vocational rehabilitation agencies. Specific findings were: 1) that severely disabled clients differed from the nonseverely disabled clients with respect to several case movement characteristics, e.g., they tended to remain longer in referral status, plan completed status, physical restoration status, and services interrupted status than their nonseverely disabled counterparts, 2) that nonseverely disabled clients in the research sample who were eligible for services were more likely to be closed in competitive employment that severely disabled clients, and 3) that severely disabled clients had services interrupted more often and they were more often closed unsuccessfully from services interrupted status.

In the second part of the study the case flow model was used as the basis for predictions of case flow parameters under the three alternative outreach policies regarding severely disabled clients that are described above, i.e., 10%, 48%, and 90% severely disabled caseloads. It was predicted that an increased emphasis on severely disabled clients would result in fewer successful closures, would require more counselor time for counseling and guidance, and would result in fewer cases receiving physical restoration services. Additional analyses are required to estimate potential changes in cost. For example, although the total number of clients receiving physical restoration services may decrease, the actual cost to the agency may increase because physical restoration costs for severely disabled clients are likely to be higher, on the average, than for nonseverely disabled clients.

An Evaluation of a RIDAC Unit

The rationale for the RIDAC concept, which was briefly described in Chapter 1, was the realization that successful movement of cases during the referral period is often dependent to a great extent upon the expeditious provision of relevant diagnostic services. The Arkansas RIDAC Project (Bolton & Davis, 1979) was initiated for the primary purpose of accelerating the diagnostic process for severely disabled clients. The specific objectives of the Arkansas RIDAC project were:

1. To reduce the time lag between referral of clients for services and their movement into active status.
2. To reduce the number of applicants who are closed in 08 status, i.e., closed from referral.
3. To increase the relevance of client diagnostic information for counselors' uses in planning with their clients, or in justifying 08 closures.
4. To increase the number of severely disabled clients accepted for services.
5. To increase client participation in, and satisfaction with, the rehabilitation process.

Method   Variables measuring client characteristics, service provision, and client outcomes were selected from the R-300 records for the purposes of describing patterns of counselors' uses of the RIDAC unit and evaluating the impact of the RIDAC services on caseload management and client outcomes, as specified in the major objectives of the project. The research design entailed comparisons between the clients referred to the RIDAC unit for evaluations and those clients who received traditional (purchased) evaluation services. In addition to the statistical analyses of caseload data, two other types of evaluation data were collected: the counselors' opinions on the value of RIDAC and the clients' reactions to the RIDAC unit.

It is important to note, however, that counselors' uses of RIDAC services and the effectiveness of their uses of the RIDAC evaluations were confounded in this investigation. This is so because the counselors decided which of their clients would receive RIDAC evaluations, rather than following a rigorous experimental design that would have entailed random assignment of clients to the RIDAC unit as was done in the Houston Project. (See Chapter 1.)

Important Results and Conclusions   Statistical analysis of the client service data for 1,357 referrals to the RIDAC unit by 10 general caseload counselors supported the following conclusions:

1. A much smaller proportion of RIDAC clients were closed 08 from referral/applicant status (16.9% compared to 49.8% of the 2,863 non-RIDAC clients in the comparison group).
2. The average cost for the 08 RIDAC closures was $180, compared to an average cost of $82 for the 08 closures in the non-RIDAC comparison group. It appeared that the referring counselors were using the RIDAC evaluations to justify 08 closures for selected clients.
3. Of the 1,128 RIDAC clients who were accepted for services, a greater proportion were severely disabled, multiply disabled, mentally retarded, psychiatrically disabled, unemployed at referral, and receiving public assistance at referral. These data suggest that, in comparison to the 1,436 non-RIDAC clients accepted for services, the RIDAC referrals tended to be more difficult cases.
4. As of October 1, 1978, 29.5% of the RIDAC clients who were accepted for services had been closed successfully in contrast to 38.6% of the non-RIDAC sample. Despite the slightly longer time required to serve the RIDAC clients, which probably reflected their higher average case difficulty, the average costs were about the same ($1,079 versus $1,169). Although almost one-half of the status 26 RIDAC closures were severely disabled, 91.9% were placed in competitive employment, which was slightly higher than the non-RIDAC comparison group.
5. While more of the RIDAC clients were closed in 28 or 30 status, the difference was not large (11.9% versus 7.5%), and the average cost for the RIDAC client was less ($651 versus $1,302). However, the latter figure was inflated by a small proportion of relatively high-cost cases.
6. Counselors' evaluations of the RIDAC unit were overwhelmingly positive, and included perceived improvement in the following areas:

case planning, case management, client benefits, financial benefits, time considerations, and convenience.

Evaluation of a Rehabilitation Service Project

An example of an evaluation of a new rehabilitation service project is the study by Cook (1978; Cook & Roessler, 1977). This project provided specialized services over 3 years to the spinal cord injured in Arkansas. The goals of the project were to: 1) establish an outreach system for identification and referral of spinal cord injured persons, 2) establish treatment related interagency linkages, 3) develop comprehensive rehabilitation treatment strategies, and 4) conduct a detailed evaluation of the project's effectiveness.

Method   Evaluation of the project was conducted at two levels, the extent to which project goals were achieved (program goal attainment), and the research on client characteristics and client outcome (evaluation research). The evaluation methodology consisted of documenting project goal achievement, e.g., Were specialized staff assigned to the project? Was the outreach system effective in identifying the spinal cord injured (SCI) to be served by the project? The evaluation design also assessed client economic, social, and psychological status from entry into the project, through treatment at an intermediary medical facility, to treatment at a comprehensive rehabilitation center. Clients completed selected psychometric instruments including the Human Service Scale and the Mini-Mult (see Chapter 5), various goal scaling instruments, and specialized questionnaires.

Important Results and Conclusions   Through project monitoring it was determined that the first project goal was achieved. Project staff were strategically assigned across the state, a registry of spinal cord injured persons in the state was in existence, and the staff were active in publicizing the project. In fact, the staff assisted in the formation of the Arkansas Spinal Cord Commission (ASCC), an agency charged with assisting all SCI in the state regardless of vocational potential. In assessing attainment of the second project objective, the establishment of treatment-related interagency linkages, it was discovered that project innovations such as helicopter evacuation from the site of injury were nonfeasible, largely due to terrain and prevailing weather conditions. The project staff did, however, arrange ground and air ambulance service for about 23% of the cases served. In measuring the project's development of "comprehensive rehabilitation strategies" it was discovered that only 20% of the project caseload enrolled at the comprehensive rehabilitation center, and that only 7% of all clients served followed the expected progression of services: injury, referral to vocational rehabilitation, enrollment at the intermediary medical center, and enrollment at the comprehensive rehabilitation center. The evaluation of the fourth objective included detailed descriptions of the psychosocial status of the spinal cord injured and comparisons of the vocational rehabilitation outcomes of project clients to the outcomes of clients served preproject. A major finding was that the project increased referrals of the spinal cord injured to vocational rehabilitation; however, case closures, especially 26 closures, decreased during the project.

SUMMARY

Program evaluation is a generic term that includes various models and methodologies that generate information that enables policy decisions to be made in a knowledgeable manner. Two broad classes of program evaluation models are formative evaluations and summative evaluations. Summative evaluations may make use of an evaluation research model or a goal attainment model. In vocational rehabilitation the goal attainment model, where program worth is established when a program meets stated goals, is popular. Four types of measurement procedures can be adapted to program evaluation studies: questionnaires, rating scales, inventories, and existing records.

As a result of the emphasis placed on standards for program evaluation by the Rehabilitation Act of 1973, the development of criteria for the evaluation of VR programs has received considerable attention. The current evaluation criteria include 12 performance and procedural standards that were formulated by the Berkeley Planning Associates. To illustrate some of the problems in implementing the evaluation standards, the literature on the measurement of client satisfaction with rehabilitation services is reviewed and several recommendations for assessing client satisfaction are made. Five program evaluation studies are summarized to illustrate different purposes and methodologies: an assessment of undue service delays, an evaluation of the annual review of ineligibles and nonrehabilitants, an evaluation of case flow modeling as a program planning technique, an evaluation of the effectiveness of a RIDAC diagnostic unit, and an evaluation of a demonstration project for spinal cord injured patients.

chapter nine
Case Weighting Systems

Paul G. Cooper and Jim N. Harper

The lack of suitability of "number of successful rehabilitations" (or 26 closures) as a criterion for the evaluation of vocational rehabilitation service delivery has stimulated the quest for more adequate evaluation methods. Case weighting has been widely accepted in the literature as an appropriate alternative. Although a wide diversity of approaches to case weighting have been suggested (Cooper, Harper, Vest & Pearce, 1978) in the context of vocational rehabilitation, most approaches represent attempts to provide information relative to the evaluation of the service delivery system. Generally, a case weighting system refers to any procedure designed to give differential value to the work done by the agency service units with clients having different characteristics, service needs, or outcomes (Noble, 1973; Conley, 1973). Thus, the concept of case weighting is closely related to the topics of outcome assessment (Chapter 5) and the prediction of outcome (Chapter 6). Research from all three areas has enhanced the development of technology designed to more adequately assess the quality and quantity of the work being done by vocational rehabilitation service units.

ISSUES IN CASE WEIGHTING

The most general definition of a case weighting system includes such single index approaches as those proposed by Conley (1973), Noble (1973), and Worrall (1978), as well as the multiple criteria approach suggested by Walls and Moriarty (1977). Also included are systems that emphasize case difficulty and systems that incorporate client outcome. Some systems, such as those suggested by Worrall (1978) and Rubin and Cooper (1977), emphasize the probability of success and compare rehabilitation clients' earnings at closure to those of the general population. Other systems, such as the Oklahoma Service Outcome Measure (Westerheide & Lenhart, 1973), focus on the gains achieved by clients. Moreover, the

Oklahoma Service Outcome Measure System tends to emphasize psycho-social client benefits while other approaches, such as that proposed by Worrall (1978), focus on the vocational/economic benefits associated with traditionally defined successful rehabilitation. The successful closure criterion has been used for many years to assess the effectiveness of the service delivery system at all levels from the entire state/federal program to the component service units of a state rehabilitation agency.

The Criterion of Successful Closure

Despite its widespread use, the literature is replete with sound arguments against the use of the number of successful rehabilitations, or 26 closures, as a sole measure of program or counselor effectiveness (see Conley, 1973; Lenhart, Westerheide & Miller, 1972; Silver, 1969; Thomas, Henke & Poole, 1976; Viaille, 1968; Walls & Moriarty, 1977). However, from the perspective of sound program evaluation, there is little or no reference to the most significant shortcoming of the 26 closure criterion, i.e., the comparison of the client employment status *before* program participation with the client employment status *after* program participation, when the client's employment status is used as a criterion for selection into the program. In a review of two studies in the criminal justice field, Mullen (1975) has noted that when clients are selected on the criterion of unemployment and the program is evaluated on the criterion of client employment, the program will appear to result in client improvement, if for no other reason than that the clients have nowhere to go but up.

These arguments do not imply that the 26 closure status should not be an important measure of outcome, but rather that it is not, in and of itself, an appropriate index of effort, efficiency, or adequacy for a program. Nor is it a comprehensive measure of client "success." Similarly, case weighting systems cannot become a substitute for the 26 closure status or serve as the sole criterion for program evaluation. Rather, case weighting systems and the 26 closure criterion are compatible with each other (Bassett, 1974) and are both potentially effective tools for program evaluation.

Uses of Case Weighting

A theme that is common to much of the literature describing case weighting systems is the assumption that the utility of such systems is limited to input into decision-making processes. That is, a case weighting system cannot constitute the sole basis for decision making. Thus, any system must be integrated within the structure of the total planning and evaluation information network and take its place as one component in the decision-making process. Specific uses of case weighting systems include the evaluation of counselors or other service units in the overall service delivery system, as well as improved utilization of management information (Cooper & Harper, 1979).

Counselor Evaluation   The enhancement of technology for the assessment of counselor performance is one of the more obvious evaluative functions of a case weighting system. Because phrases such as "counselor evaluation" or "assessment of counselor performance" are notably unpopular among rehabilitation counselors, the probability that a case weighting system will be successful may be increased if the emphasis of the agency is placed on the recognition of differential effort, on the identification of outstanding performance, or on the insurance of equal credit for equal work. Although the *process* of assessing counselor performance may be identical to the *process* of identifying outstanding performance, the more positive emphasis by the agency is important to the success of a case weighting system.

A second evaluative function of a case weighting system in an agency is the evaluation of service units other than the counselor caseload. A service unit may be a supervisory area, a special program, or any other subset of clients defined by a common program parameter or demographic characteristic. For any given special service program, a case weighting system may be used as a tool to assess program effectiveness and, thus, to justify the program to agency administrators. Likewise, a case weighting system may be used as a means of assessing total agency accomplishment or comparing rehabilitation service units, such as supervisory areas, with respect to their relative service effectiveness.

Management Information   Another category of uses of case weighting systems includes those functions resulting from the accumulation of utilization of management information. First, such a system may be used as a basis for the selection of cases for administrative review and audit. This may be accomplished simply by providing the case review team with summary weighted case data. Second, through construction of caseload weights, it is possible to use a case weighting system for the purpose of a more equitable assignment of cases to caseloads. Although this may have limited application in rural localities, it could be a useful aid in balancing caseloads among counselors in metropolitan areas. Third, by changing the relative importance of the criteria on which cases are weighted corresponding to agency policy changes, the behavior of counselors may be effectively modified to reflect new agency priorities. For example, if the proportion of severely disabled cases on the caseload were abruptly increased in importance, i.e., received greater weight in a counselor evaluation scheme, it is reasonable to expect that counselors would attempt to increase this proportion in their own caseloads. Finally, a case weighting system may also be used to provide management information, such as increased knowledge of the service correlates of successful closure, characteristics of difficult cases, or needs in the vocational rehabilitation system.

Types of Weights

It has been suggested that a case weighting system may be used to define three different types of weights (Cooper & Harper, 1979). *Case weights* generally reflect the expected agency effort that is required for successful rehabilitation of a client with specified demographic and disability characteristics. The weight of a given case may be associated with the difficulty of that case (Meyer & Taylor, 1970; Sermon, 1972). *Caseload weights* generally reflect the total difficulty of a given caseload. Included in the concept of caseload weight are average case weight (Sermon, 1972), caseload size, and effort required for effective caseload management. *Case closure weights* refer to the differential values given to the various types of closures for cases, which vary in difficulty. The latter weights are the kind traditionally generated by weighted case closure systems (Conley, 1973; Miller & Barillas, 1967; Noble, 1973; Worrall, 1978). They are typically a function of the case weight and selected outcome variables such as closure status, work status at closure, or earnings at closure.

Components of a Case Weighting System

These three types of weights may be defined in terms of three general constructs — case difficulty, agency effort, and service outcome. Therefore, these constructs must be operationally defined, then, the technology to measure the constructs must be developed. Unfortunately, the current state of the art in measurement precludes simultaneous resolutions to both problems. For example, suppose the concept of vocational handicap is included in the construct "case difficulty." Even if the meaning of various levels of vocational handicap can be precisely specified, time limitations may preclude accurate assessment of the level of a given client. Thus the researcher is restricted to operationally defining the factors important to a case weighting system in terms of specific variables for which measurement technology exists. That is, present technology requires a compromise between the conceptual clarity of a construct, such as case difficulty, and the precision with which that construct may be measured.

Difficulty   Specific indicators of difficulty, effort, and outcome have been suggested by Cooper and Harper (1979). It is convenient to require that all variables defined as contributing to case difficulty be preexisting client or environmental conditions that decrease the probability of eventual vocational rehabilitation. The probability of successful rehabilitation computed for subgroups defined by client demographic characteristics and disability is a popular indicator of difficulty. Although derived directly from the much criticized 26 closure criterion, it does enjoy much support from proponents of so-called "actuarial systems." The severity of a client's disability, although difficult to measure, remains an intuitively appealing index of case difficulty. Other variables that bear some intuitive relationship to the concept of case difficulty include earnings prior to the onset of disability, unemployment rate in the client's area, and the presence or absence of multiple disabilities.

Effort   Counselor or agency effort is somewhat easier to conceptualize than case difficulty. Indicators of counselor effort may include the time that the counselor spends working with the case or the number of counseling and guidance interviews that are conducted. Other indicators of effort are direct case service expenditures, facility services, and placement services provided to the client.

Outcome   Vocational rehabilitation services traditionally have been beneficial to society, as well as to the individual client. Because some of the benefits to society (such as increased revenue from taxation) resulting from the rehabilitation of a single client are difficult to assess, it is reasonable to limit indicators of service outcome to variables reflecting client benefit. Three types of benefit have traditionally received the most attention from agency administrators as well as researchers. Clearly, the most desirable outcome of vocational rehabilitation services (under current federal regulations) is financially rewarding employment in a position suitable to the client's capabilities. The client's earnings, work status, and public assistance status at closure give some indication of these benefits. Second, with increased emphasis on the severely disabled, more importance has recently been attached to nonvocational benefits, such as the acquisition of independent living skills or psychosocial adjustment. However, these benefits may be difficult to assess and the time requirements of current technology may render their measurement infeasible in a vocational rehabilitation context. A third type of benefit, client satisfaction, has achieved importance partially as a result of the renewed emphasis on consumer involvement in rehabilitation. Unfortunately, not only is client satisfaction measurement often flawed with formidable methodological problems (see Chapter 8), but the importance of client satisfaction as a program goal is still questionable to many rehabilitation professionals due to its lack of emphasis in current legislation. Yet, it is the difficulty of measurement that may preclude the inclusion of client satisfaction and other nonvocational benefits in a case weighting system.

FIVE APPROACHES TO CASE WEIGHTING

Most rehabilitation professionals would favor a case weighting system that provides all the needed evaluation and management information, takes no additional time to implement, and costs little. Although it is unlikely that any system could simultaneously meet all three criteria, it is not inconceivable that some more realistic qualities may be achieved. First, the counselor should not be overburdened with additional paperwork. Second, relevance of the case weighting system to its stated goals and purposes should be maintained. Third, data collected for such a system should be reliable and valid. Finally, a case weighting system should be compatible with the data processing hardware currently available to the agency, although data processing software and procedures must be capable of refinement to meet the changing needs and priorities of program administrators.

There are several feasible alternative approaches to case weighting systems that have been investigated. These approaches include rating forms (Lenhart, Westerheide & Miller, 1972), goal attainment scaling techniques (Goodyear & Bitter, 1974), profiles (Walls & Moriarty, 1977), single index actuarial systems (Worrall, 1978), and a caseload weighting approach.

The Rating Form

The rating form approach typically involves counselors' ratings of clients at acceptance and at closure as a basis for evaluation of client gain in areas such as vocational skill level, psychosocial adjustment, or independent living skills. Usually the ratings at acceptance are construed to be some indication of case difficulty, with the ratings at closure being indicators of service outcome. Agency or counselor effort is not a typical component of rating form systems (Lenhart et al., 1972; Harper, 1978). This approach is not completely satisfactory for the evaluation of service unit performance due to the questionable reliability of the data and the possibility of manipulation of the system. Also, this type of system can be very expensive relative to the benefits obtained.

Goal Attainment Scaling

Goal attainment scaling (Kiresuk & Sherman, 1968) has been described as a quantitative measure of client progress through a program defined by weighting objectives that reflect expected results (Goodyear & Bitter, 1974; Research Utilization Laboratory, 1976). Specific program objectives are established either by the individual client or by the client in cooperation with the counselor. Weights are systematically assigned for each objective and specific values are assigned to the various degrees of accomplishment of each objective, ranging from the most unfavorable outcome likely to the most favorable outcome likely. A 5-point scale is favored by the proponents of this system with the middle value being assigned to the outcome that is most realistically expected to occur. Higher values are given to the more favorable outcomes, and lower values are given to the less favorable outcome.

The Goal Attainment Scale is a potentially useful tool for a counselor, particularly when coupled with the individualized written plan. However, it does have some shortcoming with regard to its utility as a program evaluation tool. The system is relative, as it is geared toward individual client expectations, thus making comparisons across populations difficult to assess.

Like the rating form approach, agency or counselor effort is not a component of Goal Attainment Scaling (GAS). Furthermore, the GAS system is independent of methods specified by the planned rehabilitation program to reach a specified goal. Since the system is based totally on outcome, process problems cannot be identified. Without measures of process, the causes of program failure cannot be isolated. Therefore, when a rehabilitation program does fail, it is difficult to determine whether faulty program design or inadequate program inplementation constituted the primary cause of the failure.

A Profile Approach

The profile techniques and the single index approach seem to be complementary. The profile approach (Walls & Moriarty, 1977) involves, in lieu of univariate statistics such as a single change score or index, a vector of success indicators as the basis for the determination of differential case closure credit. The components of this vector of success indicators could, for example, include clients' earnings, work status, and public assistance status at closure, as well as other indicators of client benefit. The results of a profile technique can be difficult to interpret since the evaluator is left to reduce the many profile points into a unified picture of the case.

Actuarial Approach

The single index, or actuarial, approach, on the other hand, tends to oversimplify the problem and the result in a one-dimensional view of a multifaceted problem. This approach focuses on a single number computed by the use of a prescribed formula, which may take into account factors such as the client's earnings, average earnings in the client's manufacturing sector, or the client's cost to the agency (Worrall, 1978). This approach stresses the computation of case closure weights based on specified indicators of case difficulty, agency effort, and client outcome. Although the integration of several factors into a single index may result in an oversimplification, it may be appropriate for some aspects of program evaluation.

A Caseload Weighting System

A fifth approach to case weighting is to synthesize the rating form, the profile technique, and the single index approach into a single integrated system for program evaluation. Counselor ratings may be used to assess areas of client difficulty or outcome that are not amenable to more precise or objective measurement. These ratings may then be used as additional points in caseload profiles that give indicators of caseload difficulty, expended effort, and observed outcome. Additionally, a subset of the profile points may be used to define a single weighted closure index, which provides an overall measure of service outcome adjusted for caseload difficulty and effort. In this way, three basic approaches to case weighting form complementary components of a single program evaluation system. Such a system is described more fully in the following section.

FIVE EXAMPLES OF CASE WEIGHTING SYSTEMS

A Rating Form Approach

The Oklahoma Department of Rehabilitation has developed and implemented a service outcome rating form (Westerheide, Lenhart & Miller, 1974). The main purposes of this system are to measure the relative difficulty of cases and to assess the degree of client change resulting from vocational rehabilitation services. The rating form consists of a series of items divided into five basic areas: psychosocial status, economic/vocational status, family relationships, physical functioning, and education. Counselors rate clients with respect to all items at the time of acceptance and again at closure. The acceptance ratings are interpreted as indicators of case difficulty, and the closure ratings are indicators of service outcome and client gain. In this system, as in the caseload profile developed by Walls and Moriarty, the concept of agency effort is missing. Despite this, the rating form has been successfully integrated into the Oklahoma client data collection system and is being used both in program evaluation and as a counselor information feedback tool.

As a result of the Oklahoma effort, the Arkansas Rehabilitation Service adapted the service outcome measure for use in the Arkansas agency.

(See Chapter 5 and Harper, 1978.) The agency is currently revising the rating forms and the entire client data collection and retrieval system. The resulting system is expected to be an integrated management information system incorporating aspects of the rating form, the actuarial approach, and the profile method of case weighting.

Goal Attainment Scaling

The Research Utilization Laboratory of the Chicago Jewish Vocational Service (1976) completed a pilot study of a goal attainment scaling system in two vocational rehabilitation facilities. The purpose of the study was to test the hypothesis that Goal Attainment Scaling was a tool applicable to the rehabilitation field. The facilities chosen for the study were the Community Work and Development Center in Hibbing, Minnesota, and the Madison Opportunity Center in Madison, Wisconsin. Goal Attainment Scaling instruments were developed by VR personnel and facility staff for each client in the experimental facilities. A pilot study included questionnaires completed by the facilities' staff on the specific instruments, the amount of staff time required for scale development and monitoring client demographic information, as well as overall staff reactions to the Goal Attainment Scaling System.

Study results reflected acceptance of the system at both administration and staff levels. While not viewed as a panacea, Goal Attainment Scaling was felt to be very flexible and capable of being adapted to most caseload situations. The most difficult aspect of the system was that it required specific, realistic goals for each client, given in measurable terms, that would be truly indicative of client progress.

A Profile Approach

Moriarty and his associates (Moriarty, Walls, Stuart & Tseng, 1974) introduced a technique called the profile analysis technique (PAT) as a method for assessing counselor performance based on data currently existing in state agency files. However, rather than using a single index as proposed by Worrall (1978), Moriarty and his associates advocated the use of a multiple-point profile. That is, several caseload characteristics are plotted on a single graph. To facilitate interpretation and comparability of different caseload profiles, each profile point is plotted in terms of a stanine score in the distribution of all caseloads in the agency. In this way, a single caseload may be evaluated relative to the agency averages on the profile variables, and different caseloads may be compared to each other.

Like Worrall's (1978) system, Moriarty's (Walls & Moriarty, 1977) caseload profile emphasizes the economic aspects of rehabilitation service outcome. The 13 profile variables are of four general types: 1) success indicators (number of 26 closures, percent rehabilitated, number of SSI and SSDI rehabilitations, and number of severely handicapped rehabilitations); 2) placement indicators (number placed in competitive employment, self-employed, or in state agency managed business enterprises, and as homemakers or unpaid family workers); 3) economic indicators (weekly earnings at closure, gain in weekly earnings, public assistance amount per month, and reduction in monthly public assistance amount); and 4) caseload characteristics (percent referrals accepted for services). Although Walls and Moriarty (1977) do consider aspects of service outcome other than earnings at closure, the concepts of case difficulty and agency effort present in Worrall's single index approach are missing in the caseload profile. It is clear, however, that the basic profile concept can be extended to include variables reflecting these additional dimensions.

An Actuarial Approach

Worrall (1978) has extended the actuarial approach suggested by Noble (1973) to a stratified cost-benefit case closure weighting model focusing on the economic benefits of rehabilitation. The variables utilized in the model include age, race, sex, education, major disability, earnings at closure, and cost of rehabilitation. After forming 380 subgroups based on the possible combinations of the first five variables, frequency distributions for earnings at closure and for cost of rehabilitation are calculated for each subgroup. Formation of these subgroups represents an assumption of different earnings potential and expected cost of rehabilitation for clients with differing demographic characteristics. Thus, the concepts of case difficulty and agency effort are effectively introduced with the system. Worrall suggests two methods for computing case closure weights using these distributions.

The first method requires the computation of a raw weight statistic for each closed case in the population under consideration. This raw weight statistic is basically a ratio of the client's earnings index to the cost of his/her rehabilitation, where the earnings index is the client's earnings at closure divided by the average wage of similar people in the same manufacturing sector. The precise formula for computation of the raw weight is given by Worrall (1978, p. 332). The final case closure weight is defined as the percentile of the raw weight in the distribution of all raw weights. With this index the economic status of the client at closure is emphasized as the primary benefit from rehabilitation services. Further, the value of a specific level of earnings at closure is adjusted for the cost of rehabilitation, for the differences in client characteristics, and for the average earnings of persons in the general population with similar demographic characteristics. That is, a wage of $100 per week at closure for a client in a demographic group earning $150 per week on the average is given less value than the same wage for a client in a demographic group earning only $75 per week. Likewise, for similar clients earning identical wages at closure, the client with the lower cost of rehabilitation would reflect the more desirable outcome.

Worrall's second method represents a more straightforward cost-benefit ratio and also requires the computation of a raw weight for each closed case. The raw weight for this method is simply the ratio of the client's earnings percentile to his/her cost percentile. Again, the final weight is defined to be the percentile of the client's raw weight in the distribution of all raw weights. As in Worrall's first method, this second approach also represents an adjustment of the value of a given level of earnings on the basis of client characteristics and cost of rehabilitation.

A Caseload Weighting System

As part of a comprehensive research program conducted by the Arkansas Rehabilitation Research and Training Center to refine the Arkansas case weighting system, an approach to case weighting has been developed that is a synthesis of the actuarial, rating form, and profile methods (Cooper & Harper, 1979). The system has two basic components, an integrated data collection/retrieval system and a method for analyzing the data.

The data collection system includes an expanded group of objective indicators of case difficulty (e.g., presence/absence of multiple disabilities), agency effort (e.g., number of counseling and guidance interviews), and service outcome (e.g., completion/noncompletion of vocational training). Additionally, there are a group of rating items designed to indicate case difficulty and client gain in the areas of independent living skills, vocational skills, and psychosocial status. Client motivation and family stability are rated as indicators of case difficulty.

The data analysis system includes four components. The first is a caseload profile consisting of profile variables indicating caseload difficulty, cumulative effort, and cumulative service outcome. The second component is a weighted closure index based on outcome variables adjusted for difficulty and effort. The third and fourth components are indices of caseload difficulty and caseload effort, respectively. Both the profiles and indices are scaled as percentiles to facilitate interpretation and comparability between caseloads. Monthly reports are made available to the counselors, the supervisors, and the agency program evaluation staff.

OTHER LITERATURE RELATING TO CASE WEIGHTING SYSTEMS

In addition to the methods described in the previous section, many other authors have made valuable contributions to the area of weighting case closures. In a pioneering effort, Miller and Barillas (1967) suggested that the construction of weights be based on the percentage of clients who are rehabilitated within subgroups defined by demographic characteristics such as education, disability, age, and referral source. However, in a subsequent study using a similar method of defining weights, Wallis and Bozarth (1972) found no support for the use of such a weighted closure system. Conley (1973) expanded on the concept by recommending that case closures be given weights based on: the probability of success for clients having similar characteristics, the time spent by the counselor with the client, the case cost, and the extent of client change. In a concurrent research effort, Noble (1973) outlined a weighting system using the federal minimum wage as a fixed standard of reference. In his system, successfully closed cases are weighted positively to the extent that the rehabilitant's hourly wage exceeds the national minimum and, conversely, weighted negatively when the rehabilitant's wage is below the national minimum wage. Rubin and Cooper (1977) used a similar approach when they suggested an index of placement suitability. The suitability of placement index is the ratio of a client's earnings at closure to the mean earnings of a person in the general population having similar demographic characteristics. Average suitability of placement indices may be computed for the service units in a rehabilitation agency so that they may be rank ordered according to placement effectiveness.

Three other issues that are closely related to the problem of case weighting are reviewed below: 1) the assessment of case difficulty, 2) the measurement of service outcome, and 3) the evaluation of counselor performance.

Case Difficulty

Many researchers have contended that case difficulty is an important factor to consider when assessing the quality of services received by a client. That is, a specified level of outcome for a very difficult case may reflect higher quality services than a higher level of outcome for a less complex case. The main problems are, of course, the determination of the factors that constitute case difficulty and the measurement of these factors. Opinions vary greatly among both researchers and practitioners. From a strictly economic point of view, case difficulty may be indicated by case cost. On the other hand, many counselors seem to feel that the most important indicators of case difficulty are client motivation and attitude. The type and severity of disability obviously affect the difficulty of successfully rehabilitating a client, while for some researchers case difficulty is simply a matter of computing a probability of successful rehabilitation. Although there are many approaches to defining the concept of case difficulty, nearly all are plagued with a common problem — measurement. It is always an arduous task to develop appropriate technology for measuring case difficulty once it has been defined. Thus, by including a concept of case difficulty in a system for weighting cases, researchers are, of necessity, forced into a position of either compromising their definition of difficulty or sacrificing the precision and validity of measurement.

Kunce, Cope, Miller, and Lesowitz (1973) have investigated case difficulty via computation of a "feasibility score" designed to measure the extent to which a vocational rehabilitation client possesses characteristics known to influence case outcome. The investigators found that severely disabled clients having extensive education and/or experience are as likely to become successfully rehabilitated as their less-impaired but less-educated counterparts. Zawada (1972), Meyer and Taylor (1970), and Sermon (1972) have suggested the use of a similar "difficulty index" as a component of counselor evaluation. Sermon's procedure includes the computation of a Total Weighted Closure Index (TWCI) as the sum of all case difficulty indices for the cases in a caseload. For comparison between caseloads, Sermon suggests computation of an Average Weighted Closure Index (AWCI) by dividing the TWCI by the caseload size. The California Department of Rehabilitation (Mueller, 1975) has investigated the Sermon difficulty index and noted that it is based on nationwide statistics that may not be applicable to an individual agency. Mueller suggests that the Sermon index may be computed using statistics from only the agency in which it is to be used. It is worthwhile to note that most of the measures of case difficulty depend to some extent upon the idea of probability of successful rehabilitation. In all of the approaches mentioned here, this probability is computed separately for subgroups of clients defined by multiple demographic characteristics. This implies that many researchers and practitioners do indeed believe that client characteristics are related to case difficulty.

Service Outcome

A basic component of virtually all case weighting systems is some concept of outcome. Closure status (26 or non-26), work status at closure, earnings at closure, and several other routinely collected variables have all been used as operational definitions of outcome. Outcome has also been stressed via rating forms completed by the counselor at closure, indicating the client's status with respect to such constructs as psychosocial adjustment, interpersonal maturity, vocational maturity, and functional limitations. As with case difficulty, the problems of actually measuring the constructs chosen to define client outcome are often formidable.

A common endeavor related to the measurement of outcome is the search for measurable correlates of successful outcome. Correlates or predictors of rehabilitation outcome provide valuable information regarding the characteristics of successful clients, as well as clarifying some of the constructs used to define outcome. Many researchers have viewed this as their primary objective. Ben-Yishay, Gerstman, Diller, and Haas (1970) documented the importance of psychometric data as predictors of rehabilitation criteria. Tseng (1972b) identified psychometric attributes and work behaviors that were correlated with rehabilitation outcome as indicated by the completion, completion without certification, or noncompletion of a vocational rehabilitation program. Weiner (1964) found that for tuberculosis patients, the process of physical rehabilitation (getting well) was relatively independent of personal-social factors, whereas the process of vocational rehabilitation (obtaining employment) was influenced by the clients' psychosocial characteristics.

Other researchers have emphasized client demographic variables as correlates of rehabilitation outcome. DeMann (1963) and Eber (1966) identified client demographic and disability variables as correlates of outcome. Kunce and his associates (Kunce, Cope, Miller & Lesowitz, 1973; Kunce & Miller, 1972) used client demographic characteristics to identify exceptional clients and to predict successful rehabilitation. Kunce, Miller, and Cope (1974) have shown that two outcome criteria, number of successful rehabilitations and average earnings at closure, may be incompatible.

Many researchers have emphasized the multivariate nature of rehabilitation outcome. Hawryluk (1972) criticized the prevailing trend toward one-factor vocational rehabilitation outcome measurement. Because the current 26 closure criterion makes no distinction between a weak closure and a good closure, because it stresses numerical quotas, and because it does not consider the quality or stability of client employment,

Hawryluk advocates a multiple criteria index that includes not only vocational and economic outcome but also the client's psychosocial functioning and employment stability. Anderson, McClure, Athelstan, Anderson, Crewe, Arndts, Ferguson, Baldridge, Gullickson, and Kottke (1974) have examined the feasibility of evaluating the quality and effectiveness of the rehabilitation of stroke victims by assessing both physical and vocational outcomes of patients, as opposed to reviewing only the processes of rehabilitation. The development and utilization of a functional limitation scale to assess the physical aspects of client outcome constitutes the significant contribution of this research to the case weighting problem.

Counselor Evaluation

For many years the operational objective of rehabilitation agencies has been to maximize the number of successful rehabilitations. Hence, counselors have been evaluated on the basis of their individual contributions to this objective. Much literature has been written criticizing the number of 26 closures as a counselor evaluation criterion (Lawlis & Bozarth, 1972: Thomas, Henke & Pool, 1976; Silver, 1969). Further, significant work has been done toward the development of new evaluation criteria. Muthard and Miller (1964) suggested eight performance measures, six of which were clustered into two groups — case management measures and performance ratings. Bozarth (1970) advocated a system that includes directly observable client changes, indirectly observed changes inferred from improved psychosocial functioning, changes as perceived by trained raters, and changes perceived by the client. Levinson (1975) suggested computation of an index of counselor effort to indicate efficiency of the counselor's resource utilization. Struthers (1976) emphasized the need for an evaluation system in which both quantity and quality are considered as success criteria. Such a system would include factors of counselor competence, case difficulty, and client need in the final assessment of counselor performance.

In addition to work on specific criteria for counselor evaluation, there has been significant research dealing with the methodological problems of evaluating counselor performance. Bolton (1978e) has reviewed several approaches to counselor evaluation from a methodological perspective. Greenwood and Cooper (1976) studied case review as a sole indicator of counselor performance. Cooper (1976) has questioned the use of rating forms as performance evaluation tools due to their potential lack of reliability.

SUMMARY

Successful rehabilitation as indicated by the 26 closure status has traditionally been the single most important goal of the vocational rehabilitation system. However, continuously changing program goals and an expanded concept of successful rehabilitation have now rendered the 26 closure status inappropriate as the sole measure of program success. Newer and more sophisticated goals require more advanced measurement and program evaluation technology. The development of case weighting systems is one approach to the problem.

Case weighting systems may be used for the collection and utilization of management information, specifically that information used for the evaluation of individual program service units. Such weighting systems may be used to define individual case weights, caseload weights, and case closure weights. These three types of weights are defined in terms of the three basic components of a case weighting system — case difficulty, agency effort, and client outcome. Although all three of the basic components are important, different approaches to case weighting tend to emphasize different components. Five approaches are outlined and illustrated: the rating form, goal attainment scaling, caseload profile, actuarial systems, and a caseload weighting system incorporating salient aspects of each of the other four approaches. Other literature related to case weighting is reviewed under three categories — case difficulty, service outcome, and counselor evaluation.

chapter ten
Research Utilization

Rehabilitation research is conducted for the purpose of discovering useful knowledge that can be applied in rehabilitation programs to improve services to disabled persons. If the results of research cannot be translated into conclusions that foster more effective practice, the value of the research should be seriously questioned. In fact, there is scant evidence that the tremendous amount of money and energy expended on research projects has had any significant impact on the efficacy of rehabilitation practice. This realization has provided the impetus for intensive study of the research utilization process during the last 10 years. The basic problem is simply that of getting the results of research projects incorporated into rehabilitation counseling practice.

RESEARCH UTILIZATION STRATEGIES

It is only recently that researchers and administrators in rehabilitation came to the realization that research findings were not being automatically adopted by practitioners. Translating research into implications for practice and preparing for innovation in service procedures must be an integral part of the research function.

The origins of the research utilization effort in rehabilitation can be traced to three events: 1) the convening of a national conference held in Miami Beach in 1966 on the theme "Communication, Dissemination, and Utilization of Rehabilitation Research Information," 2) the establishment of a research utilization task force in 1967 within the Rehabilitation Services Administration (RSA) on "Implementation of Research Utilization," and 3) the creation and staffing of a new unit, the Research Utilization Branch, within the RSA in 1968. Readers interested in a comprehensive review of the rehabilitation literature dealing with research utilization are referred to the article by Murphy (1975).

Three basic strategies for converting research findings into improved services to handicapped clients can be identified:

1. Practitioners can be educated in research methodology in order to prepare them to critically evaluate research reports and to translate the results into techniques that can be integrated into their personal counseling styles.
2. Research utilization specialists can act as intermediaries between researchers and practitioners by translating reports into various forms that can be used by practitioners, e.g., research abstracts or summaries, training manuals, and audio-visual presentations.
3. Researchers and practitioners can be brought together at workshops and conferences to discuss research findings that are relevant to service delivery problems that counselors have identified. The visiting consultant and RULE projects, which are described later in this chapter, illustrate the strategy of direct interpersonal interaction.

The first strategy has been traditionally employed in graduate training programs for rehabilitation counselors and other practitioners, and it has generally failed. This failure has probably been due to the formal mode of instruction, which was designed to prepare researchers, rather than to any defect in the logic of the approach. The second strategy has become a major component of the RSA research utilization program and is discussed in subsequent sections. The third strategy, which relies on direct contact between researchers and users, is also illustrated later in the chapter. It should be emphasized that these three strategies are really complementary; the tremendous amount of research information currently available necessitates the use of multiple RU approaches.

BARRIERS TO RESEARCH UTILIZATION

Three major barriers to the utilization of research results can be identified. These obstacles serve as a starting point for solving research utilization problems and provide a framework for the topics presented in this chapter.

1. Research projects are often designed without any input or participation from the practitioners who will ultimately constitute the vehicle for the application of the research findings. When practitioners are not active participants in the design of studies, questions of major significance may be overlooked or inappropriately framed and, thus, the eventual results may be inapplicable. The study by Glaser and

Taylor (1973) strongly suggests that the involvement of practitioners and administrators in planning and conducting research is the major factor in determining the eventual success of a research project.

2. Research findings are generally not reported in a form that encourages the utilization of results. Most reports (e.g., journal articles, monographs, and books) are written for researchers and other academically oriented persons, and *not* for practitioners. Clearly, the mode of dissemination must be appropriate for the needs and professional interests of the target audience. (This is not to suggest that research reports should be "watered down" for practitioners; studies must be reported carefully in order to minimize the possibility that results will be misinterpreted or overgeneralized.) The Rehabilitation Services Administration (RSA) has developed a comprehensive program for the dissemination and utilization of research results that is designed to accelerate the translation of research into practice.

3. Resistance to change is a natural characteristic of individuals and organizations that often impedes the utilization of research findings. Halpert (1966) pointed out that practitioners, who derive their satisfaction from meeting people's needs, are motivated against changing from practices that apparently have been successful. Thus, the results of research must be presented to potential consumers in convincing and nonthreatening ways.

FACTORS INFLUENCING THE SUCCESS OF RESEARCH

Glaser and Taylor (1973) reported the results of an intensive follow-up study of 10 research projects that had been funded by the National Institute of Mental Health (NIMH). The Applied Research Branch of NIMH had rated five of the projects high on a success criterion, which included 1) the extent to which the objectives were met, 2) the quality of the final report, and 3) the dissemination of the findings. The other five projects had been rated relatively low on the criterion. The purpose of the follow-up study was to discover variables that may have been associated with the degree of project success.

The principal research instrument for the study was a comprehensive interview schedule administered to key people associated with each project. These key people included the principal investigator, other staff members, administrators, and persons who would be most likely to be utilizers of the findings of the research project. The main results of the follow-up study were organized into six stages in the life cycle of a research project:

1. *Idea*   Successful projects actively solicited reactions and contributions from other persons during the early idea stage; the research idea was more likely to be directly relevant to pertinent practical issues of concern to the host agency.
2. *Design*   Successful projects evidenced a more dynamic, issue-laden interaction which frequently led to conflict and the need for revisions and compromise. In contrast, the less successful projects were comparatively calm and uneventful.
3. *Funding*   Successful projects more frequently availed themselves of the consultative services of NIMH regional offices and were more likely to have had their NIMH grant supplemented by contributions from the host agency.
4. *Research*   Successful projects characteristically solicited consultation, involvement, and expertise from many different sources while the studies were under way; problems were recognized and dealt with through discussions and the use of consultants.
5. *Dissemination*   Successful projects were more active in making use of conventional outlets for dissemination (journal publications, etc.), but these channels were judged to be only moderately effective. Furthermore, the successful projects were encouraged by involved persons to disseminate their findings through publications and presentations.
6. *Utilization*   Successful projects were able to identify more instances in which their research findings were utilized by practitioners and other researchers. If the practitioners in the host agency were actively involved in the development and conduct of the project, then there was greater likelihood that they would use the findings in their practice and would encourage practitioners elsewhere to do the same.

It can be concluded that the primary dimension that distinguishes the five highly rated projects from those rated low is the extent to which the active *involvement* of others (e.g., administrators, practitioners, and consultants) was obtained. Applied social research usually takes place in conjunction with ongoing service programs and it is imperative for the researcher to respect the existing organizational environment. If the research project does not have the support of the personnel and administration in the cooperating agency, a successful outcome may be impossible to achieve.

Before moving on, it may be instructive to consider the Glaser and Taylor study from the perspective of research design. Is the study an experiment? Did the investigators manipulate the independent variables (the various factors that discriminated between the successful and unsuccessful projects)? The study is clearly an ex post facto design because the investigators studied the relationship between the factors and success, retrospectively. How confident can we be that the factors were *causally* related to the degree of success of the projects? Is it possible that the success of a project influences the involvement (or perceived involvement) of persons who are working with the research project? (After all, it's nice to be involved with something successful.) Finally, could the differences be due to chance? Would another sample of 10 projects, if studied the same way, lead to similar conclusions?

Definitive answers to these questions could be obtained by carrying out experimental studies in which the independent variables would be manipulated. When considered in the context of cost and benefit, the potential value of such experimental studies is seen to be minimal. The results of the Glaser and Taylor study are further supported by its consistency with other research findings and social psychological theory. It would be much more efficient to prepare a set of guidelines, based on the results of the study, for use by researchers who propose to conduct research in service settings. (See Engstrom's suggestions that are summarized in the next section.) In other words, the results of this ex post facto study make good sense and therefore should be utilized to improve the quality and usefulness of future applied research projects.

THE RSA RESEARCH UTILIZATION PROGRAM

An important distinction exists between the dissemination of research results and their utilization. Dissemination refers to the distribution process, and utilization is concerned with the actual usage of the results by practitioners. Dissemination is a *necessary* prerequisite for utilization, but widespread availability of research reports does not *guarantee* that they will be read or used by the target audience. Thus, a comprehensive utilization program must include techniques for helping individuals and organizations adopt new ideas and alter service procedures. The RSA research utilization program encompasses a variety of dissemination and utilization components (Garrett, 1970):

1. All RSA-supported research and demonstration (R&D) grants must conclude with a final project report, which states the *Significant Findings and Implications for Rehabilitation Practice* on the inside cover.

2. Research BRIEFs (Bring Research Into Effective Focus) are distributed separately to disseminate project findings to a wider audience. The BRIEFs' uncomplicated format and minimal length (front and back of a looseleaf notebook page) are intended to be attractive to the busy counselor or administrator.

3. Research Utilization Specialists (RUSs) have been employed and trained in nine states in conjunction with a nationwide program to implement and evaluate the "county agent" concept that the U.S. Department of Agriculture has successfully used for many years.

4. Research Utilization Laboratories (RULs) have been established at the Chicago Jewish Vocational Service and at The Institute for the Crippled and Disabled in New York City to study and enhance the utilization process.

5. Rehabilitation Research and Training Centers (RRTCs) in four areas (medical, vocational, mental retardation, and deafness) conduct applied research and translate results into training programs, which are conducted for rehabilitation practitioners in a variety of settings.

6. Regional Rehabilitation Research Institutes (RRIs) conduct programmatic research on designated topics of broad interest (e.g., counselor functioning, job placement, and attitudinal barriers) and disseminate their findings nationally.

The RSA research and demonstration (R&D) program emphasizes the importance of research utilization from the initial conceptualization of projects through the actual implementation of research findings (Engstrom, 1975). Specifically, the RSA R&D program is premised on the development of working relationships between researchers and practitioners, referred to as "participatory planning," as the foundation for successful applied research projects. (This concept was derived from the Glaser and Taylor study.)

In addition, the RSA R&D program requires that projects have direct relevance to rehabilitation practice, that they be technically sound, and that strategies for the implementation of results be planned in advance. Some dissemination approaches that are recommended in addition to written reports are short-term training institutes, audiovisual briefs, and telecommunication systems. Written reports should incorporate the concept of "targeted communications," which means simply that the research findings must be communicated in different ways to different users.

Engstrom (1975) concluded his review of the RSA R&D program with a number of suggestions for increasing the "transferability" of research results to program operations. Some of his excellent suggestions are:

Conceptualization and Design

To the researcher   Know your interests and the needs of your clientele. Do they match? Can you translate their needs into researchable issues? Have you set mutually agreed-upon performance criteria?

To the user   Be an active participant in need assessment, and be ready to thoroughly orient the researcher to your program operations. Be prepared for the frustrations that the research designs may impose.

Conduct

To the researcher   Spend ample time on the project. Set milestones and reset them when they are unmet. Bring users into project policy decisions. Prepare interim briefings for users at both periodic and milestone intervals. Also, arrange for regular reviews by users.

To the user   Apportion your time to give ample attention to the project. Assure that agency resources are available to meet deadlines. Participate in periodic briefings, being sure to include management councils that can make policy decisions as well as allocate agency resources.

Implementation

To the researcher   Be sure that your findings are relevant to your audiences. Present findings in operational and cost-benefit terms whenever possible. Be careful to point out any changes in policy, professional practice, or organizational structure that may be required to implement the findings. Package your results in various ways that will be meaningful to user audiences at different levels of interest in terms of project outcomes.

To the user   Be prepared to assume the greater share of project responsibility during this phase. Redefine objectives and operational plans on the basis of knowledge acquired. Use project staff as consultants in implementing findings, since they will be most aware of the pitfalls as well as the advantages that may be encountered. (pp. 362-363)

EIGHT PROPOSITIONS ABOUT RESEARCH UTILIZATION

Rogers (1971) conceptualized the research utilization (RU) process in terms of three social systems and eight propositions about the interrelationships among the systems. The social systems are: 1) the *research system,* which creates and develops research results or innovations; 2) the *linking systems,* which perform the function of translating practitioner needs to researchers and of diffusing research results and innovations to practitioners; and 3) the *practitioner system,* which recognizes needs for research and thus leads to its initiation, and which later adopts the innovations that may result (Rogers, 1971, p. 251).

Based on an examination of the research literature concerned with research utilization, Rogers outlined a series of eight propositions that serve to integrate many of the seemingly disparate findings that are discussed in this chapter:

1. Communication between the research system and practitioner system is facilitated by a linking system between them.
2. The effectiveness of communicating research results and/or practitioner needs between a research system and a linking system is facilitated by the degree of similarity (homophily) between researchers and linkers.
3. The effectiveness of communicating research results and/or practitioner needs between a linking system and a practitioner system is facilitated by the degree of homophily between linkers and practitioners.
4. The effectiveness of communicating research results and/or practitioner needs between a linking system and a practitioner system is facilitated by opinion leaders who bridge the heterophily (dissimilarity) gap between linkers and practitioners.
5. The effectiveness of communicating research results and/or practitioner needs between a linking system and a practitioner system is facilitated by increasing the technical competence of practitioners, so that linker-practitioner heterophily is decreased.
6. The effectiveness of communicating research results and/or practitioner needs is facilitated by the degree to which researchers and linkers make use of feedback from practitioners.
7. The effectiveness of research utilization efforts is increased by training administrators in methods of managing change.
8. Research utilization is increased by orienting research activities towards the needs of practitioners. (pp. 256–262)

While many of these propositions appear to be "self-evident truths," they are for the most part research hypotheses. It should be obvious that the "linker systems" are synonymous with the research utilization specialists. Also, it is important to note that there are exceptions to the "linker" model, outlined by Rogers, that have been demonstrated to be successful, i.e., the visiting consultant and RULE projects. Finally, the reader should recognize the fifth proposition as the fundamental premise on which this textbook was designed and written.

THE RESEARCH UTILIZATION SPECIALIST[11]

At the conference of rehabilitation administrators and counselor educators held in Miami Beach in 1966, Everett Rogers, a leading expert on research utilization, proposed a novel approach to research utilization in rehabilitation, the Research Utilization Specialist (RUS). Based on the highly successful model of the county agricultural extension agent, the RUS would serve as a link between researcher and practitioner. Rogers' suggestion, that a nationwide program be initiated to evaluate the feasibility of the RUS concept in state vocational rehabilitation (VR) agencies, was accepted by the RSA as part of their concerted effort to improve communications between producers and users of knowledge.

In 1969, the national RUS demonstration program was initiated with nine states participating: Alabama, California, Massachusetts, Missouri, New Jersey, Texas, Utah, Virginia, and Wisconsin. All regions were represented except the Pacific Northwest. In each state, the RUS was located in the state office of the VR agency with the general goal of serving as a catalyst for innovations within the state agency structure that could be based on promising research findings.

Roles and Functions of the RUS

In 1974, 5 years of project operation were synthesized into seven goals for the RUS. These goals include both the job functions of the RUS and the benefits that such an individual brings to an operating agency:

1. To determine systematically the relevant needs of the state agency's staff for program and practice knowledge in order to focus RUS efforts toward meeting those needs.
2. To mobilize knowledge utilization resources and activities within the state agency, which includes building storage and retrieval capability for reports and abstracts and disseminating appropriate useful information to prospective users.
3. To encourage and facilitate the use of promising cross-validated R&D findings or of other knowledge by staff and personnel of the VR state agency or collaborating agencies.
4. Through collaboration with staff, or in some instances on the RUS's own initiative, to start small projects that introduce new methods and knowledge into program and practice.
5. To help assure that research within the agency is planned, conducted, and reported to maximize the likelihood of useful results.

[11]The material in this section and the two that follow is abstracted from the referenced articles, which were published in Bolton, B. (Ed.), Research utilization in rehabilitation. *Rehabilitation Counseling Bulletin*, 1975, *19*, 353–448 (Special Issue).

6. To stimulate within the state agency a general atmosphere conducive to the thoughtful consideration of promising new knowledge; a willingness to use available resources and knowledge; and, through that *modus operandi,* a thrust toward ongoing renewal within agency and program.
7. To assess the impact of various RUS techniques or processes used. (Hamilton & Muthard, 1975, pp. 378–379)

During the first two years, RSA training staff and research utilization consultants conducted four 3-day training sessions aimed at providing the RUSs with skills in communication, human relations, organizational problem solving, consultation, and field interviewing. Three theoretical models of the RU process were presented during the training sessions as possible frameworks within which the RUSs might build workable roles: the research, development, and diffusion (RD&D) model, the social interaction (S-I) model, and the problem solver (P-S) model. The P-S model, a need-reduction cycle emphasizing collaboration with the consumer system and the diagnosis of the system's needs before action is structured or attempted, became the primary framework for the RUS roles, functions, and activities. The steps in the P-S model — felt need, need articulated as a problem, search for a solution, choice of solution, application of solution, and reduction of need or search for a new solution — correspond remarkably well with the steps in the rehabilitation process.

A distinguishing feature of the P-S model, need sensing, was a major part of the RUS role. Need-sensing mechanisms included advisory committees, studies, and surveys and access to the agency decision-making process. Less interactive need-sensing techniques included examining documents to determine new policy developments and targeting unsolicited information on that basis, and watching for patterns in information requests from the field.

Because of resource limitations and a lack of training utilization strategies, the RUSs focused primarily on information dissemination. The major means of communication was the project newsletter. A variety of methods were employed to distribute literature, research reviews, and information packets. Consultation workshops and seminars, as well as formal inservice training programs, were vehicles used to link research knowledge to agency program planning and development, evaluation, and research activity.

Each of the RUSs initiated and developed novel approaches to pressing problems within the agency. Some examples of the successful "blue-ribbon projects" are the introduction of counselor aides in New Jersey after earlier attempts had failed; a systematic program for developing and testing placement innovations in Massachusetts; and the application of behavior modification techniques by the staff of a comprehensive rehabilitation facility operated by the Virginia state agency. In each instance, the RUSs' initiative and advocacy backed by the knowledge of successful application in other settings led to applications which, although proven elsewhere, were novel for their organization.[12]

Hamilton and Muthard concluded from their review of the activities and products of the nine RUS programs that a wide variety of procedures and techniques can be used by state agency personnel for strengthening the agency's delivery of VR services. Their conclusion was confirmed by the results of a formal evaluation of the RUS program by Glaser and Backer (1975).

Evaluating the RUS

Working under a contract from RSA, Glaser and Backer (1975) conducted a 3-year evaluation of the nine RUS demonstration projects. For their evaluation they conceptualized five general classes of RUS project activities: knowledge search, conduct of special projects, consultation to agency staff, holding conferences and workshops, and information dissemination. The common thread in these activities is a mechanism of action by which RUSs attempted to produce some impact on service delivery operations in their state VR agencies — that mechanism is *personal contact*.

A growing body of evidence on research utilization and organizational change suggests that well-informed key individuals in given fields of knowledge or practice can help greatly in selecting the most usable knowledge from the flood of research information that increases every day. Moreover, interactions with a person knowledgeable (and enthusiastic) about a given innovation can help increase staff receptivity to the potential use of the innovation. Personal contact thus can be a vital spark that helps get worthwhile innovations adopted and continued.

The methodology employed by Glaser and Backer (1975) was based on a "clinical" approach to evaluation that they devised; three types of measurement strategies were used:

1. Field visits in which clinically-oriented interviews (each employing a semi-structured depth interview schedule) with rehabilitation agency staff and some direct observation were used to learn about the RUS programs and their impact.

[12]Details concerning the RUSs' dissemination and utilization strategies are available in Hamilton, L. S. and Muthard, J. E. *Research Utilization Specialists in vocational rehabilitation.* Gainesville: University of Florida Rehabilitation Research Institute, 1975.

2. A questionnaire survey of more than 1,500 rehabilitation professionals in the nine state agencies, concerning whether they had had some contact with the RUSs and their projects, what the nature of that contact had been, what impact may have resulted, and how the respondent regarded organizational change and research utilization efforts in general.

3. Intensive document analysis, in which progress reports and other materials provided by the RUSs or by RSA were scrutinized in order to develop an on-paper understanding of the demonstration program. (p. 391)

The data collection phase of the evaluation required 2 years of work by a five-member research team, headed by Glaser and Backer. During the first year, the document analysis was performed, field visits were conducted in each project state, and the questionnaire survey was completed. Near the beginning of the second year, a conference was held with all the RUSs to discuss the findings to date and to plan the second round of data gathering. Then the nine field visits were repeated, after which all the data were analyzed.

The results of the data analysis produced a number of kinds of evidence of the impact of the RUS projects:

1. *Survival*   Eight of the nine projects continued in full-scale operation to the end of the 5-year demonstration period.

2. *Visibility*   Questionnaire survey results showed that, on the average, 51% of all agency personnel had some direct contact or experience with RUSs and the services that their projects provided.

3. *Endorsement*   Both questionnaire findings and interviews revealed that many agency staff were favorably impressed with the work of the RUSs and supported the continuation of the project in their state.

4. *System Operation*   All RUSs were able to set up and maintain an information retrieval system, which was used by at least some of the personnel in their agency.

5. *Subprojects Leading to Change*   Some "blue-ribbon projects" initiated by RUSs led to enduring, seemingly productive changes in the VR agency's operation.

6. *Visibility for Other RU Efforts*   The very existence of the RUS helped the nine state agencies involved become much more aware of the overall RSA program of research utilization (RU) activities and the resources it could provide.

7. *Consultation*   Some RUSs were able to offer considerable direct assistance to decision makers in their VR agency. The result was in-

creased credibility for the RUS effort, and sometimes genuine impact on operating procedures.

Glaser and Backer concluded that, for at least some of the RUS programs, the overall impact was the establishment of a valued new resource in the state agency that helped stimulate worthwhile change. The evaluation findings suggested that many worthwhile ideas, procedures, and products grew out of the national RUS demonstration program. In fact, six of the nine projects were continued under regular state agency funding.

TWO OTHER UTILIZATION PROJECTS

At the same time that the RUS demonstration program was being conducted and evaluated, two other RU approaches, both relying on the mechanism of interpersonal contact, were being carried out. The visiting consultant project provided research consulting services to state agencies by sending expert consultants to the agencies, while the RULE project arranged for rehabilitation practitioners to visit facilities and agencies to learn about innovative practices.

Visiting Consultant Project

The visiting consultant project, which was conducted by the University of Wisconsin RRI, focused on the direct delivery of consultation services by the researcher to consumer agencies (Butler, 1975). The overall objective of the 3-year project was to demonstrate and evaluate the effectiveness of visiting research consultants for state VR and social welfare agencies in the five-state region including Illinois, Indiana, Michigan, Minnesota, and Ohio.

Unique aspects of the project stemmed from the simultaneous application of the following concepts: 1) basing RU programming upon systematic assessment of agency needs for consultation, 2) active consumer (agency) involvement in the interpretation of needs, 3) systematic selection of consultants to match specific needs of agencies, and 4) bypassing the middleman in the research utilization process and stressing direct communication between researcher and practitioner.

During the first year, each state agency was visited by project personnel to assess the agency's interest and to determine the most appropriate strategy for the assessment of needs and the delivery of consultation services. Each agency director appointed a liaison officer who coordinated activities with project staff. Simultaneously, an extensive consultant file of more than 280 individuals was developed for use in meeting consultation needs.

The processing of requests for consultation services by the agencies was standardized in order to provide the maximum amount of information for the fulfillment of consultation objectives and the evaluation of consultation visits. The liaison officer was required to specify the purpose of the consultation in reasonable detail, the number and type of recipients, the amount of time, and the type of consultation, e.g., group interaction, or individual visits. It was estimated that 120 consultation visits would be completed by the end of the project. The four most popular consultation topics by far were: need assessment and service planning; multiagency service delivery, coordination, and integration; public relations relative to service delivery; and measurement, monitoring, and evaluation of services.

A preliminary evaluation of the effectiveness of the project indicated that the consultation visits were beneficial to the agencies, focused on agency needs, and aided progress toward goals. Two potential facilitators of outcome emerged: an openness to new ideas and the support of top management. One potential barrier was identified as "institutional inertia." Both the perceived competence of the consultants and their knowledge of, and familiarity with, rehabilitation were also associated with positive outcomes. Butler concluded with a series of implications and recommendations for research utilization by direct consultation.

The RULE Project

The RULE project (Research Utilization through Learning Experiences), which was carried out by the University of Missouri RRI, expedited informational exchange to encourage positive program management changes through purposeful, planned meetings (Kunce & Hartley, 1975). The goal of the 3-year project was to assist rehabilitation practitioners in Iowa, Kansas, Missouri, and Nebraska to obtain information relevant to their programmatic interests and activities that might be in need of special improvement or modification.

The RULE project arranged for designated agency staff, or others approved by the state rehabilitation agency, to make site visits to locations where their observations and interactions might provide information useful to a specific topic or problem. Informational visits could be arranged suitable for a number of different types of problems or activities, such as unique rehabilitation facility practices, agency organizational structures, client evaluation programs, and special rehabilitation services to persons with severe disabilities.

The administrative procedures for setting up, approving, and executing a site visit had psychological implications for facilitating an individual's adoption of ideas. Specifically, the visitor had personal *involvement* as a direct consequence of making the visit, a *purpose* or goal in mind before making the trip, a *commitment* to consider ideas that might be relevant to his/her agency's own unique situation, and a *responsibility* to inform others about any tangible results of the visit.

The RULE project sponsored 220 study visits during a 30-month period. Virtually all the participants were satisfied with site visits as a means of obtaining new information and ideas. Results of follow-up surveys immediately following, 3 months later, and 1 year later provided tangible evidence that about two-thirds of the visits led to identifiable changes in program services or activities. Even when visitors were unable to point to specific changes, they were often able to identify less tangible evidence. The authors concluded that program adaptation and modification of innovations that someone else has experimented with can be easily accomplished through interpersonal information exchange.

RESEARCH UTILIZATION LABORATORIES

As noted previously, two Research Utilization Laboratories (RULs) were established in conjunction with the RSA research utilization program. The Chicago Jewish Vocational Service (CJVS) RUL focuses on the processes of dissemination, innovation, and utilization in vocational workshops. The Institute for the Crippled and Disabled (ICD) RUL disseminates information and provides a consultative function in the rehabilitation of special client populations.

Chicago Jewish Vocational Service RUL

The purpose of the CJVS RUL is to take research and other information out of the libraries, the archives, and people's heads and apply it to problems in the field of vocational rehabilitation in the six states in close proximity to Chicago (Soloff, Goldston, Pollack & White, 1975).

The CJVS-RUL's principal function is linkage. To help rehabilitation organizations solve problems, it links facilities and agencies to knowledge. The knowledge searched for is determined by the problems of the agencies and the facilities that are served. Packages are developed to effectively link the agencies to the knowledge chosen. Seminars are conducted to help each agency or facility form the kinds of links that should lead to solving each problem. A fundamental tenet of the RUL is that research results must be modified to fit into different organizations and services.

Four innovative practices have been identified, evaluated, and packaged in the form of manuals or guidelines for practitioners:

1. "Observation and Client Evaluation in Workshops" was based on research on the relationship between clients' workshop behavior and their success in subsequent employment.
2. "Agency-Community Relations" was developed in three cooperating agencies that used different procedures for dealing directly with employers or preparing clients to deal with employers.
3. "Structured Role-playing as a Supplementary Work Adjustment Technique" was developed through studies conducted in two workshops. A manual, sample role plays, a videotape demonstration, and other materials were assembled.
4. "The Meaning of Work" uses the Minnesota Importance Questionnaire (see Appendix 1, page 64) to assess an important aspect of client functioning in vocational rehabilitation programs.

Each package has three elements: research content, preparation of research for presentation, and techniques used to present the package and train practitioners in its use. In general, packaging is converting research results or ideas underlying practices into easily understandable and adequate procedures. The packager rewrites research results or practical ideas into the practitioner's language. Four generalizations summarize the CJVS-RUL's experience in creating packages for a large, varied audience:

1. Practitioners do not like to read, especially technical materials. To avoid causing them to ignore written materials, the RUL provides practitioners with information regularly and in highly readable prose. A special effort is made to make the vehicle, *RUL Lab Notes,* visually attractive and clearly written.
2. Written material should play down the research aspect of the total presentation. For practitioners, the most important considerations are what is to be done, by whom, and to what purpose. The major question raised about background is usually "How do I know it will work?"
3. The interest of users is enhanced by their awareness of other practitioners' positive experience with a package. In seminars on each RUL study, participants have been most interested in hearing reactions from facilities where the innovation was tested.
4. Personal contact between the RUL and users increases the value of the package to the user. Because of the size of the RUL's potential constituency, such contact is not always possible, and packages must be written so that they carry their own weight. (Soloff et al., 1975, pp. 418–419)

Institute for the Crippled and Disabled RUL

The ICD-RUL was established for the general purposes of disseminating useful knowledge culled from RSA R&D projects and collaborating with other rehabilitation facilities in cross-validation, improvement, and adaption of apparently useful research results prior to their being promoted for widespread adoption (Robinault & Weisinger, 1975).

The RUL has focused on the rehabilitation of special client populations, starting with disabled public assistance recipients (PA/VR clients). Activities conducted in conjunction with this target group included: 1) the National PA/VR Information Center, 2) training in information dissemination procedures for the RSA Research Information System (RIS) and for PA/VR projects, 3) development of materials pertinent to the PA/VR national expansion grant effort, and 4) resource consultants for a variety of special needs of the RSA central office.

In 1975 the RUL shifted its major thrust to that of demonstrating how management practices can be improved in programs for vocationally vulnerable populations. Implementation involved: 1) the development of a National Information Center for dissemination of program evaluation (PE) materials to vocational rehabilitation agencies, and 2) the initiation of field studies to develop and disseminate innovative service delivery techniques for vocationally vulnerable populations served by VR agencies. Activities relevant to these goals included: 1) the publication of a quarterly PE newsletter, 2) the development and distribution of PE abstracts, bibliographies, and monographs, and 3) the conduct of special training seminars for state VR agency personnel participating in the implementation of model techniques.

Field-test projects employing model development principles have included group discussion units for job-sample assessments, placement preparation audiovisual packages, PA/VR project resource packets, and a leaderless group audiotape kit. In summary, the ICD-RUL has collected and disseminated materials through two National Information Centers, developed training manuals, handbooks, and audiovisual aids for improving services to special client populations, conducted training seminars, and provided consultative assistance on a wide variety of service-oriented topics.

UNIVERSITY OF FLORIDA RRI

Under the direction of John Muthard, the University of Florida Rehabilitation Research Institute (UF-RRI) has pursued a core research program focused on research utilization in vocational rehabilitation since 1971. However, the UF-RRI's work on information retrieval began in 1968 with the preparation of several indices and directories. Muthard and his colleagues initially assembled bibliographies of the rehabilitation counseling literature and vocational rehabilitation research reports that incorporated *keyword indices* for locating topics by subject. The popularity of these indexed bibliographies led to the development of additional RU tools.

The first of these was a comprehensive keyword index to all RSA R&D project reports published up to that time, *Rehabilitation Research and Demonstration Projects 1955–1970.* Also organized according to the keyword indexing scheme, the *Directory of Rehabilitation Consultants: 1971* was designed to aid in locating rehabilitation specialists for advice and consultation. A third volume, the *Guide to Information Centers for Workers in the Social Sciences,* describes the resources of 44 primary and 113 secondary information resources for the social service field. Because of the rapid expansion of the research literature in vocational rehabilitation, an updated index, including R&D reports completed between 1955 and 1973 and articles published in 11 rehabilitation journals between 1968 and 1973, was published under the title *Vocational Rehabilitation Index: 1974.* A supplementary volume, *Vocational Rehabilitation Index: 1977,* updated the previous index by listing about 2,000 additional project reports and journal articles.

Referred to as a "Handbook of Useful R&D Projects," *Research Applied to Policy and Practice* (Wells, Crocker & Muthard, 1976) contains four- to six-page reviews of 25 carefully selected RSA sponsored R&D projects. Each review includes a description of the project, a critique of its methodology, discussion of significant findings, and citations of the impact of the project. The details of the impact assessment are described by Wells, Crocker, and Muthard (1976). A companion volume, *Research in Action,* contains one-page journalistic versions of each review written for field administrators and practitioners.

In 1977, the UF-RRI assumed responsibility for the preparation, dissemination, and evaluation of the usage of REHAB BRIEFs. The BRIEFs, which are published at a rate of about 12 each year, are two to four pages in length and follow a standard format: background information, methodology, results, discussion, limitations, and implications for practitioners. Three styles are employed: question and answer, magazine or news feature, and vignettes on related studies. Earlier, Muthard, Crocker, and Wells (1973) conducted a survey of rehabilitation practitioners in state and private agencies to determine the usefulness of REHAB BRIEFs. Almost all (90%) respondents found that the material in the BRIEFs included sufficient detail to be useful to them. The authors concluded that short descriptive summaries of research reports may be an effective way to disseminate important research findings to practitioners.

A recent investigation by Muthard and Felice (1978) that was directed toward measuring and improving the utilization of rehabilitation research produced several important findings. In collaboration with three research and training centers, six dissemination packages were developed and their usefulness to VR counselors was evaluated. Among the conclusions reached by the investigators were the following:

1. Using appropriate practices during the conduct of a project will increase the impact of that project's results on users.
2. To some extent dissemination through personal contact between researchers and users will have greater impact than will publication alone.
3. Communications that translate a project's results for use by a specific audience will result in greater user impact than general research publications.
4. Short reports of research results are well received by rehabilitation professionals and do lead to increased knowledge of topics covered.
5. Slide-cassette training packages presented to small groups in district offices are effective means for increasing counselor knowledge of research results related to counseling practices with the disabled.
6. Although short reports are easier to prepare and less costly to distribute, training packages using videotape and/or slide-cassette presentations hold promise for more effective and continued use.

Other relevant activities of the UF-RRI include participation in the planning for, and training of, the RUSs, preparation of a report summarizing the 5-year RUS program (described above), and studies of the information-use practices of VR counselors and supervisors.

OTHER DISSEMINATION VEHICLES

In addition to the resources for the dissemination of rehabilitation-relevant knowledge that have already been described in this chapter are several others that practitioners should be familiar with. The National Rehabilitation Information Center (NARIC), which is located at Catholic University in Washington, D.C., supports rehabilitation practitioners by supplying copies of all types of relevant publications, preparing bibliographies tailored to specific requests, and locating answers to factual or statistical questions. The National Clearing House of Rehabilitation

Training Materials at Oklahoma State University maintains a large collection of training materials and information for use by rehabilitation educators, agency training personnel, and other rehabilitation professionals. A memorandum listing new acquisitions and announcing other available materials is mailed periodically to approximately 2,000 users to facilitate awareness of resources.

Several state agencies distribute newsletters or similar publications that are designed to make practitioners aware of new knowledge in rehabilitation. For example, *The Linker* is a monthly listing of articles, books, and research reports that are available on a loan basis from the Research Utilization Branch of the Virginia Department of Vocational Rehabilitation. Interestingly, *The Linker* originated with the nationwide RUS project in 1969. *The Innovator,* which is "dedicated to the innovative use of research in rehabilitation," is published monthly by the Research Utilization Section of the California Department of Rehabilitation. Included are book reviews, abstracts of articles, citations of new publications, and a variety of announcements. The format and writing style emphasize readability.

The final dissemination vehicle to be mentioned is the Institute on Rehabilitation Issues (IRI), which is a cooperative effort by state VR agencies, research and training centers, consumers, and the RSA to develop resource materials on rehabilitation issues of common concern. The primary function of IRI is to identify and study issues and problems that are barriers to optimal rehabilitation services and to develop methods or recommendations for resolving these problems. Each year three study groups are convened and priority topics are assigned by the RSA, e.g., consumer involvement, post-employment services, the severely handicapped homebound, and counselor evaluation. The results of the IRI studies are published as resource documents for staff development personnel and rehabilitation practitioners.

SUMMARY

Rehabilitation research is conducted for the purpose of improving rehabilitation counseling practice. Three strategies for converting research findings into practice are: 1) educating practitioners to be research consumers, 2) using research utilization specialists to translate research into usable forms, and 3) bringing researchers and practitioners together to discuss the application of research results to service delivery problems. Three barriers to the utilization of research are: 1) failure to include practitioners in the planning of projects, 2) research reports that are not written for practitioners, and 3) the natural tendency of individuals and organizations to resist change.

Glaser and Taylor conducted a follow-up study of 10 NIMH-funded research projects and concluded that the successful projects were characterized by the active involvement of practitioners and administrators in the cooperating agencies. The RSA research utilization program includes six components: dustjacket summaries on research reports, BRIEFs of research projects, Research Utilization Specialists, Research Utilization Laboratories, Rehabilitation Research and Training Centers, and Rehabilitation Research Institutes. The RSA R&D program advocates "participatory planning" as the foundation for successful applied research projects. Rogers conceptualized the research utilization process in terms of three social systems — the research system, the linking system, and the practitioner system — and outlined eight propositions that define the interrelationships among the systems.

The national Research Utilization Specialist (RUS) demonstration program was carried out from 1969 to 1974 in nine participating states. The RUS position was designed to serve as a link between researchers and practitioners. Independent evaluations of the RUS program concluded that the project was successful in improving service delivery procedures. Two other innovative projects, the visiting consultant project and the RULE project, demonstrated that direct, interpersonal contact between researchers and practitioners can facilitate the use of knowledge by practitioners and administrators. Two Research Utilization Laboratories (RULs) at the Chicago Jewish Vocational Service and at the Institute for the Crippled and Disabled focus on research utilization in vocational workshops and with special client populations, respectively. The University of Florida Rehabilitation Research Institute has emphasized information retrieval and dissemination in vocational rehabilitation for the last 10 years and has also conducted studies of the research utilization process.

Glossary

Analysis of variance (ANOVA)   A statistical procedure that partitions the total variability into two major components, systematic variance and error variance.

Automatic interaction detection   A statistical procedure that analyzes the relationship between several independent variables and a criterion by sorting the subjects into homogeneous groups.

Case difficulty index   A measure of the difficulty of rehabilitating a particular client, usually based on the probability of successful rehabilitation computed for clients with similar demographic characteristics.

Coefficient of determination   The square of a correlation coefficient, which is interpreted as the proportion of variance shared by two variables.

Concurrent validity   Refers to the simultaneous collection of test scores and criterion data.

Construct validity   The all-encompassing set of procedures that are concerned with determining the underlying trait that an instrument measures.

Content validity   Refers to the adequacy or representativeness of the sample of items that comprise a test.

Correlation coefficient   An index that summarizes the relationship between two variables; the coefficient ranges from -1.0 (perfect negative relationship), through 0 (no relationship), to $+1.0$ (perfect positive relationship).

Criterion   The measure of outcome or success that is used to validate an instrument.

Cross-validation   A procedure for empirically verifying the results of a statistical analysis by applying the prediction equation to an independent sample of subjects.

Dependent variable   The variable that is measured by the experimenter; any changes (or differences) are presumed to be the result of the manipulation of the independent variable.

Descriptive statistics   Methods of organizing, summarizing, and presenting data.

251

Dispersion   The extent of variability in a distribution of scores.

Distribution   The total set of values or scores for any variable.

Error variance (measurement)   Represents the errors of measurement or unreliability of the instrument.

Error variance (statistical)   Represents all variability that is not systematic, including unreliability and unexplained individual differences.

Ex post facto design   A retrospective design that is not a true experimental design because the independent variable is not manipulated by the experimenter.

Factor analysis   A statistical procedure that reduces a large number of variables to a small number of more fundamental, underlying dimensions (factors).

Frequency distribution   Summarizes a set of scores by showing the number of times each score occurs.

Goal attainment scaling   Refers to an evaluation technique in which goals are specified and the degree to which those goals are met is assessed.

Homogeneity of variance   The variability of the scores on the dependent variable is the same for all populations.

Independent variable   The variable that is manipulated by the experimenter; the presumed cause of measured change (or differences) in the dependent variable.

Inferential statistics   Procedures for reaching tentative conclusions from data based on samples by translating the data into probability statements.

Interaction   Two variables interact when the relationship between one independent variable and the dependent variable is contingent upon knowing the level of the second independent variable.

Intercorrelation matrix   The systematic arrangement of all possible correlations among a set of variables.

Item analysis   Refers to statistical procedures used to select the best subset of items from a larger pool of trial items; the selection criterion is correlation with the total score.

Mean   An arithmetical average that takes into account the absolute magnitude of each of the scores in the distribution.

Median   The middle score in a distribution.

Measurement   The assignment of numbers to objects or events according to rules.

Multiple regression analysis   A procedure for analyzing the relationship between several independent variables and a criterion; the independent variables are weighted so as to minimize errors of prediction.

Non-parametric test   A statistical significance test that requires minimal assumptions about the distributional properties of the variables.

Oblique rotation   A technique of factor analysis that allows the factors to be correlated.

Operationalism   The doctrine that constructs and theories have no other meaning than the meaning that is yielded by the methods of observation or investigation used to arrive at them.

Orthogonal rotation   A technique of factor analysis that maintains independent factors.

Parameter   An unknown population characteristic that may be estimated by the appropriate statistic.

Practical significance   The assessment of the importance of the actual magnitude of change or difference that is produced by an experimental treatment.

Predictive validity   Refers to the situation where the criterion scores are obtained at some future time.

Probability   A predictive value that represents the outcome of an idealized experiment; the values range from 0 (impossible) to 1 (certainty) and are interpreted as relative frequencies.

Profile analysis technique   A data transformation technique that converts routinely collected program data into normed scores.

Program evaluation   The application of measures of program effectiveness and efficiency to decisions regarding a service program.

Random selection   Refers to a procedure for choosing a sample of subjects from a defined population; a random sample is representative of the population on all characteristics.

Range   The difference between the highest score and the lowest score.

Raw change score   A difference score that is calculated by subtracting the pretest score from the posttest score.

Reliability   The precision of a measurement; a reliable measurement produces similar results when repeated.

Residual change score   A difference score that results from subtracting the average posttest score for all subjects with the same pretest score from each posttest score.

Sampling distribution   A theoretical distribution of a statistic for samples of a given size drawn from the population distribution.

Skewed distribution   An asymmetrical distribution with one tail truncated.

Standard deviation   An index of dispersion that has a direct interpretation in terms of the normal distribution; the square root of the variance.

Statistic   A measured sample characteristic used to estimate a population parameter.

Statistical regression   An apparent improvement from pretest to posttest that occurs because the subjects were selected for their extreme scores on related measures.

Statistical significance   The probability that a given result would occur if the null hypothesis were true.

Validity   The extent to which an instrument measures what it purports to measure.

Variance   The average squared deviation of a set of scores from the mean of the distribution.

Weighted case closure   Refers to any procedure designed to give differential credit for case closures based on the difficulty of the case.

References

Ackoff, R. L., Gupta, S., & Minas, J. S. *Scientific method: Optimizing applied research decision.* New York: Wiley, 1962.

Adcock, N. V. Testing the test: How adequate is the 16PF with a N. Z. student sample? *New Zealand Psychologist,* 1974, *3,* 2-10.

Adcock, N. V., & Adcock, C. J. An item factor analysis of the 16PF based on a large New Zealand sample. Paper presented at the New Zealand Psychological Society Conference, Wellington, August 1975.

Adcock, N. V., Adcock, C. J., & Walkey, F. H. Basic dimensions of personality. *International Review of Applied Psychology,* 1974, *23,* 131-136.

Aiken, W. J., Smits, S. J., & Lollar, D. J. Leadership behavior and job satisfaction in state rehabilitation agencies. *Personnel Psychology,* 1972, *25,* 65-73.

Albrecht, G. L., & Higgins, P. C. Rehabilitation success: The interrelationships of multiple criteria. *Journal of Health and Social Behavior,* 1977, *18,* 36-45.

Allport, G. W. *Personality: A psychological interpretation.* New York: Holt, 1937.

American Rehabilitation Counseling Association. A statement of policy on the professional preparation of rehabilitation counselors. In B. Bolton & M. E. Jaques (Eds.), *Rehabilitation counseling: Theory and practice.* Baltimore: University Park Press, 1978.

Anastasi, A. Faculties versus factors: A reply to Professor Thurstone. *Psychological Bulletin,* 1938, *35,* 391-395.

Anderson, T. P., McClure, W., Athelstan, G., Anderson, E., Crewe, N., Arndts, L. G., Ferguson, M. B., Baldridge, M., Gullickson, G., Jr., & Kottke, F. J. *Evaluating quality of rehabilitation using outcomes assessment.* Minneapolis: University of Minnesota Hospitals, Department of Physical Medicine and Rehabilitation, 1974.

Anthony, W. A. Human relations skills and training: Implications for rehabilitation counseling. *Rehabilitation Counseling Bulletin,* 1973, *16,* 181-188.

Anthony, W. A., & Buell, G. J. Predicting psychiatric rehabilitation outcome using demographic characteristics: A replication. *Journal of Counseling Psychology,* 1974, *21,* 421-422.

Anthony, W. A., Buell, G. J., Sharatt, S., & Althoff, M. E. Efficacy of psychiatric rehabilitation. *Psychological Bulletin,* 1972, *78,* 447-456.

Anthony, W. A., & Carkhuff, R. R. Effects of training on rehabilitation counselor trainee functioning. *Rehabilitation Counseling Bulletin,* 1970, *13,* 333-342.

Anthony, W. A., Cohen, M. R., & Vitalo, R. The measurement of rehabilitation outcome. *Schizophrenia Bulletin,* 1978, *4*(3), 365-383.

Arkansas Rehabilitation Research and Training Center. *Consumer involvement:*

Rehabilitation issues. Fayetteville: Arkansas Rehabilitation Research and Training Center, 1975.

Armstrong, J. A., & Soelberg, P. On the interpretation of factor analysis. *Psychological Bulletin,* 1968, *70,* 361–364.

Arnholter, E. G. The validity of Fisher's maladjustment and rigidity scales as an indicator of rehabilitation. *Personnel and Guidance Journal,* 1962, *40,* 634–637.

Athelstan, G. T., Crewe, N. M., & Meadows, G. K. Legitimizing non-vocational goals in rehabilitation counseling. Paper presented at the American Psychological Association meeting, Montreal, September 1973.

Ayer, M. J., Thoreson, R. W., & Butler, A. J. Predicting rehabilitation success with the MMPI and demographic data. *Personnel and Guidance Journal,* 1966, *44,* 631–637.

Azrin, N. H. A strategy for applied research: Learning based but outcome oriented. *American Psychologist,* 1977, *32,* 140–149.

Azrin, N. H., Flores, T., & Kaplan, S. J. Job-finding club: A group-assisted program for obtaining employment. *Rehabilitation Counseling Bulletin,* 1977, *21,* 130–140.

Azrin, N. H., & Philip, R. A. The job club method versus a lecture-discussion-role-play method of obtaining employment for clients with job-finding handicaps. *Rehabilitation Counseling Bulletin,* 1979.

Backer, T. E. A reference guide for psychological measures. *Psychological Reports,* 1972, *31,* 751–768.

Backer, T. E. *New directions in rehabilitation outcome measurement.* Washington, D.C.: Institute for Research Utilization, 1977.

Bakan, D. The test of significance in psychological research. *Psychological Bulletin,* 1966, *66,* 423–437.

Barbee, M. S., Berry, K. L., & Micek, L. A. Relationship of work therapy to psychiatric length of stay and readmission. *Journal of Consulting and Clinical Psychology,* 1969, *33,* 735–738.

Barker, R. G., Wright, B. A., Meyerson, L., & Gonick, M. R. *Adjustment to physical handicap and illness: A survey of the social psychology of physique and disability* (Rev. ed.). New York: Social Science Research Council, 1953.

Barry, J. R., Dunteman, G. H., & Webb, M. W. Personality and motivation in rehabilitation. *Journal of Counseling Psychology,* 1968, *15,* 237–244.

Bassett, P. *Measurement of outcomes.* Institute: West Virginia Research and Training Center, 1974.

Bauman, M. K., & Yoder, N. M. *Adjustment to blindness — Re-viewed.* Springfield, Ill.: Charles C Thomas, 1966.

Baumeister, A. A., & Bartlett, C. J. A comparison of the factor structure of normals and retardates on the WISC. *American Journal of Mental Deficiency,* 1962, *66,* 641–646. (a)

Baumeister, A. A., & Bartlett, C. J. Further factorial investigations of WISC performance of mental defectives. *American Journal of Mental Deficiency,* 1962, *67,* 257–262. (b)

Baumeister, A. A., Bartlett, C. J., & Hawkins, W. F. Stimulus trace as a predictor of performance. *American Journal of Mental Deficiency,* 1963, *68,* 726–729.

Becker, W. C. A comparison of the factor structure and other properties of the 16PF and the Guilford-Martin personality inventories. *Educational and Psychological Measurement,* 1961, *21,* 393–404.

Bennett, E. C., & Weisinger, M. (Eds.). *Program evaluation: A resource handbook for vocational rehabilitation.* New York: Institute for the Crippled and Disabled, Research Utilization Laboratory, 1974.

Ben-Yishay, Y., Gerstman, L., Diller, L., & Haas, A. Prediction of rehabilitation outcomes from psychometric parameters in left hemiplegics. *Journal of Consulting and Clinical Psychology,* 1970, *34,* 436–441.

Bereiter, C. E. Some persistent dilemmas in the measurement of change. In C. W. Harris (Ed.), *Problems in measuring change.* Madison: University of Wisconsin Press, 1963.

Berkeley Planning Associates. The VR evaluation standards: A system for data collection, validation, processing and analysis. *Working Paper No. 5.* Berkeley, Cal.: Berkeley Planning Associates, 1978. (a)

Berkeley Planning Associates. The VR evaluation standards: A guide for implementation. *Working Paper No. 6.* Berkeley, Cal.: Berkeley Planning Associates, 1978. (b)

Berkowitz, M., Englander, V., Rubin, J., & Worrall, J. D. *An evaluation of policy-related rehabilitation research.* New York: Praeger, 1975.

Berkowitz, M., Englander, V., Rubin, J., & Worrall, J. D. A summary of "An evaluation of policy-related rehabilitation research." *Rehabilitation Counseling Bulletin,* 1976, *20,* 29–45.

Berven, N. L., & Hubert, L. J. Complete-link clustering as a complement to factor analysis: A comparison to factor analysis used alone. *Journal of Vocational Behavior,* 1977, *10,* 69–81.

Berzins, J. I., Bednar, R. L., & Severy, L. J. The problem of intersource consensus in measuring therapeutic outcomes: New data and multivariate perspectives. *Journal of Abnormal Psychology,* 1975, *84,* 10–19.

Betz, N. E., & Weiss, D. J. Validity. In B. Bolton (Ed.), *Handbook of measurement and evaluation in rehabilitation.* Baltimore: University Park Press, 1976.

Bitter, J. A. Bias effect on validity and reliability of a rating scale. *Measurement and Evaluation in Guidance,* 1970, *3,* 70–75.

Bitter, J. A., & Bolanovich, D. J. WARF: A scale for measuring job-readiness behaviors. *American Journal of Mental Deficiency,* 1970, *74,* 616–621.

Bitter, J. A., Kunce, J. T., Lawver, D. L., Miller, D. E., & Ray, C. C. Follow-up: A methodological note. *Rehabilitation Counseling Bulletin,* 1972, *16,* 64–70.

Bloom, B. S. *Stability and change in human characteristics.* New York: Wiley, 1964.

Bolton, B. A factor analytic study of communication skills and nonverbal abilities of deaf rehabilitation clients. *Multivariate Behavioral Research,* 1971, *6,* 485–501.

Bolton, B. Psychometric validation of a clinically derived typology of deaf rehabilitation clients. *Journal of Clinical Psychology,* 1972, *28,* 22–25. (a)

Bolton, B. The prediction of rehabilitation outcomes. *Journal of Applied Rehabilitation Counseling,* 1972, *3,* 16–24. (b)

Bolton, B. Factor analytic studies of communication skills, intelligence, and other psychological abilities of young deaf persons. *Rehabilitation Psychology,* 1972, *19*(2), 71–79. (c)

Bolton, B. An alternative solution for the factor analysis of communication skills and nonverbal abilities of deaf clients. *Educational and Psychological Measurement,* 1973, *33,* 459–463.

Bolton, B. A behavior-oriented treatment program for deaf clients in a comprehensive rehabilitation center. *American Journal of Orthopsychiatry,* 1974, *44,* 376–385. (a)

Bolton, B. A factor analysis of personal adjustment and vocational measures of client change. *Rehabilitation Counseling Bulletin,* 1974, *18,* 99–104. (b)

Bolton, B. Three verbal interaction styles of rehabilitation counselors. *Rehabilitation Counseling Bulletin,* 1974, *18,* 34–40. (c)

Bolton, B. Teaching ANOVA models via miniature numerical examples. *Improving College and University Teaching,* 1975, *23,* 241–242. (a)

Bolton, B. Factors contributing to successful rehabilitation of deaf clients. *Journal of Rehabilitation of the Deaf,* 1975, *9,* 36–43. (b)

Bolton, B. A brief instrument for assessing psychopathology in rehabilitation clients. *Research Report.* Fayetteville: Arkansas Rehabilitation Research and Training Center, 1975. (c)

Bolton, B. Rehabilitation programs. In B. Bolton (Ed.), *Psychology of deafness for rehabilitation counselors.* Baltimore: University Park Press, 1976. (a)

Bolton, B. (Ed.). *Handbook of measurement and evaluation in rehabilitation.* Baltimore: University Park Press, 1976. (b)

Bolton, B. Factorial validity of the Tennessee Self-Concept scale. *Psychological Reports,* 1976, *39,* 947–954. (c)

Bolton, B. Case performance characteristics associated with three counseling styles. *Rehabilitation Counseling Bulletin,* 1976, *19,* 464–468. (d)

Bolton, B. Homogeneous subscales for the Mini-Mult. *Journal of Consulting and Clinical Psychology,* 1976, *44,* 684–685. (e)

Bolton, B. Evidence for the 16PF primary and secondary factors. *Multivariate Experimental Clinical Research,* 1977, *3*(1), 1–15. (a)

Bolton, B. Teaching research in rehabilitation counseling: Reactions and issues. *Rehabilitation Counseling Bulletin,* 1977, *20,* 290–293. (b)

Bolton, B. Psychologist versus client perspectives in the assessment of psychopathology. *Applied Psychological Measurement,* 1977, *1,* 533–542. (c)

Bolton, B. Rehabilitation client needs and psychopathology. *Rehabilitation Counseling Bulletin,* 1977, *21,* 7–12. (d)

Bolton, B. Client psychological adjustment associated with three counseling styles. *Rehabilitation Counseling Bulletin,* 1977, *20,* 247–253. (e)

Bolton, B. Review of the Sixteen Personality Factor Questionnaire. In O. K. Buros (Ed.), *The eighth mental measurement yearbook.* Highland Park, N.J.: Gryphon Press, 1978. (a)

Bolton, B. Review of the Hiskey-Nebraska Test of Learning Ability. In O. K. Buros (Ed.), *The eighth mental measurement yearbook.* Highland Park, N.J.: Gryphon Press, 1978. (b)

Bolton, B. Client and counselor perspectives in the assessment of client adjustment. *Rehabilitation Counseling Bulletin,* 1978, *21,* 282–288. (c)

Bolton, B. Dimensions of client change: A replication. *Rehabilitation Counseling Bulletin,* 1978, *22,* 8–14. (d)

Bolton, B. Methodological issues in the assessment of rehabilitation counselor performance. *Rehabilitation Counseling Bulletin,* 1978, *21,* 189–193. (e)

Bolton, B. Rehabilitation needs. In R. Woody (Ed.), *Encyclopedia of clinical assessment.* San Francisco: Jossey-Bass, 1979. (a)

Bolton, B. Rehabilitation clients' psychological adjustment: A six-year longitudinal investigation. *Journal of Applied Rehabilitation Counseling,* 1979, *9,* 133–141 (Special Feature). (b)

Bolton, B. Longitudinal stability of the primary and secondary dimensions of the 16PF-E. *Multivariate Experimental Clinical Research,* 1979, *4,* 67–71. (c)

Bolton, B. F., Butler, A. J., & Wright, G. N. Clinical versus statistical prediction of client feasibility. *Monograph No. 7.* Madison: University of Wisconsin, 1968.

Bolton, B., & Davis, S. Rehabilitation counselors' uses of an experimental RIDAC unit. *Journal of Rehabilitation,* 1979, *45*(4).

Bolton, B., Lawlis, G. F., & Brown, R. H. Scores and norms. In B. Bolton (Ed.), *Handbook of measurement and evaluation in rehabilitation.* Baltimore: University Park Press, 1976.

Bolton, B., & Rubin, S. A research model for rehabilitation counselor performance. *Rehabilitation Counseling Bulletin,* 1974, *18,* 141–148.

Bolton, B., & Soloff, A. To what extent is research utilized? A ten-year follow-up study. *Rehabilitation Research and Practice Review,* 1973, *4*(2), 75–79.

Bonjean, C. M., Hill, R. J., & McLemore, S. D. *Sociological measurement: An inventory of scales and indexes.* San Francisco: Chandler, 1967.

Borgen, F. H., Weiss, D. J., Tinsley, H. E. A., Dawis, R. V., & Lofquist, L. H. The measurement of occupational reinforcer patterns. *Minnesota Studies in Vocational Rehabilitation,* No. 25. Minneapolis: University of Minnesota, 1968.

Bouchard, T. J. Review of the Sixteen Personality Factor Questionnaire. In O. K. Buros (Ed.), *Personality tests and reviews II.* Highland Park, N.J.: Gryphon Press, 1975.

Bozarth, J. D. (Ed.). *Symposium: New developments in assessments of vocational rehabilitation.* Fayetteville: Arkansas Rehabilitation Research and Training Center, 1970.

Bozarth, J. D., Rubin, S. E., Krauft, C. C., Richardson, B. K., & Bolton, B. Client counselor interaction, patterns of service, and client outcome: Overview of project, conclusions, and implications. *Arkansas Studies in Vocational Rehabilitation,* No. 19. Fayetteville: Arkansas Rehabilitation Research and Training Center, 1974.

Bronson, W. H., Butler, A. J. Thoreson, R. W., & Wright, G. N. A factor analytic study of the rehabilitation counselor role: Dimensions of professional concern. *Rehabilitation Counseling Bulletin,* 1967, *11,* 87–97.

Buell, G. J., & Anthony, W. A. Demographic characteristics as predictors of recidivism and posthospital employment. *Journal of Counseling Psychology,* 1973, *20,* 361–365.

Burdsal, C. A., & Bolton, B. An item factoring of 16PF-E: Further evidence concerning Cattell's normal personality sphere. *Journal of General Psychology,* 1979, *100,* 103–109.

Burdsal, C. A., & Vaughn, D. S. A contrast of the personality structure of college students found in the questionnaire medium by items as compared to parcels. *The Journal of Genetic Psychology,* 1974, *125,* 219–224.

Burisch, M. Construction strategies for multiscale personality inventories. *Applied Psychological Measurement,* 1978, *2,* 97–111.

Buros, O. K. (Ed.). *Tests in print I.* Highland Park, N.J.: Gryphon Press, 1961.

Buros, O. K. The story behind the Mental Measurements Yearbooks. *Measurement and Evaluation in Guidance,* 1968, *1,* 86–95.

Buros, O. K. (Ed.). *Tests in print II*. Highland, Park, N. J.: Gryphon Press, 1974.

Buros, O. K. (Ed.). *Personality tests and reviews II*. Highland Park, N.J.: Gryphon Press, 1975.

Burstein, A. G., Soloff, A., Gillespie, H., & Haase, M. Prediction of hospital discharge of mental patients by psychomotor performance: Partial replication of Brooks and Weaver. *Perceptual and Motor Skills*, 1967, *24*, 127–134.

Burstein, A. G., Soloff, A., & Mitchell, J. Psychomotor performance and prognosis of chronic mental patients: An extension of the work of Brooks and Weaver. *Perceptual and Motor Skills*, 1968, *26*, 491–498.

Butler, A. J. Visiting consultant program for research utilization. *Rehabilitation Counseling Bulletin*, 1975, *19*, 405–415.

Byrd, E. K. The use of the Automatic Interaction Detector in evaluation of a state vocational rehabilitation program. *Rehabilitation Counseling Bulletin*, 1978, *21*, 350–353.

Campbell, D. P. *Handbook for the Strong Vocational Interest Blank*. Stanford, Cal.: Stanford University Press, 1971.

Campbell, D. T., & Fiske, D. W. Convergent and discriminant validation by the multitrait-multimethod matrix. *Psychological Bulletin*, 1959, *56*, 81–105.

Carroll, B. J., Fielding, J. M., & Blashki, T. G. Depression rating scales. *Archives of General Psychiatry*, 1973, *28*, 361–366.

Carver, R. P. Two dimensions of tests: Psychometric and edumetric. *American Psychologist*, 1974, *29*, 512–518.

Casselman, B. On the practitioner's orientation toward research. *Smith College Studies in Social Work*, 1972, *42*, 211–233.

Cattell, R. B. *The description and measurement of personality*. New York: World, 1946.

Cattell, R. B. *Personality and motivation structure and measurement*. New York: World, 1957.

Cattell, R. B. The structuring of change by P-technique and incremental R-technique. In C. W. Harris (Ed.), *Problems in measuring change*. Madison: University of Wisconsin Press, 1963.

Cattell, R. B. Factor analysis: An introduction to essentials. *Biometrics*, 1965, *21*, 190–210. (a)

Cattell, R. B. Factor analysis: An introduction to essentials. *Biometrics*, 1965, *21*, 405–435. (b)

Cattell, R. B. (Ed.). *Handbook of multivariate experimental psychology*. Chicago: Rand-McNally, 1966.

Cattell, R. B. The 16PF and basic personality structure: A reply to Eysenck. *Journal of Behavioral Science*, 1972, *1*, 169–187.

Cattell, R. B. *Personality and mood by questionnaire*. San Francisco: Jossey-Bass, 1973.

Cattell, R. B. A large sample cross-check on 16PF primary structure by parcelled factoring. *The Journal of Multivariate Experimental Personality and Clinical Psychology*, 1975, *1*, 79–95.

Cattell, R. B. *The scientific use of factor analysis*. New York: Plenum, 1978.

Cattell, R. B., & Dickman, K. A dynamic model of physical influences demonstrating the necessity of oblique simple structure. *Psychological Bulletin*, 1962, *59*, 389–400.

Cattell, R. B., Eber, H. W., & Delhees, K. H. A large sample cross validation of the 16PF with some clinical implications. *Multivariate Behavioral Research,* 1968, *3,* 107–132. (Special Issue)

Cattell, R. B., Eber, H. W., & Tatsuoka, M. M. *Handbook for the Sixteen Personality Factor Questionnaire (16PF).* Champaign, Ill.: Institute for Personality and Ability Testing (IPAT), 1970.

Cattell, R. B., & Gibbons, B. D. Personality factor structure of the combined Guilford and Cattell personality questionnaires. *Journal of Personality and Social Psychology,* 1968, *9,* 107–120.

Cattell, R. B., & Sullivan, W. The scientific nature of factors: A demonstration by cups of coffee. *Behavioral Science,* 1962, *7,* 184–193.

Cattell, R. B., & Tsujioka, B. The importance of factor trueness and validity versus homogeneity and orthogonality in test scales. *Educational and Psychological Measurement,* 1964, *24,* 3–30.

Cattell, R. B., & Vogelmann, S. A comprehensive trial of the scree and KG criteria for determining the number of factors. *Multivariate Behavioral Research,* 1977, *12,* 289–325.

Caywood, T. A quadriplegic young man looks at treatment. *Journal of Rehabilitation,* 1974, *49,* 22–25.

Chun, K., Cobb, S., & French, J. R. P. *Measures for psychological assessment.* Ann Arbor, Mich.: Institute for Social Research, 1975.

Clowers, M. R., & Belcher, S. A. A service-delivery model for the severely disabled individual: Accountability data-collection system. *Rehabilitation Counseling Bulletin,* 1978, *22,* 53–59.

Collingwood, T. R. *Survival camping: A therapeutic mode for rehabilitation problem youth.* Fayetteville: Arkansas Rehabilitation Research and Training Center, 1972.

Collins, H. A., Burger, G. K., & Doherty, D. D. Self-concept of EMR and nonretarded adolescents. *American Journal of Mental Deficiency,* 1970, *75,* 285–289.

Comrey, A. L. *A first course in factor analysis.* New York: Academic Press, 1973.

Comrey, A. L., Backer, T. E., & Glaser, E. M. *A sourcebook for mental health measures.* Los Angeles: Human Interaction Research Institute, 1973.

Conley, R. Weighted case closures. *Rehabilitation Record,* 1973, *14*(5), 29–33.

Cook, D. W. Psychological aspects of spinal cord injury. *Rehabilitation Counseling Bulletin,* 1976, *19,* 535–543.

Cook, D. W. Guidelines for conducting client satisfaction studies. *Journal of Applied Rehabilitation Counseling,* 1977, *8,* 107–115.

Cook, D. W. Rehabilitation of the spinal cord injured in Arkansas. *Research Report.* Fayetteville: Arkansas Rehabilitation Research and Training Center, 1978.

Cook, D. W. Psychological adjustment to spinal cord injury: Incidence of denial, depression, and anxiety. *Rehabilitation Psychology,* 1979.

Cook, D. W., & Cooper, P. G. *Fundamentals of evaluation research in vocational rehabilitation.* Fayetteville: Arkansas Rehabilitation Research and Training Center, 1978.

Cook, D. W., & Roessler, R. Spinal cord injury in Arkansas: Rehabilitation service provision and client characteristics. *Research Report.* Fayetteville: Arkansas Rehabilitation Research and Training Center, 1977.

Cooper, P. G. The assessment of rehabilitation facility service in Arkansas. *Research Report*. Fayetteville: Arkansas Rehabilitation Research and Training Center, 1976.

Cooper, P. G., & Davis, S. Case flow modeling: A program innovation for planning services to the severely disabled. *Journal of Rehabilitation Administration*, 1979, *3*, 22-28.

Cooper, P. G., & Greenwood, R. Timeliness of service delivery in vocational rehabilitation agencies. *Journal of Applied Rehabilitation Counseling*, 1976, *7*(3), 142-148.

Cooper, P. G., Greenwood, R., & Davis, S. An investigation of the results of the annual review of ineligible and nonrehabilitants. *Journal of Applied Rehabilitation Counseling*, 1979, *10*(1), 32-34.

Cooper, P. G., & Harper, J. N. Issues in the development and implementation of a case weighting system. *Journal of Applied Rehabilitation Counseling*, 1979, *10*(1), 7-11.

Cooper, P. G., Harper, J. N., Vest, L., & Pearce, R. Case weighting systems in vocational rehabilitation: Selected abstracts. *Research Report*. Fayetteville: Arkansas Rehabilitation Research and Training Center, 1978.

Craighead, W. E., Kazdin, A. E., & Mahoney, M. J. *Behavior modification: Principles, issues, and applications*. Boston: Houghton Mifflin, 1976.

Crites, J. *Vocational psychology*. New York: McGraw-Hill, 1969.

Cronbach, L. J. Test validation. In R. L. Thorndike (Ed.), *Educational measurement* (2nd ed.). Washington, D.C.: American Council on Education, 1971.

Cronbach, L. J. Dissent from Carver. *American Psychologist*, 1975, *30*, 602-603.

Cronbach, L. J., & Furby, L. How we should measure "change": Or should we? *Psychological Bulletin*, 1970, *74*, 68-80.

Cureton, E. E. The principal compulsions of factor-analysts. *Harvard Educational Review*, 1939, *9*, 287-295.

Dahlstrom, W. G., Welsh, G. S., & Dahlstrom, L. E. *An MMPI handbook: Volume 2: Research applications* (Rev. ed.). Minneapolis: University of Minnesota Press, 1975.

Darlington, R. B. Reduced-variance regression. *Psychological Bulletin*, 1978, *85*, 1238-1255.

Dawis, R. V. The Minnesota Theory of Work Adjustment. In B. Bolton (Ed.), *Handbook of measurement and evaluation in rehabilitation*. Baltimore: University Park Press, 1976.

DeCencio, D. V., Leshner, M., & Leshner, B. Personality characteristics of patients with chronic obstructive pulmonary emphysema. *Archives of Physical Medicine and Rehabilitation*, 1968, *49*, 471-475.

DeGeyndt, W., Hammond, J., Ouradnik, N., & Parkinson, J. Methodological adequacy of SRS FY74 R&D continuation grants and contracts (Final report on contract SRS-74-20). Washington, D.C.: Department of Health, Education and Welfare, Rehabilitation Services Administration, Social and Rehabilitation Services, 1974.

Dellario, D. J. Rehabilitation research: A need for perspective. *Journal of Rehabilitation*, 1978, *44*(3), 37-39.

DeMann, M. M. A predictive study of rehabilitation counseling outcomes. *Journal of Counseling Psychology*, 1963, *10*(4), 340-343.

Dembo, T., Leviton, G. L., & Wright, B. A. Adjustment to misfortune — A problem of social psychological rehabilitation. *Artificial Limbs,* 1956, *3,* 4–62. (Reprint in *Rehabilitation Psychology,* Special Monograph Issue, 1975, *22,* 1–100)

DeYoung, G. E. Standards of decision regarding personality factors in questionnaires. *Canadian Journal of Behavioral Science,* 1972, *4,* 253–255.

Dielman, T. E. A note on Howarth and Browne's item factor analysis of the 16PF. *Personality,* 1974, *4.*

Drasgow, J., & Dreher, R. G. Predicting client readiness for training and placement in vocational rehabilitation. *Rehabilitation Counseling Bulletin,* 1965, *8,* 94–98.

Eber, H. W. Multivariate analysis of a vocational rehabilitation system. *Multivariate Behavioral Research Monographs,* No. 66-1, 1966.

Eber, H. W. Multivariate Analysis as a rehabilitation tool: An application of complex research findings. *Studies in Rehabilitation Counselor Training,* 1967, *5,* 59–71.

Eber, H. W. Computer-assisted prediction in rehabilitation counseling. Paper presented at the American Psychological Association Convention, September, San Francisco, 1968.

Eber, H. W. Multivariate methodologies for evaluation research. In E. L. Struening & M. Guttentag (Eds.), *Handbook of evaluation research* (Vol. 1). Beverly Hills, Cal.: Sage Publications, 1975.

Edwards, W., Guttentag, M., & Snopper, K. A decision-theoretic approach to evaluation research. In E. L. Struening & M. Guttentag (Eds.), *Handbook of evaluation research* (Vol. 1). Beverly Hills, Cal.: Sage Publications, 1975.

Ehrle, R. A. Quantification of biographical data for predicting vocational rehabilitation success. *Journal of Applied Psychology,* 1964, *48,* 171–174.

Ellsworth, R. B., Foster, L., Childers, B., Arthur, G., & Kroeker, D. Hospital and community adjustment as perceived by psychiatric patients, their families, and staff. *Journal of Consulting and Clinical Psychology Monograph Supplement,* 1968, *32*(5, Pt. 2).

Engelkes, J. R., Livingston, R., & Vandergoot, D. *Guidelines for conducting follow-up studies to measure the sustention of rehabilitation client benefits in state vocational rehabilitation agencies.* East Lansing: Michigan State University, 1975.

Engstrom, G. A. Research and research utilization — A many faceted approach. *Rehabilitation Counseling Bulletin,* 1975, *19,* 357–364.

Evans, J. H. Changing attitudes toward disabled persons: An experimental study. *Rehabilitation Counseling Bulletin,* 1976, *19,* 572–579.

Eysenck, H. J. Uses and abuses of factor analysis. *Applied Statistics,* 1952, *1,* 45–49.

Eysenck, H. J. The logical basis of factor analysis. *American Psychologist,* 1953, *8,* 105–114.

Eysenck, H. J. On the choice of personality tests for research and prediction. *Journal of Behavioral Science,* 1971, *1,* 85–89.

Eysenck, H. J. Primaries or second-order factors: A critical consideration of Cattell's 16PF battery. *British Journal of Social and Clinical Psychology,* 1972, *11,* 265–269.

Eysenck, H. J. An exercise in mega-silliness. *American Psychologist,* 1978, *33,* 517.

Eysenck, H. J., White, P. O., & Soueif, M. I. Factors in the Cattell personality inventory. In H. J. Eysenck, S. B. G. Eysenck et al., *Personality structure and measurement*. San Diego: Robert R. Knapp, 1969.

Faschingbauer, T. R., & Newmark, C. S. *Short forms of the MMPI*. Lexington, Mass.: Heath, 1978.

Fiske, D. W. Strategies in the search for personality constructs. *Journal of Experimental Research in Personality,* 1971, *5,* 323-330. (a)

Fiske, D. W. *Measuring the concepts of personality*. Chicago: Aldine, 1971. (b)

Fiske, D. W. Can a personality construct be validated empirically? *Psychological Bulletin,* 1973, *80,* 89-92.

Fiske, D. W. Can a personality construct have a singular validational pattern? Rejoinder to Huba and Hamilton. *Psychological Bulletin,* 1976, *83,* 877-879.

Fitts, W. H. *Manual for the Tennessee Self-Concept Scale*. Nashville: Counselor Recording and Tests, 1965.

Flynn, R. J. Determinants of rehabilitation rate: A causal analysis. *Rehabilitation Counseling Bulletin,* 1975, *18,* 181-191.

Flynn, R. J. Rehabilitation dynamics: A system dynamics computer simulation model of the U.S. state-federal vocational rehabilitation program, 1921-2000. Unpublished doctoral dissertation, Syracuse University, 1978.

Flynn, R. J., & Salomone, P. R. Performance of the MMPI in predicting rehabilitation outcome: A discriminant analysis, double cross-validation assessment. *Rehabilitation Literature,* 1977, *38,* 12-15.

Fox, S., Miller, G. A., & Lawrence, R. The rehabilitant: A follow-up study. *Rehabilitation Counseling Bulletin,* 1967, *10,* 99-107.

Franklin, J. L., & Thrasher, J. H. *An introduction to program evaluation*. New York: Wiley, 1976.

Fraser, R. T., & Wright, G. N. Improving rehabilitation personnel management. *Journal of Rehabilitation,* 1977, *43*(3), 22-24.

Furth, H. G. *Thinking without language*. New York: Free Press, 1966.

Furth, H. G. Linguistic deficiency and thinking: Research with deaf subjects 1964-1969. *Psychological Bulletin,* 1971, *76,* 58-76.

Garrett, J. Using research findings to enhance services to people. In D. Patrick (Ed.), *Expanding services to the disabled and disadvantaged: Implications for research utilization in delivery of services and manpower planning*. Birmingham: University of Alabama Research and Training Center, 1970.

Gay, D. A., Reagles, K. W., & Wright, G. N. Rehabilitation client sustention: A longitudinal study. *Wisconsin Studies in Vocational Rehabilitation,* No. 16. Madison: University of Wisconsin, 1971.

Gay, E. G., Weiss, D. J., Hendel, D. D., Dawis, R. V., & Lofquist, L. H. Manual for the Minnesota Importance Questionnaire. *Monograph No. 28.* Minneapolis: University of Minnesota Industrial Relations Center, 1971.

Gellman, W., Stern, D., & Soloff, A. A scale of employability for handicapped persons *Chicago Jewish Vocational Service Monograph,* No. 4. Chicago: Jewish Vocational Service, 1963.

Giangreco, C. The Hiskey-Nebraska Test of Learning Aptitude (revised) compared to several achievement tests. *American Annals of the Deaf,* 1966, *111,* 566-567.

Gibbons, B. D. A study of the relationships between factors found in Cattell's 16PF questionnaire and factors found in the Guilford personality inventories. Unpublished doctoral dissertation, University of Southern California, 1966.

Gibson, D. L., Weiss, D. J., Dawis, R. V., & Lofquist, L. H. Manual for the Minnesota Satisfactoriness Scales. *Monograph No. 27.* Minneapolis: University of Minnesota Industrial Relations Center, 1970.

Glaser, E. M., & Backer, T. E. Evaluating the research utilization specialist. *Rehabilitation Counseling Bulletin,* 1975, *19,* 387-395.

Glaser, E. M., & Taylor, S. H. Factors influencing the success of applied research. *American Psychologist,* 1973, *28,* 140-146.

Glass, G. V. Primary, secondary, and meta-analysis of research. *The Educational Researcher,* 1976, *10,* 3-8.

Glass, G. V. Integrating findings: The meta-analysis of research. *Review of Research in Education,* 1978.

Goldberg, L. R. Parameters of personality inventory construction and utilization: A comparison of prediction strategies and tactics. *Multivariate Behavioral Research Monographs,* No. 72-2, 1972.

Goldenson, R. M. (Ed.). *Disability and rehabilitation handbook.* New York: McGraw-Hill, 1978.

Goldiamond, I. Coping and adaptive behaviors of the disabled. In G. L. Albrecht (Ed.), *The sociology of physical disability and rehabilitation.* Pittsburgh: University of Pittsburgh Press, 1976.

Golding, S. L. Method variance, inadequate constructs, or things that go bump in the night? *Multivariate Behavioral Research,* 1977, *12,* 89-98.

Goldman, B. A., & Busch, J. C. (Eds.). *Directory of unpublished experimental mental measures* (Vol. 2). New York: Human Sciences Press, 1978.

Goldman, B. A., & Saunders, J. L. (Eds.). *Directory of unpublished experimental mental measures* (Vol. 1). New York: Human Sciences Press, 1974.

Goldston, M. H., & Hefley, R. J. *Project Expedite: An investigation of accelerated and diagnostic services in a local vocational rehabilitation office.* Houston: Texas Rehabilitation Commission, 1975.

Goodyear, D. L., & Bitter, J. A. Goal attainment scaling as a program evaluation measure in rehabilitation. *Journal of Applied Rehabilitation Counseling,* 1974, *5*(1), 19-26.

Gorsuch, R. L. *Factor analysis.* Philadelphia: Saunders, 1974.

Goss, A. M. Predicting work success for psychiatric patients with the Kuder Preference Record. *Educational and Psychological Measurement,* 1968, *28,* 571-576.

Green, B. L., Gleser, G. C., Stone, W. N., & Seifert, R. F. Relationships among diverse measures of psychotherapy outcome. *Journal of Consulting and Clinical Psychology,* 1975, *43,* 689-699.

Greenwood, R., & Cooper, P. The case review technique for assessing rehabilitation counselor performance. *Journal of Applied Rehabilitation Counseling,* 1976, *7,* 124-127.

Greif, S. Untersuchungen zur deutschen U'bersetzung des 16PF Fragebogens. *Psychol. Beitr.,* 1970, *12,* 186-213.

Gressett, J. D. Prediction of job success following heart attack. *Rehabilitation Counseling Bulletin,* 1969, *13,* 10-14.

Growick, B. S. Rehabilitation outcome as a function of differential service patterns. *Rehabilitation Counseling Bulletin,* 1976, *20,* 110-117.

Growick, B. S. Another look at the relationship between vocational and nonvocational client change. *Rehabilitation Counseling Bulletin,* 1979.

Growick, B. S., Butler, A. J., & Sather, W. S. Validation of the Human Service Scale as a program evaluation tool. *Rehabilitation Counseling Bulletin,* 1979, *22,* 347–351.

Growick, B. S., & Strueland, D. The relationship between differential service patterns and change in weekly earnings for three disability groups. *Rehabilitation Counseling Bulletin,* 1979.

Guilford, J. P. When not to factor analyze. *Psychological Bulletin,* 1952, *54,* 26–37.

Guilford, J. P. *Fundamental statistics in psychology and education* (4th ed.). New York: McGraw-Hill, 1965.

Guilford, J. P. Factors and factors of personality. *Psychological Bulletin,* 1975, *82,* 802–814.

Guilford, J. P. The invariance problem in factor analysis. *Educational and Psychological Measurement,* 1977, *37,* 11–19.

Haakmeester, P. "Catch 26" or the need to improve our measurement system of rehabilitation gain. *Journal of Applied Rehabilitation Counseling,* 1975, *6,* 178–182.

Hakstian, A. R. A comparative evaluation of several prominent methods of oblique factor transformation. *Psychometrika,* 1971, *36,* 175–193.

Hakstian, A. R., & Abell, R. A. A further comparison of oblique factor transformation methods. *Psychometrika,* 1974, *39,* 429–444.

Hall, C., & Lindzey, G. *Theories of personality* (Rev. ed.). New York: Wiley, 1970.

Halpert, H. P. Communications as a basic tool in promoting utilization of research findings. *Community Mental Health Journal,* 1966, *2,* 231–236.

Hamilton, L. S., & Muthard, J. E. Research utilization specialists in vocational rehabilitation: Five years of experience. *Rehabilitation Counseling Bulletin,* 1975, *19,* 377–386.

Hansen, C. E., & Parker, R. M. A factor analytic study of attitudes toward income maintenance plans. *Rehabilitation Counseling Bulletin,* 1972, *16,* 86–93.

Harman, H. *Modern factor analysis* (3rd ed.). Chicago: University of Chicago Press, 1976.

Harper, J. N. A description and assessment of the Arkansas service outcome measure system. *Research Report.* Fayetteville: Arkansas Rehabilitation Research and Training Center, 1978.

Harrison, R. H., & Budoff, M. A factor analysis of the Laurelton Self-Concept Scale. *American Journal of Mental Deficiency,* 1972, *76,* 446–459.

Hawryluk, A. Rehabilitation gain: A better indicator needed. *Journal of Rehabilitation,* 1972, *38,* 22–25.

Hawryluk, A. Rehabilitation gain: A new criterion for an old concept. *Rehabilitation Literature,* 1974, *35,* 322–328.

Hays, W. *Statistics for psychologists.* New York: Holt, 1963.

Hensen, M., & Barlow, D. H. *Single case experimental designs: Strategies for studying behavior change.* New York: Pergamon, 1976.

Herzberg, P. A. The parameters of cross-validation. *Psychometrika Monograph Supplement,* 1969, *34*(16).

Hill, C. E. Differential perceptions of the rehabilitation process: A comparison of client and personnel incongruity in two categories of chronic illness. *Social Science and Medicine,* 1978, *12,* 57–63.

Hinman, S., & Bolton, B. *Factor analytic studies: 1971–1975*. Troy, N.Y.: Whitson, 1979.

Hiskey, M. A study of the intelligence of deaf and hearing children. *American Annals of the Deaf*, 1956, *101*, 329–339.

Hiskey, M. *Manual for the Hiskey-Nebraska Test of Learning Aptitude*. Lincoln: Union College Press, 1966.

Holt, R. R. Clinical and statistical prediction: A reformulation and some new data. *Journal of Abnormal and Social Psychology*, 1958, *56*, 1–12.

Holtzman, W. H. Statistical models for the study of change in the single case. In C. W. Harris (Ed.), *Problems in measuring change*. Madison: University of Wisconsin Press, 1963.

Horn, J. L. On subjectivity in factor analysis. *Educational and Psychological Measurement*, 1967, *29*, 3–23.

Horn, J. L., & Knapp, J. R. On the subjective character of the empirical base of Guilford's structure-of-intellect model. *Psychological Bulletin*, 1973, *80*, 33–43.

Horst, P., Wallin, P., & Guttman, L. *The prediction of personal adjustment*. New York: Social Science Research Council, 1941.

Howarth, E., & Browne, J. A. An item-factor-analysis of the 16PF. *Personality*, 1971, *2*, 117–139.

Howarth, E., Browne, J. A., & Marceau, R. An item analysis of Cattell's 16PF. *Canadian Journal of Behavioral Science*, 1972, *4*, 85–90.

Huba, G. J., & Hamilton, D. L. On the generality of trait relationships: Some analyses based on Fiske's paper. *Psychological Bulletin*, 1976, *83*, 868–876.

Hummel-Rossi, B., & Weinberg, S. L. Practical guidelines in applying current theories to the measurement of change. *Catalog of Selected Documents in Psychology*, 1975, *5*, 226.

Ingwell, R. H., Thoreson, R. W., & Smits, S. S. Accuracy of social perception of physically handicapped and nonhandicapped persons. *Journal of Social Psychology*, 1967, *72*, 107–116.

Institute for Personality and Ability Testing. *Interim manual supplement for Form E of the 16PF*. Champaign, Ill.: Institute for Personality and Ability Testing, 1971.

Institute for Personality and Ability Testing. *Manual for Form E of the 16PF*. Champaign, Ill.: Institute for Personality and Ability Testing, 1976.

Institute on Rehabilitation Issues. Critical issues in rehabilitating the severely handicapped. *Rehabilitation Counseling Bulletin*, 1975, *18*, 205–213.

Jackson, D. N. Multimethod factor analysis in the evaluation on convergent and discriminant validity. *Psychological Bulletin*, 1969, *72*, 30–49.

Jackson, D. N. Multimethod factor analysis: A reformulation. *Multivariate Behavior Research*, 1975, *10*, 259–275.

Jackson, D. N. Distinguishing trait and method variance in multitrait-multimethod matrices: A reply to Golding. *Multivariate Behavioral Research*, 1977, *12*, 99–110.

Jackson, S. K., & Butler, A. J. Prediction of successful community placement of institutionalized retardates. *American Journal of Mental Deficiency*, 1963, *68*, 211–217.

Jaques, M. E., & Patterson, K. M. The self-help group model: A review. *Rehabilitation Counseling Bulletin*, 1974, *18*, 48–58.

Jenkins, C. D., & Zyzanski, S. J. Dimensions of belief and feeling concerning three diseases, poliomyelitis, cancer, and mental illness: A factor analytic study.

Behavioral Science, 1968, *13,* 372-381.

Karson, S., & O'Dell, J. W. Is the 16PF factorially valid? *Journal of Personality Assessment,* 1974, *38,* 104-114.

Kasl, S. V. Epidemiological contributions to the study of work stress. In C. L. Cooper & R. Payne (Eds.), *Stress at work.* New York: Wiley, 1978.

Kassebaum, G. G., & Baumann, B. O. Dimensions of the sick role in chronic illness. *Journal of Health and Human Behavior,* 1965, *6,* 16-27.

Kauppi, D. R., & Brummer, E. Proposed goals and curricular modifications to provide training in research for MA students in rehabilitation counseling. Unpublished manuscript, State University of New York at Buffalo, 1970.

Kazdin, A. E., & Wilson, G. T. *Evaluation of behavior therapy: Issues, evidence, and research strategies.* Cambridge, Mass.: Ballinger, 1978.

Keil, E. C., & Berry, K. L. The vocational rehabilitation counselor on mental patient treatment teams. *Personnel and Guidance Journal,* 1969, *47,* 531-535.

Keith, R. D., Engelkes, J. R., & Winborn, B. B. Employment-seeking preparation and activity: An experimental job-placement training model for rehabilitation clients. *Rehabilitation Counseling Bulletin,* 1977, *21,* 159-165.

Kemeny, J. G., Snell, J. L., & Thompson, G. L. *Introduction to finite mathematics.* Englewood Cliffs, N.J.: Prentice-Hall, 1957.

Kilburn, K. L., & Sanderson, R. E. Predicting success in a vocational rehabilitation program with the Raven Coloured Progressive Matrices. *Educational and Psychological Measurement,* 1966, *26,* 1031-1034.

Kincannon, J. Prediction of the standard MMPI scale scores from 71 items: The Mini-Mult. *Journal of Consulting and Clinical Psychology,* 1968, *32,* 319-325.

Kiresuk, T. J., & Sherman, R. E. Goal attainment scaling: A general method for evaluating comprehensive community mental health programs. *Community Mental Health Journal,* 1968, *4*(6), 443-453.

Kirk, S. A., Asmalov, M., & Fischer, J. Social workers' involvement in research. *Social Work,* 1976, *21,* 121-124.

Kohler, E. T., & Graves, W. H. Factor analysis of the disability factor scales with the Little Jiffy Mark III. *Rehabilitation Psychology,* 1973, *20,* 102-107.

Kravetz, S. Rehabilitation need and status: Substance, structure, and process. Unpublished doctoral thesis, University of Wisconsin, 1973.

Kunce, J. T. Prediction and statistical overkill. *Measurement and Evaluation in Guidance,* 1971, *4,* 38-42.

Kunce, J. T., Cope, C. S., Miller, D. E., & Lesowitz, N. Identification of the exceptional rehabilitation client. *Rehabilitation Record,* 1973, *14*(1), 37-39.

Kunce, J. T., & Hartley, L. B. Planned interpersonal informational exchanges: The RULE project. *Rehabilitation Counseling Bulletin,* 1975, *19,* 443-446.

Kunce, J. T., Iacono, C. U., & Miller, D. E. Determination of caseload feasibility. *Journal of Applied Rehabilitation Counseling,* 1974, *5,* 215-219.

Kunce, J. T., & Miller, D. E. Simplified prediction: A following study. *Journal of Counseling Psychology,* 1972, *19*(6), 505-508.

Kunce, J. T., Miller, D. E., & Cope, C. S. Macro data analysis and rehabilitation program evaluation. *Rehabilitation Counseling Bulletin,* 1974, *17*(3), 132-140.

Kunce, J. T., & Worley, B. Simplified prediction of occupational adjustment of distressed clients. *Journal of Counseling Psychology,* 1970, *17,* 326-329.

Kutner, B. The social psychology of disability. In W. S. Neff (Ed.), *Rehabilitation Psychology.* Washington, D.C.: American Psychological Association, 1971.

Lake, D. G., Miles, M. B., & Earle, R. B. (Eds.). *Measuring human behavior.* New York: Columbia University Teachers College Press, 1973.

Lasky, R. G., & Salomone, P. R. A modification of the Handicap Problems Inventory. *Rehabilitation Counseling Bulletin,* 1971, *15,* 105–115.

Laughlin, J. E. Comment on "Estimating coefficients in linear models: It don't make no nevermind." *Psychological Bulletin,* 1978, *85,* 247–253.

Lawlis, G. F., & Bozarth, J. D. *Evaluation of case closures as a criterion of counselor effectiveness.* Fayetteville: Arkansas Rehabilitation Research and Training Center, 1972.

Lawshe, C. H. Statistical theory and practice in applied psychology. *Personnel Psychology,* 1969, *22,* 117–124.

Lenhart, L., Westerheide, W. J., & Miller, C. Description of service outcome measurement project: Two approaches to measuring case difficulty and client change. *Rehabilitation Research and Practice Review,* 1972, *4*(1), 27–33.

Levinson, P. A look at the utilization of available resources. In S. E. Rubin (Ed.), *Studies of the evaluation of state vocational rehabilitation agency programs.* Fayetteville: Arkansas Rehabilitation Research and Training Center, 1975.

Leviton, G. Professional and client viewpoints on rehabilitation issues. *Rehabilitation Psychology,* 1973, *20*(1). (Special Monograph)

Levonian, E. A statistical analysis of the 16 Personality Factor Questionnaire. *Educational and Psychological Measurement,* 1961, *21,* 589–596.

Lewis, J. Differential evaluation of selected tests when utilized with institutionalized and non-institutionalized trainable mentally retarded. Unpublished doctoral dissertation, University of Nebraska, 1969.

Lindemann, J. E., Fairweather, G. W., Stone, G. B., & Smith, R. S. The use of demographic characteristics in predicting length of neuropsychiatric hospital stay. *Journal of Consulting Psychology,* 1959, *23,* 85–89.

Lindenberg, R. E. Work with families in rehabilitation. *Rehabilitation Counseling Bulletin,* 1977, *21,* 67–76.

Linkowski, D. C. A scale to measure acceptance of disability. *Rehabilitation Counseling Bulletin,* 1971, *14,* 236–244.

Linkowski, D. C., & Dunn, M. A. Self-concept and acceptance of disability. *Rehabilitation Counseling Bulletin,* 1974, *18,* 28–32.

Linn, M. W., & Greenwald, S. R. Student attitudes, knowledge, and skill related to research training. *Journal of Education for Social Work,* 1974, *10,* 48–54.

Lorei, T. W. Prediction of community stay and employment for released psychiatric patients. *Journal of Consulting Psychology,* 1967, *31,* 349–357.

Lorr, M., & Gilberstadt, H. A comparison of two typologies for psychotics. *The Journal of Nervous and Mental Diseases,* 1972, *155,* 145–148.

Lowe, C. M. Prediction of posthospital work adjustment by the use of psychological tests. *Journal of Counseling Psychology,* 1967, *14,* 248–252.

Lykken, D. T. Multiple factor analysis and personality research. *Journal of Experimental Research in Personality,* 1971, *5,* 161–170.

MacGuffie, R. A., Jansen, F. V., Samuelson, C. O., & McPhee, W. M. Self-concept and ideal-self in assessing the rehabilitation applicant. *Journal of Counseling Psychology,* 1969, *16,* 157–161.

Marrow, A. J. *The practical theorist: The life and work of Kurt Lewin.* New York: Columbia University Teachers College Press, 1969.

Massimo, J. L., & Shore, M. F. The effectiveness of a vocationally oriented psychotherapeutic program for delinquent boys. *American Journal of Orthopsychiatry,* 1963, *33,* 634–642.

Mathews, J. B. *The psychological impact of physical disability upon vocationally handicapped individuals.* Unpublished doctoral thesis, University of Wisconsin, 1966.

May, P. R., & Tuma, A. H. Choice of criteria for the assessment of treatment outcomes. *Journal of Psychiatric Research,* 1964, *2,* 199–209.

McClelland, D. C., Constantian, C. A., Regalado, D., & Stone, C. Making it to maturity. *Psychology Today,* 1978, *12,* 42–53.

McCord, J. A. A thirty-year follow-up of treatment effects. *American Psychologist,* 1978, *33,* 284–289.

McDaniel, J. *Physical disability and human behavior* (2nd ed.). New York: Pergamon, 1976.

McNemar, Q. The factors in factoring behavior. *Psychometrika,* 1951, *16,* 353–359.

McNemar, Q. *Psychological statistics* (4th ed.). New York: Wiley, 1969.

McWilliams, J. M., & Eldridge, L. W. A 6-year study with a 4-year follow-up. *Journal of Rehabilitation,* 1973, *39,* 18–20.

Meehl, P. E. *Clinical versus statistical prediction.* Minneapolis: University of Minnesota Press, 1954.

Meehl, P. E. A scientific, scholarly, nonresearch doctorate for clinical practitioners. In R. R. Holt (Ed.), *New horizon for psychotherapy.* New York: International Universities Press, 1971.

Menninger, W. C. The meaning of work in western society. In H. Borrow (Ed.), *Man in a world at work.* Boston: Houghton Mifflin, 1964.

Meyer, H. A., & Taylor, J. G. *A comparison of the annual production of the states of region IV by using the difficulty index.* Tallahassee: Florida Department of Health and Rehabilitative Services, Division of Vocational Rehabilitation, 1970.

Miller, D. E., & Kunce, J. T. Prediction and statistical overkill revisited. *Measurement and Evaluation in Guidance,* 1973, *6,* 157–163.

Miller, D. E., Kunce, J. T., & Getsinger, S. H. Prediction of job success for clients with hearing loss. *Rehabilitation Counseling Bulletin,* 1972, *16,* 21–28.

Miller, L. A., & Allen, G. The prediction of future outcomes among OASI referrals using NMZ scores. *Personnel and Guidance Journal,* 1966, *45,* 349–352.

Miller, L. A., & Barillas, M. G. Using weighted 26-closures as a more adequate measure of counselor and agency effort in rehabilitation. *Rehabilitation Counseling Bulletin,* 1967, *11*(2), 117–121.

Miller, L. R. Abilities structure of congenitally blind persons: A factor analysis. *Journal of Visual Impairment and Blindness,* 1977, *71,* 145–153.

Mira, M. The use of the Arthur Adaption of the Leiter International Performance Scale and the Nebraska Test of Learning Aptitude with preschool deaf children. *American Annals of the Deaf,* 1962, *107,* 224–228.

Mischel, W. *Introduction to personality* (2nd ed.). New York: Holt, 1976.

Moran, M. F. The effects of differential training on the risk variable in the counselor decision-making process. *Rehabilitation Research and Practice Review,* 1971, *2*(3), 9–15.

Moran, M. F., Winter, M., & Newman, J. A scale for measuring the risk-taking variable in rehabilitation counselor decision-making. *Rehabilitation Counseling*

Bulletin, 1972, *15,* 211–219.

Moriarty, J. B. Profile analysis technique. In J. E. Muthard (Ed.), *Counselor and program evaluation methods in vocational rehabilitation.* Gainesville: University of Florida Rehabilitation Research Institute, 1977.

Moriarty, J. B., Walls, R. T., Stuart, J. D., & Tseng, M. S. *Resource for evaluating VR programs.* Morgantown: West Virginia Research and Training Center, 1974.

Mortenson, B. F. The relationship of certain biographical information to the successful vocational rehabilitation of psychiatric patients. Unpublished doctoral dissertation, University of Utah, 1960.

Mueller, P. F. C. *Development of case difficulty weights for the clients of the California State Department of Rehabilitation.* Sacramento: Department of Rehabilitation, 1975.

Muhlern, T. J. Use of the 16PF with mentally retarded adults. *Measurement and Evaluation in Guidance,* 1975, *8,* 26–28.

Mulaik, S. A. *The foundations of factor analysis.* New York: McGraw-Hill, 1972.

Mullen, J. *The dilemma of diversion: Resource materials on adult pretrial intervention programs.* Washington, D.C.: Department of Justice, Law Enforcement Assistance Administration, National Institute of Law Enforcement and Criminal Justice, 1975.

Murphy, S. T. Problems in research utilization: A review. *Rehabilitation Counseling Bulletin,* 1975, *19,* 365–376.

Murphy, S. T. A critical view of job-placement inquiry. *Rehabilitation Counseling Bulletin,* 1977, *21,* 166–175.

Muthard, J. E., Crocker, L. M., & Wells, S. A. Rehabilitation workers' use and evaluation of research and demonstration BRIEF reports. *Technical Report No. 1.* Gainesville: University of Florida Rehabilitation Research Institute, 1973.

Muthard, J. E., & Felice, K. A. Measuring and improving research utilization practices in rehabilitation. *Rehabilitation Monograph No. 10.* Gainesville: University of Florida Rehabilitation Research Institute, 1978.

Muthard, J. E., & Miller, L. A. Criteria for rehabilitation counselor performance in state vocational rehabilitation agencies. *Journal of Counseling Psychology,* 1964, *11,* 123–128.

Muthard, J. E., & Salomone, P. The roles and functions of the rehabilitation counselor. *Rehabilitation Counseling Bulletin,* 1969, *13,* 81–168.

Neff, W. S. The success of a rehabilitation program: A follow-up study of clients of the Vocational Adjustment Center. *Chicago Jewish Vocational Service Monograph,* No. 3. Chicago: Jewish Vocational Service, 1959.

Neff, W. S. Rehabilitation and work. In W. S. Neff (Ed.), *Rehabilitation psychology.* Washington, D.C.: American Psychological Association, 1971.

Neff, W. S. *Work and human behavior* (Rev. ed.). Chicago: Atherton, 1978.

Neff, W., & Kultov, M. *Work and mental disorder: A study of factors involved in the rehabilitation of the vocationally disadvantaged former mental patient.* New York: Institute for the Crippled and Disabled, 1967.

Nesselroade, J. R., & Baltes, P. B. Higher order factor convergence and divergence of two distinct personality systems: Cattell's HSPQ and Jackson's PRF. *Multivariate Behavioral Research,* 1975, *10,* 387–407.

Nesselroade, J. R., & Cable, D. G. "Sometimes, it's okay to factor differences scores" — The separation of state and trait anxiety. *Multivariate Behavioral Re-*

search, 1974, *9,* 273–281.

Noble, J. H. Actuarial system for weighting case closures. *Rehabilitation Record,* 1973, *14*(5), 34–37.

Nunnally, J. *Psychometric theory.* New York: McGraw-Hill, 1967.

O'Connor, E. F. Extending classical test theory to the measurement of change. *Review of Educational Research,* 1972, *42,* 73–97.

O'Leary, K. D., & Wilson, G. T. *Behavior therapy: Application and outcome.* Englewood Cliffs, N.J.: Prentice-Hall, 1975.

Osgood, C. E. On the whys and wherefores of E.P.A. *Journal of Personality and Social Psychology,* 1969, *12,* 194–199.

Overall, J. E. Note on the scientific status of factors. *Psychological Bulletin,* 1964, *61,* 270–276.

Park, L. C., Uhlenhuth, E. H., Lipman, R. S., Rickels, K., & Fisher, S. A comparison of doctor and patient improvement ratings in a drug (meprobamate) trial. *British Journal of Psychiatry,* 1965, *111,* 535–540.

Parker, R. Methodological pitfalls in predicting counseling success. *Journal of Vocational Behavior,* 1974, *5,* 31–39.

Pervin, L. A. *Personality: Theory, assessment, and research* (Rev. ed.). New York: Wiley, 1975.

Peterson, D. R. Scope and generality of verbally defined personality factors. *Psychological Review,* 1965, *72,* 48–59.

Pickerel, E. W. *The relative predictive efficiency of three methods of utilizing scores from biographical inventories* (Research bulletin AFPTRC-TR-54-73). Lackland Air Force Base, Tex.: Air Force Personnel and Training Research Center, 1954.

Prusoff, B. A., Klerman, G. L., & Paykel, E. S. Concordance between clinical assessments and patients' self-report in depression. *Archives of General Psychiatry,* 1972, *26,* 546–552.

Pruzek, R. M., & Frederick, B. C. Weighting predictors in linear models: Alternatives to least squares and limitations of equal weights. *Psychological Bulletin,* 1978, *85,* 254–266.

Randolph, A. The Rehabilitation Act of 1973: Implementation and implications. *Rehabilitation Counseling Bulletin,* 1975, *18,* 200–204.

Reagles, K. W. *Follow-up studies: A handbook for human service professionals.* New York: Institute for the Crippled and Disabled, 1978.

Reagles, K. W., & Butler, A. J. The Human Service Scale: A new measure for evaluation. *Journal of Rehabilitation,* 1976, *42,* 34–38.

Reagles, K. W., & O'Neill, J. Single-subject designs for client groups: Implications for program evaluation. *Rehabilitation Counseling Bulletin,* 1977, *21,* 13–22.

Reagles, K. W., Wright, G. N., & Butler, A. J. A scale of rehabilitation gain for clients of an expanded vocational rehabilitation program. *Wisconsin Studies in Vocational Rehabilitation,* No. 13. Madison: University of Wisconsin, Regional Rehabilitation Research Institute, 1970. (a)

Reagles, K. W., Wright, G. N., & Butler, A. J. Correlates of client satisfaction in an expanded vocational rehabilitation program. *Wisconsin Studies in Vocational Rehabilitation,* No. 12. Madison: University of Wisconsin Regional Rehabilitation Research Institute, 1970. (b)

Reagles, K. W., Wright, G. N., & Butler, A. J. Rehabilitation gain: Relationship with client characteristics and counselor intervention. *Journal of Counseling Psychology*, 1971, *18*, 490–495.

Reagles, K. W., Wright, G. N., & Butler, A. J. Toward a new criterion of vocational rehabilitation success. *Rehabilitation Counseling Bulletin*, 1972, *15*, 233–241.

Reagles, K. W., Wright, G. N., & Thomas, K. R. Development of a scale of client satisfaction for clients receiving vocational rehabilitation counseling services. *Rehabilitation Research and Practice Review*, 1972, *3*(2), 15–22. (a)

Reagles, K. W., Wright, G. N., & Thomas, K. R. Client satisfaction as a function of interventive counselor behaviors. *Rehabilitation Research and Practice Review*, 1972, *3*(2), 23–29. (b)

Research Utilization Laboratory. Goal attainment scaling in rehabilitation. *Chicago Jewish Vocational Service Monograph*, No. 5. Chicago: Jewish Vocational Service, 1976.

Rice, B. D., & Glenn, V. L. Identification of personality groups in a comprehensive rehabilitation center population. *Journal of Applied Rehabilitation Counseling*, 1973, *4*, 15–22.

Richardson, B. K., & Rubin, S. E. Analysis of rehabilitation counselor subrole behavior. *Rehabilitation Counseling Bulletin*, 1973, *17*, 47–57.

Robinault, I. P., & Weisinger, M. A brief history of the ICD research utilization laboratory. *Rehabilitation Counseling Bulletin*, 1975, *19*, 426–432.

Roehlke, H. J. Predicting outcome of rehabilitation of psychiatric patients. Unpublished doctoral dissertation, University of Missouri, 1965.

Roessler, R., & Bolton, B. *Psychosocial adjustment to disability*. Baltimore: University Park Press, 1978.

Roessler, R., Cook, D., & Lillard, D. Effects of systematic group counseling on work adjustment clients. *Journal of Counseling Psychology*, 1977, *24*, 313–317.

Roessler, R., & Mack, G. Strategies for expanded interagency linkages: Rehabilitation implications. *Rehabilitation Counseling Bulletin*, 1975, *19*, 344–352. (a)

Roessler, R., & Mack, G. Service integration final report. *Research Monograph*. Fayetteville: Arkansas Rehabilitation Research and Training Center, 1975. (b)

Rogers, E. M. Research utilization in rehabilitation. In W. S. Neff (Ed.), *Rehabilitation Psychology*. Washington, D.C.: American Psychological Association, 1971.

Rorer, L. G. Review of the Sixteen Personality Factor Questionnaire. In O. K. Buros (Ed.), *Personality Tests and Reviews II*. Highland Park, N.J.: Gryphon Press, 1975.

Rosen, M., Kivitz, M. S., Clark, G. R., & Floor, L. Prediction of postinstitutional adjustment of mentally retarded adults. *American Journal of Mental Deficiency*, 1970, *74*, 726–733.

Rosen, S. D., Weiss, D. J., Hendel, D. D., Dawis, R. V., & Lofquist, L. H. Occupational reinforcer patterns (second volume). *Monograph No. 29*. Minneapolis: University of Minnesota Industrial Relations Center, 1972.

Rosenberg, M. B., & Colarelli, N. J. Behavioral styles and ego competencies. St. Louis: St. Louis University, Department of Psychology, 1969.

Rosillo, R. H., & Fogel, M. L. Emotional support. *Psychosomatics*, 1970, *11*, 194–196.

Rubin, S. E. (Ed.). *Studies in the Evaluation of State Vocational Rehabilitation Programs*. Fayetteville: Arkansas Rehabilitation Research and Training Center, 1975.

Rubin, S. E., Bolton, B., Krauft, C. C., Richardson, B. K., & Bozarth, J. D. Rehabilitation counselor behavior and client intermediate-term personality change. *Monograph No. 12*. Fayetteville: Arkansas Rehabilitation Research and Training Center, 1974.

Rubin, S. E., Bolton, B., & Salley, K. A review of the literature on the prediction of rehabilitation client outcome and the development of a research model. *Monograph No. 5*. Fayetteville: Arkansas Rehabilitation Research and Training Center, 1973.

Rubin, S. E., & Cooper, P. G. A placement suitability measure for assessing rehabilitation service units. *Rehabilitation Counseling Bulletin*, 1977, *21*(1), 23–30.

Rubin, S. E., Richardson, B. K., & Bolton, B. Empirically derived rehabilitation counselor subgroups and their biographical correlates. *Monograph No. 6*. Fayetteville: Arkansas Rehabilitation Research and Training Center, 1973.

Salomone, P. R. Placement in the rehabilitation process. *Rehabilitation Counseling Bulletin*, 1977, *21*, 81–176. (Special Issue)

Sankovsky, R., & Newman, J. Follow-up in rehabilitation. *Rehabilitation Research and Practice Review*, 1972, *3*, 41–45.

Sarason, S. B. *Work, Aging, and Social Change: Professionals and the One Life-One Career Imperative*. New York: Free Press, 1977.

Saunders, D. R. Moderator variables in prediction. *Educational and Psychological Measurement*, 1956, *16*, 209–222.

Sawyer, J. Measurement and prediction, clinical and statistical. *Psychological Bulletin*, 1966, *66*, 178–200.

Schletzer, V. M., Dawis, R. V., England, G., & Lofquist, L. H. A follow-up study of placement success. *Minnesota Studies in Vocational Rehabilitation*, No. 3. Minneapolis: University of Minnesota, 1958.

Schmitt, N., Coyle, B. W., & Rauschenberger, J. A Monte Carlo evaluation of three formula estimates of cross-validated multiple correlation. *Psychological Bulletin*, 1977, *84*, 751–758.

Schmitt, N., Coyle, B. W., & Saari, B. A review and critique of analyses of multitrait-multimethod matrices. *Multivariate Behavioral Research*, 1977, *12*, 447–448.

Schurr, K. T., Joiner, L. M., & Towne, R. C. Self-concept research on the mentally retarded: A review of empirical studies. *Mental Retardation*, 1970, *8*, 39–43.

Schwab, J. J., Bialow, M. R., & Holzer, C. E. A comparison of two rating scales for depression. *Journal of Clinical Psychology*, 1967, *23*, 94–96.

Schwartz, M. L., Dennerll, R. D., & Lin, Y. Neuropsychological and psychological predictors of employability in epilepsy. *Journal of Clinical Psychology*, 1968, *24*, 174–177.

Science News. Thirty-year follow-up: Counseling fails. *Science News*, 1977, *122*(22), 357.

Scott, T. B., Dawis, R. V., England, G. W., & Lofquist, L. H. A definition of work adjustment *Minnesota Studies in Vocational Rehabilitation*, No. 10. Minneapolis, University of Minnesota, 1958.

Sears, P. S., & Barbee, A. H. Career and life satisfaction among Terman's gifted women. In J. Stanley, W. George, & C. Solano (Eds.), *The Gifted and the Creative: Fifty-year perspective.* Baltimore: Johns Hopkins University Press, 1977.

Sears, R. R. Sources of life satisfactions of the Terman gifted men. *American Psychologist,* 1977, *32,* 119–128.

Sells, S. B., Demaree, R. G., & Will, D. P. Dimensions of personality: I. Conjoint factor structure of Guilford and Cattell trait markers. *Multivariate Behavioral Research,* 1970, *5,* 391–422.

Sells, S. B., Demaree, R. G., & Will, D. P. Dimensions of personality: II. Separate factor structure in Guilford and Cattell trait markers. *Multivariate Behavioral Research,* 1971, *6,* 135–186.

Serban, G., & Katz, G. Schizophrenic performance on form E of Cattell's 16PF test. *Journal of Personality Assessment,* 1975, *39,* 169–177.

Sermon, D. T. The difficulty index — An expanded measure of counselor performance. *Research Monograph No. 1.* St. Paul: Minnesota Division of Vocational Rehabilitation, 1972.

Sheehan, D. V., & Hackett, T. P. Psychosomatic disorders. In A. M. Nicholi (Ed.), *The Harvard Guide to Modern Psychiatry.* Cambridge, Mass.: Harvard University Press, 1978.

Shontz, F. C. *Research Methods In Personality.* New York: Appleton-Century-Crofts, 1965.

Shontz, F. C. Physical disability and personality; Theory and recent research. *Psychological Aspects of Disability,* 1970, *17,* 51–69.

Shontz, F. C. Physical disability and personality. In W. S. Neff (Ed.), *Rehabilitation Psychology.* Washington, D.C.: American Psychological Association, 1971.

Shontz, F. C. *The Psychological Aspects of Physical Illness and Disability.* New York: Macmillan, 1975.

Shore, M., & Massimo, J. Comprehensive vocationally oriented psychotherapy for adolescent delinquent boys: A follow-up study. *American Journal of Orthopsychiatry,* 1966, *36,* 609–615.

Shore, M., & Massimo, J. Five years later: A follow-up study of comprehensive vocationally oriented psychotherapy. *American Journal of Orthopsychiatry,* 1969, *39,* 769–773.

Shore, M., & Massimo, J. After ten years: A follow-up study of comprehensive vocationally oriented psychotherapy. *American Journal of Orthopsychiatry,* 1973, *43,* 128–132.

Shulman, L. S. The vocational development of mentally handicapped adolescents: An experimental and longitudinal study. *Chicago Jewish Vocational Service Monograph,* No. 6. Chicago: Jewish Vocational Service, 1967.

Shurrager, H. C. *A Haptic Intelligence Scale for Adult Blind.* Chicago: Illinois Institute of Technology, 1961.

Shutt, D., & Hannon, T. The validity of the HNTLA for evaluation of the abilities of bilingual children. *Educational and Psychological Measurement,* 1974, *34,* 429–432.

Siller, J. Generality of attitudes toward the physically disabled. *Proceedings of the 78th Annual Convention of the American Psychological Association,* 1970, 697–698.

Siller, J., & Chipman, A. Factorial structure and correlates of the attitudes toward disabled persons scale. *Educational and Psychological Measurement,* 1964, *24,* 831–840.

Siller, J., Chipman, A., Ferguson, L. T., & Vann, D. H. Attitudes of the nondisabled toward the physically disabled. *Studies in Reactions to Disability,* No. 11. New York: New York University, 1967.

Siller, J., Ferguson, L. T., Vann, D. H., & Holland, B. Structure of attitudes toward the physically disabled: Disability Factor Scales — amputation, blindness, cosmetic conditions. *Studies in Reactions to Disability,* No. 12. New York: New York University, 1967.

Silver, D. L. A look at evaluation of vocational rehabilitation counselor performance. *Journal of Rehabilitation,* 1969, *35*(6), 13–14.

Skinner, B. F. The flight from the laboratory. In B. F. Skinner (Ed.), *Cumulative Record* (2nd ed.). New York: Appleton-Century-Crofts, 1961.

Smith, M. L., & Glass, G. V. Meta-analysis of psychotherapy outcome studies. *American Psychologist,* 1977, *32,* 752–760.

Soloff, A. *A Work Therapy Research Center.* Chicago: Jewish Vocational Service, 1967.

Soloff, A., & Bolton, B. *Multiple Regression Analyses of the Work Therapy Center Data.* Chicago: Jewish Vocational Service, 1968.

Soloff, A., & Bolton, B. The validity of the CJVS scale of employability for older clients in a vocational adjustment workshop. *Educational and Psychological Measurement,* 1969, *29,* 993–998.

Soloff, A., Goldston, L. J., Pollack, R. A., & White, B. Running a research utilization laboratory. *Rehabilitation Counseling Bulletin,* 1975, *19,* 416–424.

Sonquist, J. A. *Multivariate model building: The validation of a search strategy.* Ann Arbor: University of Michigan, Institute for Social Research, 1970.

Sonquist, J. A., Baker, E. L., & Morgan, J. N. *Searching for structure (ALIAS-AID-III).* Ann Arbor: University of Michigan, Institute for Social Research, 1971.

Sorokin, P. A. A criticism of the prediction of personal adjustment. *American Journal of Sociology,* 1942, *48,* 76–80.

Spitzer, R. L., Fleiss, J. L., Endicott, J., & Cohen, J. Mental Status Schedule: Properties of factor-analytically derived scales. *Archives of General Psychiatry,* 1967, *16,* 479–493.

Stanley, J. C. Reliability. In R. L. Thorndike (Ed.), *Educational measurement.* Washington, D.C.: American Council on Education, 1971.

Stein, C. I., Bradley, A. D., & Buegel, B. L. A test of basic assumptions underlying vocational counseling utilizing a differential criterion method. *Journal of Counseling Psychology,* 1970, *17,* 93–97.

Stock, D. D., & Cole, J. A. Adaptive housing for the severely physically handicapped. *Rehabilitation Counseling Bulletin,* 1975, *18,* 224–231.

Strong, E. K. Permanence of interest scores over 22 years. *Journal of Applied Psychology,* 1951, *35,* 89–91.

Struthers, R. D. *Michigan vocational rehabilitation service staff discussion paper: Quality rehabilitation services.* Lansing: Michigan Rehabilitative Services, 1976.

Suchman, E. A. *Evaluative research.* New York: Russell Sage Foundation, 1967.

Super, D. E. *The psychology of careers.* New York: Harper & Row, 1957.

Thomas, R. E., Henke, R., & Pool, D. A. Accountability in vocational rehabilitation: Difficulties with the "26 closure" as a criterion. *Journal of Applied Rehabilitation Counseling,* 1976, *7*(2), 67–75.

Thorndike, R. M. Reliability. In B. Bolton (Ed.), *Handbook of measurement and evaluation in rehabilitation.* Baltimore: University Park Press, 1976.

Thurstone, L. L. *Multiple-factor analysis.* (2nd ed.). Chicago: University of Chicago Press, 1947.

Timm, U. Reliabilitat und Faktorenstruktur von Cattells 16PF Test bei einer deutschen Stichprobe. *Z. Exp. Angew. Psychol.,* 1968, *15,* 354–373. (Cited in Eysenck (1972)).

Tinsley, H. E. A., & Gaughen, S. A cross-sectional analysis of the impact of rehabilitation counseling. *Rehabilitation Counseling Bulletin,* 1975, *18,* 147–153.

Tinsley, H. E. A., Warnken, R. G., Weiss, D. J., Dawis, R. V., & Lofquist, L. H. A Follow-up survey of former clients of the Minnesota DVR. *Minnesota Studies in Vocational Rehabilitation,* No. 26. Minneapolis: University of Minnesota, 1969.

Trantow, D. J. An introduction to evaluation: Program effectiveness and community need. *Rehabilitation Literature,* 1970, *31*(12), 2–9, 12.

Trybus, R. J. Personality assessment of entering hearing-impaired college students using the 16PF, Form E. *Journal of Rehabilitation of the Deaf,* 1973, *6*(3), 34–40.

Tseng, M. S. Self-perception and employability: A vocational rehabilitation problem. *Journal of Counseling Psychology,* 1972, *19,* 314–317. (a)

Tseng, M. S. Predicting vocational rehabilitation drop-outs from psychometric attributes and work behavior. *Rehabilitation Counseling Bulletin,* 1972, *15*(3), 154–159. (b)

Tucker, J. A. Relative predictive efficiency of multiple regression and unique patterns techniques. Unpublished doctoral thesis, Columbia University, 1950.

Underwood, B. J. *Psychological research.* New York: Appleton-Century-Crofts, 1957.

The Urban Institute. *Report of the Comprehensive Service Needs Study.* Washington, D.C.: The Urban Institute, 1975.

Usdane, W. M. Rehabilitation initial diagnostic assessment center. *Focus,* 1972, *3*(2), 1–2.

Vaillant, G. *Adaption to life.* Boston: Little, Brown & Co., 1977.

Vandergoot, D. Further evidence of the factorial validity of the service outcome measurement form. *Rehabilitation Counseling Bulletin,* 1976, *20,* 144–147.

Van Hagen, J., & Kaufman, A. S. Factor analysis of the WISC-R for a group of mentally retarded children and adolescents. *Journal of Consulting and Clinical Psychology,* 1975, *43,* 661–667.

Vaughn, D. S. The relative methodological soundness of several major personality factor analyses. *Journal of Behavioral Science,* 1973, *1,* 305–313.

Viaille, H. D. *Operations Research Program in Oklahoma Vocational Rehabilitation Agency.* Oklahoma City: Oklahoma Vocational Rehabilitation Agency, 1968.

Viaille, H. D., Hills, W. G., & Ledgerwood, D. E. Management practices in vocational rehabilitation district offices. *Monograph No. 2.* Norman: University of Oklahoma Regional Rehabilitation Research Institute, 1973.

Wagner, R. J. Rehabilitation team practice. *Rehabilitation Counseling Bulletin,* 1977, *20,* 206–217.

Wainer, H. Estimating coefficients in linear models: It don't make no nevermind. *Psychological Bulletin,* 1976, *83,* 213–217.

Wainer, H. On the sensitivity of regression and regressors. *Psychological Bulletin,* 1978, *85,* 267–273.

Wallis, J., & Bozarth, J. D. *The development and evaluation of weighted DVR case closures.* Fayetteville: Arkansas Rehabilitation Research and Training Center, 1972.

Wallis, W. A. Statistics of the Kinsey Report. *Journal of the American Statistical Association,* 1949, *44,* 463–484.

Walls, R. T., & Masson, C. Rehabilitation client problems and family communications. *Rehabilitation Counseling Bulletin,* 1978, *21,* 317–324.

Walls, R. T., & Moriarty, J. B. The caseload profile: Alternative to weighted closure. *Rehabilitation Literature,* 1977, *38*(9), 285–291.

Walsh, J. Review of the 16PF. In O. Buros (Ed.), *The eighth mental measurements yearbook.* Highland Park, N.J.: Gryphon Press, 1978.

Watley, D. J. Counselor variability in making accurate predictions. *Journal of Counseling Psychology,* 1966, *13,* 53–62.

Weiner, H. Characteristics associated with rehabilitation success. *Personnel and Guidance Journal,* 1964, *42,* 687–694.

Weiss, D. J. A technique for curvilinear multivariate prediction. Unpublished doctoral thesis, University of Minnesota, 1963.

Weiss, D. J. Factor analysis and counseling research. *Journal of Counseling Psychology,* 1970, *17*(5), 477–485.

Weiss, D. J. Further considerations in applications of factor analysis. *Journal of Counseling Psychology,* 1971, *18*(1), 85–92.

Weiss, D. J. Canonical correlation analysis in counseling psychology research. *Journal of Counseling Psychology,* 1972, *19,* 241–252.

Weiss, D. J., & Dawis, R. V. A multivariate prediction technique for problems involving multi-functional predictor-criterion relationships. *Proceedings of the Annual Convention of the American Psychological Association,* 1968, 229–230.

Weiss, D. J., Dawis, R. V., England, G. W., & Lofquist, L. H. Manual for the Minnesota Satisfaction Questionnaire. *Monograph No. 22.* Minneapolis: University of Minnesota, Industrial Relations Center, 1967.

Wells, S. A., Crocker, L. M., & Muthard, J. E. Research applied to policy and practice: A method for assessing the impact of selected research and demonstration projects. In J. G. Albert (Ed.), *Case studies of evaluation in health, education, and welfare.* New York: Sage, 1976.

Westerheide, W. J., & Lenhart, L. Development and reliability of a pretest-posttest rehabilitation services outcome measure. *Rehabilitation Research and Practice Review,* 1973, *4*(2), 15–24.

Westerheide, W. J., Lenhart, L., & Miller, M. C. Field test of a services outcome measurement form: Case difficulty. *Monograph No. 2.* Oklahoma City: Department of Institutions, Social and Rehabilitation Services, 1974.

Westerheide, W. J., Lenhart, L., & Miller, M. C. Field test of a service outcome measurement form: Client change. *Monograph No. 3.* Oklahoma City: Department of Institutions, Social and Rehabilitation Services, 1975.

Whiteman, M., & Lukoff, I. F. A factorial study of sighted people's attitudes toward blindness. *The Journal of Social Psychology,* 1964, *64,* 339–353.

Wiggins, J. S. *Personality and prediction: Principles of personality assessment.* Reading, Mass.: Addison-Wesley, 1973.

Williams, J. G., Barlow, D. G., & Agras, W. S. Behavioral measurement of severe depression. *Archives of General Psychiatry,* 1972, *27,* 330–333.

Willis, D., Wright, L., & Wolfe, J. WISC and Nebraska performance of deaf and hearing children. *Perceptual and Motor Skills,* 1972, *34,* 783–788.

Winter, M. S. The rehabilitation team: A catalyst to risky rehabilitation decisions. *Rehabilitation Counseling Bulletin,* 1976, *19,* 580–586.

Worrall, J. D. Weighted case closure and counselor performance. *Rehabilitation Counseling Bulletin,* 1978, *21*(4), 325–334.

Wright, B. A. *Physical disability — A psychological approach.* New York: Harper & Row, 1960.

Wright, B. A. Psychological snares in the investigative enterprise. In E. P. Trapp & P. Himelstein (Eds.), *Readings on the exceptional child* (2nd ed.). New York: Appleton-Century-Crofts, 1972.

Wright, G. N., & Fraser, R. T. Task analysis for the evaluation, preparation, classification, and utilization of rehabilitation counselor-track personnel *Monograph No. 22, Series 3.* Madison: University of Wisconsin, Regional Rehabilitation Research Institute, 1975.

Wright, G. N., & Remmers, H. H. *Manual for the Handicap Problems Inventory.* Lafayette, Ind.: Purdue Research Foundation, 1960.

Wright, G. N., Smits, S. J., Butler, A. J., & Thoreson, R. W. A survey of counselor perceptions. *Monograph No. 2.* Madison: University of Wisconsin Regional Rehabilitation Research Institute, 1968.

Yuker, H. E., Block, J. R., & Younng, J. H. *The Measurement of Attitudes Towards Disabled Persons.* Albertson, N.Y.: Human Resources Center, 1966.

Zadny, J. J., & James, L. F. Time spent on placement. *Rehabilitation Counseling Bulletin,* 1977, *21,* 31–35. (a)

Zadny, J. J., & James, L. F. Job placement of the vocationally handicapped: A survey of technique, Part I. Introduction to design and method *Monograph No. 2.* Portland, Ore.: Portland State University, Regional Rehabilitation Research Institute, 1977. (b)

Zawada, A. R. Rationale and derivation of a Florida difficulty index. *Research Report.* Tallahassee: Florida Department of Health and Rehabilitation Services, Division of Vocational Rehabilitation, 1972.

Zimbalist, S. E. The research component of the master's degree curriculum in social work: A survey summary. *Journal of Education for Social Work,* 1974, *10,* 118–123.

Author Index

281

Subject Index